MAGNIFICENT PRAISE FOR

The Englishman's Daughter

"A wrenching but thoroughly captivating book. In his war story, love story and mystery, Mr. Macintyre takes time to unite the strands into a compelling whole. The tempo, tension and rich imagery reminds one of the novels of Michael Ondaatje." —*The Washington Times*

"[A] lovely, affecting book . . . Macintyre has pieced together a remarkably thorough account that has the ring of truth." —*The Washington Post Book World*

"Macintyre humanizes the history of life in occupied France. . . . Reads like a novel while succeeding as a sterling piece of investigative journalism." —*The Boston Herald*

"Remarkable . . . a picaresque and, as the title suggests, romantic tale." —*The New York Times*

"Moving." —*The Baltimore Sun*

"Macintyre does a superb job of portraying the various actors in this tragedy." —*The Boston Sunday Globe*

"Heartbreaking . . . Even more piercing than the mystery of who betrayed Digby are the descriptions of last century's most savage war." —*People*

"Splendid . . . It would make a marvelous film." —*The Midwest Book Review*

"A wondrously engaging tale, which quietly proves again the cliché that fact is stranger than fiction. . . . Reads more like a novel than nonfiction." —*Richmond Times-Dispatch*

"While Macintyre is satisfyingly thorough in his attempt to solve this long-buried mystery, he is even better at re-creating the texture of day-to-day life in rural occupied France." —*Publishers Weekly*

"Powerful and evocative . . . It's a simple story, but Macintyre reports it beautifully. . . . Wrapped in well-researched history and presented in exemplary prose, this elegy of lost time recalls the verse of Wilfred Owen and Rupert Brooke." —*Kirkus Reviews* (starred review)

"A magnificent story . . . it is easy to forget that this story is absolutely true." —*Library Journal*

"A tale of immense stature that ranks as one of the books of the year. . . . Stirring, ambitious and profound, this is storytelling at its very best." —*The Sunday Times* (UK)

ALSO BY BEN MACINTYRE

The Napoleon of Crime:
The Life and Times of Adam Worth, Master Thief

Forgotten Fatherland: The Search for Elisabeth Nietzsche

The Englishman's Daughter

The Englishman's Daughter

A TRUE STORY OF LOVE AND BETRAYAL

IN WORLD WAR I

Ben Macintyre

DELTA TRADE PAPERBACKS

A DELTA BOOK
Published by
Dell Publishing
Random House, Inc.
New York, New York

Originally published in 2001 by HarperCollins, Great Britain, as *A Foreign Field: A True Story of Love and Betrayal in the Great War.* Published in hardcover in the United States by Farrar, Straus and Giroux in 2002.

Library of Congress Catalog Card Number: 2001033477

ISBN: 0-385- 33679-9

Reprinted by arrangement with Farrar, Straus and Giroux.

Manufactured in the United States of America

Published simultaneously in Canada

February 2003

10 9 8 7 6 5 4 3 2 1
BVG

In memory of Angus Macintyre

If I should die, think only this of me:
That there's some corner of a foreign field
That is for ever England. There shall be
In that rich earth a richer dust concealed . . .
          —Rupert Brooke (1887–1915)
              "The Soldier"

I have a rendezvous with Death
At some disputed barricade,
When Spring comes back with rustling shade
And apple-blossoms fill the air—
I have a rendezvous with Death
When Spring brings back blue days and fair.

It may be he shall take my hand
And lead me into his dark land
And close my eyes and quench my breath—
It may be I shall pass him still.
I have a rendezvous with Death
On some scarred slope of battered hill,
When Spring comes round again this year
And the first meadow-flowers appear.

God knows 'twere better to be deep
Pillowed in silk and scented down,
Where love throbs out in blissful sleep,
Pulse nigh to pulse, and breath to breath,
Where hushed awakenings are dear . . .
But I've a rendezvous with Death
At midnight in some flaming town,
When Spring trips north again this year,
And I to my pledged word am true,
I shall not fail that rendezvous.
          —Alan Seeger (1888–1916)
              "I Have a Rendezvous with Death"

A Note on Sources

This is a true story. It is based on official documents, letters, diaries, newspaper articles, and contemporary writings by the participants. It would have been impossible to tell without the admirable and peculiarly French habit of bureaucratic history-hoarding, which prompted local officials to amass quantities of first-hand evidence from ordinary people, describing their experiences in the region behind the lines between 1914 and 1918. This information, collected immediately after the war, was carefully stored in municipal, departmental, and academic archives, and then almost entirely forgotten.

The story has also emerged from hundreds of hours of conversation with scores of people who were directly touched by the events described, or who learned of them from their parents, grandparents, and neighbours. Their accounts are inevitably partial, in every sense, but also surprisingly consistent. Recollections of a remote time can never be perfectly accurate, but they were offered with simple honesty, and I have tried to record them faithfully. What follows, then, is partly an excavation from a distant war, but also the collective memoir of a community, an attempt to reconstruct a forgotten fragment of the past through reminiscence and oral history.

The Englishman's Daughter

ALONG THE WESTERN FRONT, 1917

N

North Sea

THE NETHERLANDS

Nieuport
• Ostend
Dunkirk
Ypres
Ghent
• Antwerp

Brussels ★

BELGIUM

Lille
Lyt
Escaut

Lens
Douai
Mons
Charleroi

Meuse
Liège

Aachen

Cologne•

Bonn•

GERMANY

Arras •
Bapaume
Albert •
Valenciennes
• Cambrai
• Le Cateau
• Le Nouvion-en-Thiérache
Péronne
Somme
Villeret •
Amiens
Saint-Quentin

Maubeuge

Moselle

Charleville-Mézières •

Noyon
• Laon
Sedan

LUXEMBOURG

Compiègne •
Aisne
Aisne
Soissons

FRANCE

Reims •

★ Paris

Verdun

Marne

• Metz

Saint-Mihiel

Nancy •

Strasbourg •

Seine

Meuse

Moselle

Rhine

Mulhouse •

Belfort •

Saône

SWITZERLAND

© 2001 Jeffrey L. Ward

International Frontiers

◄▼▼▼▼◄ The Western Front

▷△△△▷ The Hindenburg Line
(from April 1917)

0 Miles ——————————— 100

0 Kilometers ——————— 100

VILLERET AND ITS SURROUNDINGS

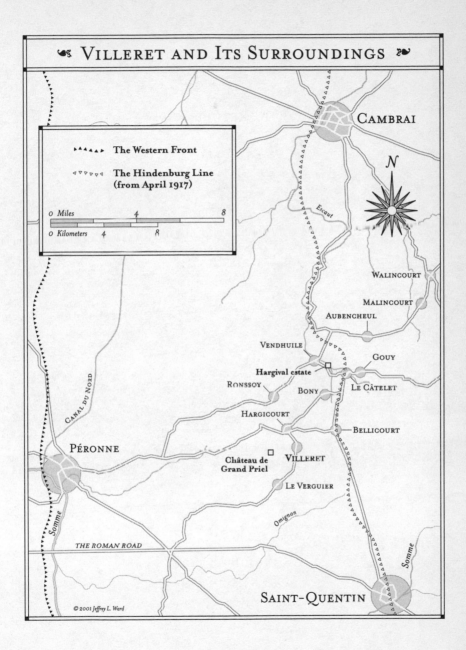

The Western Front

The Hindenburg Line
(from April 1917)

0 Miles   4   8
0 Kilometers   4   8

CAMBRAI

Escaut

N

WALINCOURT

MALINCOURT

AUBENCHEUL

VENDHUILE

GOUY

Hargival estate

RONSSOY

BONY

LE CÂTELET

HARGICOURT

BELLICOURT

CANAL DU NORD

PÉRONNE

Château de
Grand Priel

VILLERET

LE VERGUIER

Omignon

Somme

THE ROMAN ROAD

Somme

SAINT-QUENTIN

© 2001 Jeffrey L. Ward

Prologue

❦

Rain spilled from an ashen sky as the famously glutinous mud of Picardy caked on my shoe-soles like mortar, and damp seeped into my socks. In a patch of cow-trodden pasture beside the little town of Le Câtelet, we stared out from beneath a canopy of umbrellas at a pitted chalk rampart, the ivy-strangled remnant of a vast medieval castle, to which a small plaque had been nailed: *"Ici ont été fusillés quatre soldats Britanniques"* (Four British soldiers were executed by firing squad on this spot). The band from the local mental institution played "God Save the Queen," excruciatingly, and then someone clicked on a boom-box and out crackled a reedy tape-recording of French schoolchildren reciting Wilfred Owen's "Anthem for Doomed Youth."

> What passing-bells for these who die as cattle?
> Only the monstrous anger of the guns.
> Only the stuttering rifles' rapid rattle
> Can patter out their hasty orisons.

An honour guard of three old men, dressed in ragged replica First World War uniforms—one English, one Scottish, one French —clutched their toy rifles and looked stern, as the rain dripped off their moustaches. A pair of passing cattle stopped on their way to milking and stared at us.

The day before, I had received a call from the local schoolmaster at the *Times* office in Paris: "It would mean a great deal to the village to have a representative of your newspaper present when we unveil the plaque," he said. I had hesitated, fumbling for the polite French excuse, but the voice was pressing. "You must come, you will find it interesting."

Reluctantly I had set off from Paris, driving up the Autoroute du Nord past signposts—Amiens, Albert, Arras—recalling the Great War, the war to end all wars, and the very worst war, until the one that came after. Following the teacher's precise directions, I had turned off towards Saint-Quentin, across the line of the Western Front, over the River Somme, through land that had once been no-man's, and headed east along a bullet-straight Roman road into the battlefields of the war's grand finale. No place on earth has been so indelibly brutalised by conflict. The war is still gouged into the landscape, its path traced by the ugly brick houses and uniform churches thrown together with cheap cement and Chinese labour in 1919. It is written in the shape of unexploded shells unearthed with every fresh ploughing and tossed onto the roadside, and in the cemeteries, battalions of dead marching across the fields of northern France in perfect regimental order.

Early for my rendezvous, I stopped beside the British graveyard at Vadancourt and wandered among the neat Commonwealth War Graves headstones with their stock, understated laments for the multitudinous dead: some known, some unknown, and the briskly facile "Known unto God," one of the many official formulations for engraved grief worked up by Rudyard Kipling. The cemetery is a small one, just a few hundred headstones, a fraction of the 720,000 British soldiers slain, who in turn made up barely one-tenth of the carnage of that barbaric war, fought by highly civilised nations for no pressing ideological reason.

The schoolteacher, solemn of manner and strongly redolent of lunchtime garlic, was waiting for me by the Croix d'Or restaurant in Le Câtelet, where a group of about thirty people huddled under the eaves, like damp pigeons. I was introduced as *"Monsieur, le ré-dacteur du* Times," an exaggeration of my position that made me suspect he had forgotten my name. My general greeting to the assembled was met with unsmiling curiosity, and again I wondered why I had come to a ceremony for four entirely obscure soldiers, a droplet in the wave of war-blood, Known unto Nobody.

The band, drawn up in the field behind the restaurant, now broke into a hearty, rhythm-defying rendition of something French and appropriately martial. The three amateur soldiers came to attention, of sorts, as two cars pulled up. Out of the first emerged the mayor of Le Câtelet, the *préfet* of the region, and his wife; from the second an elderly white-haired woman was extracted, placed in a wheelchair, and trundled across the field to the rampart wall.

After a round of formal French handshaking, the ceremony began. The previous year I had reported on the eightieth anniversary of the Battle of the Somme, a huge, poppy-packed performance with big bands and bigwigs to celebrate the very few, very old survivors. The Le Câtelet ceremony felt somehow more apt: ill-fitting uniforms on civilians, children reciting English words they did not understand, a handful of people remembering to remember, in the pouring rain. I began to feel moved, in spite of myself. The *préfet* launched into a lofty speech about valour, honour, and death. "See the holes in the wall?" the teacher whispered, with a gust of garlic, in my ear. "Those are from the execution." As the oration rumbled on, I surveyed the assembled crowd, few under seventy and some plainly as old as the event we were here to remember. Lined peasant faces listened hard to the official version of what the war had meant.

Suddenly I had the sensation of being watched myself. The old woman in the wheelchair, placed alongside the *préfet*, had also stopped listening and was staring at me. Disconcerted, I forced a smile, and tried to feign absorption in the speech, but when I sneaked a sideways glance, I found her eyes were still fixed on me. Finally, the *préfet* wound down, and the village priest offered a hasty orison, again in English: "Our Father who art in Heaven . . ." The rain stopped, the band struck up, and the military trio shouldered plastic and marched briskly off down the street towards the town hall, where a *vin d'honneur* was on offer.

As the crowd drifted away, I looked around for the old woman, and then realised she was beside me, looking up. Before I could volunteer my name, she spoke, in a high, faint voice and a thick Picardy accent that I could barely understand. "You are the Englishman," she said. It was not a question. The eyes that had caught my attention through the drizzle were now exploring my face. They were the most intensely blue eyes I have ever seen. Unnerved again, I offered a banal observation about the improvement in the weather, but she barely allowed me to finish before piping up once more.

"Our village, Villeret"—she gestured vaguely to the west with a mottled white hand—"was over there, near the front line, on the German side. When the British were retreating, in *quatorze,* some soldiers were left behind and could not get back to their army across the trenches. They came to us for protection. We bandaged their wounds, we fed them, and we hid them from the Germans. We concealed them in our village."

Her voice was rhythmical, as if reciting a story rehearsed by heart and scored in memory. "There were seven of them, brave British soldiers, and my family and the other villagers, we kept them safe. Then, one day, the Germans came to their hiding place." The voice trailed away, and for the first time I became aware that another person was listening: I turned to find an elderly man standing behind my shoulder, an expression of undisguised alarm on his face. She pressed on, her eyes now turned to the plaque.

"Three of the British soldiers managed to escape from Villeret, and returned to England. Four did not. We were betrayed. The Germans captured them. They shot them against that wall, and we buried them beside the church." She turned back to me and smiled gravely. "That was in 1916. I was six months old."

She continued, as if the events she spoke of were the moments of yesterday, the tragedy as fresh as the rain. "Those seven British soldiers were our soldiers." She paused again, and then murmured, the faintest whisper: "One of them was my father."

CHAPTER ONE

The Angels of Mons

❧

On a balmy evening at the end of August in the year 1914, four young soldiers of the British army—two Englishmen and a pair of Irishmen—crouched in terror under a hedgerow near the Somme River in northern France, painfully adjusting to the realisation that they were profoundly and hopelessly lost, adrift in a briefly tranquil no-man's-land somewhere between their retreating comrades and the rapidly advancing German army, the largest concentration of armed men the world had ever seen.

Privates Digby, Thorpe, Donohoe, and Martin were small human shards from a mighty explosion that had been primed for years, expected by many, desired by some, and detonated just six weeks earlier when a young Bosnian Serb named Gavrilo Princip pulled a revolver in a Sarajevo back street and mortally wounded Archduke Franz Ferdinand, heir to the imperial throne of Austria-Hungary. Europe was now ablaze, and the first battles of a long and brutal war had been fought. The lamps were going out all over Europe, but in the small town of Villeret, deep in the Picardy countryside, the lamps were just being lit, watched, from under a hedge, by four pairs of hungry British eyes.

The four Tommies, of whom the oldest was only thirty-six, had barely a clue of their whereabouts, but knew well enough that they were not supposed to be there. According to official military theory, they should have been at least one hundred miles north, in Belgium, winning a swift and decisive victory against the Hun. But, then, the war was not going according to plan: neither the Schlieffen Plan, dreamed up by a dead German aristocrat, to encircle France rapidly from the north; nor France's Plan XVII, which called for the gallant French soldiery to attack the enemy with such *élan* that the Germans would immediately lose heart; nor the British plan, to defend Belgian neutrality, support the French, reinforce the might of the British Empire, and then go home.

Barely a fortnight earlier, the British Expeditionary Force, or BEF (this was a war that appreciated a clipped acronym), had begun crossing the Channel in troopships, to be met with beer and flowers in the August sun. Some of the soldiers were surprised, even a little disappointed, to discover they were not going to fight the French again. They swapped cap badges for kisses and then happily headed east and north towards Belgium to teach the Kaiser a lesson: thirty thousand jingling horses and eighty thousand men clad splendidly in khaki and self-confidence. The poet Rupert Brooke thanked God,

> Who has matched us with His hour,
> And caught our youth, and wakened us from sleeping,
> With hand made sure, clear eye and sharpened power . . .

To the east, the first of the two hundred thousand Frenchmen whose *élan* would be extinguished forever in this single summer month were already rotting into the soil of Alsace and Lorraine. And down through Belgium hurtled the German behemoth, sweeping aside the impregnable fortifications of Liège and Namur and moving on across the great industrial plains to where the unsuspecting British army was busily arranging itself into neat battalions. "The evening was still and wonderfully peaceful," recalled one British officer, scouting in advance of the main body of troops. "A dog was barking at some sheep. A girl was singing as she walked down the lane." He watched the darkness settle gently over the land. "Then, without a moment's warning, with a suddenness that made us start and strain our eyes to see what our minds could not realise, we saw the whole horizon burst into flames. To the north, outlined against the sky, countless fires were burning . . . A chill of horror came over us."

At Mons, above the Belgian border, on August 23, the British stiff upper lip was busted by a roundhouse punch that seemed to come from nowhere, as wave upon wave of field grey came crashing down from the north, three-quarters of a million German men. At first the outnumbered British fought with calm efficiency, then determination, then desperation. For some, the fear was worse than the blood-letting. Retreating inside France, three days later they turned and fought again at Le Cateau, leaving more dead on the battlefield than Wellington had lost at Waterloo. The retreat resumed. Sure hands now trembling, clear eyes clouded, the depleted army scrambled south, a pell-mell withdrawal that would last two weeks and take them to the edge of Paris.

An old Frenchwoman stood on a cottage doorstep and watched the ragged British soldiery stumbling through her village. As the mounted officer passed, she spat a livid stream of sarcasm at him: "You make a mistake," she hissed. (The young captain would never forget the sting of it.) "The enemy is *behind* you. Are you not riding in the wrong direction?"

For two hundred miles the German army pursued, looting, burning, and wielding the weapons of summary massacre and collective retribution, for this was the policy of *Schrecklichkeit*, organised ghastliness, a determination to inflict such horrific repression on the civilian population that it would never dare to resist. Hostages were shot and bayonetted, priests executed, homes and towns destroyed, and at Louvain, in a signal act of desecration, the great library of more than two hundred thousand books was put to the torch. Some German soldiers were appalled at their own might. Ernst Rosenhainer, an educated and sensitive young infantry officer, was torn between exultation and repulsion as he watched civilians fleeing from their homes: "It was heart-rending to hear a woman beg a high-ranking officer, *'Monsieur, protégez-nous!'* " he wrote.

The local people watched in disbelief as refugees, Belgian and then French, streamed through the villages of the Somme and the Aisne, a "broken torrent of dusty misery," dragging overladen donkey and dog carts, carrying their children and, along with them, lurid tales of German brutality. Behind followed the BEF: horse-drawn ambulances with mangled wounded and the long lines of exhausted and hungry soldiers, "an unthought-of confusion of men, guns, horses, and wagons. All dead-beat, many wounded, all foot sore." At their backs, plumes of smoke marked the steady German advance in a spectacular frenzy of arson. An English officer turned around from a small incline to see "the whole valley and plain burning for miles."

"We must allow the enemy no rest," declared a German battalion commander, and so the British rear-guard fought as it fled. Nerves frayed, bellies empty, minds warping from lack of sleep, some retreating soldiers dozed on the march while others began to see ghosts and castles along the way. Flight forged its own legends. The "Angels of Mons" were said to have been seen hovering over the retreat, the shimmering spectres of English bowmen killed at Agincourt in 1415, now resurrected to protect their fleeing countrymen.

The *Times* correspondent wrote: "Amongst all the straggling units that I have seen, flotsam and jetsam in the fiercest fight in history, I saw fear in no man's face. It was a retreating and broken army, but it was not an army of hunted men . . . Our losses are very great. I have seen the broken bits of many regiments." The lines stretched and snapped, authority dimmed, the stragglers multiplied, and the treasured distinctions of regiment and division blurred as units fragmented, re-formed, or broke away. Whatever the British reading public might be told, many soldiers were terrified. When the horses were allowed to rest, their legs folded. Unable to march farther, some men threw away their equipment and lay down to die or await the enemy. Officers who would have shot any man who acted thus a day or two earlier, did not now look back. "That pained look in the troubled eyes of those who fell by the way will not easily be forgotten by those who saw it.

That look imposed by circumstances on spent men seemed to demand all forgiveness from officers and comrades alike, as it conveyed a helpless and dumb farewell to arms." The neat martial simplicities of the army that had disembarked on the coast of France became hazy in retreat. Most men marched unquestioningly on. Some deserted. Some looted. Some hid. Others died of exhaustion. An officer of the Royal Fusiliers recalled a private from Hackney, "a most extraordinarily ugly little man in my company who could not march one bit . . . On the second day of the Retreat he collapsed at the side of the road and died in my arms. I have no record of his name, but as a feat of endurance and courage I cannot name his equal."

A general noted sternly that a "good many cases of unnecessary straggling and looting have taken place," and summary courts-martial were held. Some could not resist the lure of an empty home, as a hiding place or source of plunder, and hunger saw soldiers pulling chocolate from the pockets of dead men or chewing raw roots scrabbled out of a field. In Saint-Quentin, two senior British officers looked on their beaten men and agreed with the petrified city mayor that surrender would be preferable to a losing fight and the probable death of countless civilians in the crossfire. It was a most humane decision, for which both officers were cashiered and disgraced.

Later, the retreat would be rendered into history as a courageous action that had held up the Germans for long enough to scupper Field Marshal Schlieffen's plan, ensuring that the advance would finally be stopped on the line of the River Marne. But to those who took part in it, the retreat was a grim shambles, just a few shades short of a rout, "a perfect débâcle." The BEF had been severely wounded. (Most of the rest of the body would be hacked up at Ypres, a few months later.) Of the eighty thousand British men who had come to France to fight a short war, twenty thousand were killed, wounded, captured, or found to be missing on the long retreat from Mons.

In the wake of the limping army, like the detritus from some huge and bloody travelling fair, lay packs, greatcoats, limbs, canteens, makeshift graves, dead horses, and living men. In woods, ditches, homes, and haylofts, alone and in small bands, surviving shreds of the khaki army felt the battle roll over them, and then heard it rumble south. The advancing German troops were thorough in flushing out the enemy remnants: Walter Bloem, novelist, drama critic, and a captain in the Brandenburg Grenadiers, recalled how advancing German hussars, rightly suspecting that British soldiers were hiding among the newly cut corn, "did not trouble to ransack every stook, but simply found that by galloping in threes or fours through a field shouting, and with lowered lances spiking a stook here and there, anyone hiding in them anywhere in the field surrendered."

The war correspondents of the *Daily Mail* and *The Times* observed the drooping tail of the retreat: "We saw no organised bodies of troops, but we met and talked to many fugitives in twos and threes, who had lost their units in disorderly retreat and for the most part had no idea where they were."

Some of the more resourceful residue contrived to fight, wriggle, or wrench their way out. A band of Irishmen made it to Boulogne, and at one point stragglers headed west in such numbers that German intelligence was briefly confused into believing that the British army was making for the coastal ports. Bernard Montgomery and a small group of lost men from various regiments marched for three days between the marauding advance guard of German cavalry and the main infantry body. Montgomery finally outflanked the advance, linked up with the rest of the army, and went on to become Field Marshal Montgomery of Alamein.

The Expeditionary Force was a regular army, an army of professionals very different from Kitchener's volunteer force that would come later. Here were recruits from the industrial slums of the north, illiterate farm boys, some "scallywags and minor adventurers," men who were escaping trouble, and a few who were looking for it, but, unlike the conscript armies of Europe, they were well trained: some had fought in the Boer War, and most were "adepts in musketry, night operations and habits of concealment, matters about which the other belligerents had scarcely troubled." For many who found themselves lost in what was now enemy territory, concealment was the first instinct. When the army finally caught its breath, about-faced, and fought its way north again, sceptical commanders were not always easily persuaded that the men who emerged from barns and bushes were genuine stragglers rather than deserters. "It was the coward's chance," thought one war correspondent. "Was it any wonder that some of these young men who had laughed on the way to Waterloo station, and held their heads high in the admiring gaze of London crowds, sure of their own heroism, slunk now into the backyards of French farmhouses, hid behind hedges when men in khaki passed, and told wild, incoherent tales when cornered at last by some cold-eyed officer in some town of France to which they had blundered?"

Those who never reappeared were duly recorded in the regimental files. A few months later, once the full-blown trench war of stasis was under way, their families received a letter, no different from the hundreds of thousands to follow, communicating the news, with official sadness, that a husband, son, or brother was missing. And that, as far as the British army was concerned, was that.

Yet there were some who were neither dead nor captive; war had threshed through the fields of northern France, crushing homes and lives, military and civilian, and blowing human chaff into every corner of the landscape.

At dawn on August 26, 1914, Robert Digby and the other men of the Hampshire Regiment trained their rifles across the clover and beet fields north of the small town of Haucourt, and waited for the Germans. The battle of Le Cateau began, for Private No. 9368, as a distant rolling thunder, and as the day brightened the sound of shelling grew steadily louder. In the darkness of the night before battle, an officer had read aloud passages from Sir Walter Scott's poem *Marmion*, a thumping epic with all the appropriate, granite-hewn sentiments.

Where shall the traitor rest,
He, the deceiver,
Who could win maiden's breast,
Ruin, and leave her?
In the lost battle,
Borne down by the flying,
Where mingles war's rattle
With groans of the dying.

And when the mountain sound I heard
Which bids us be for storm prepar'd
The distant rustling of his wings,
As up his force the tempest brings.

At nine in the morning, the attack finally began, and the officers of the Hampshire Regiment had "the pleasure of seeing Germans coming forward in large masses." Under cover, a handful of Germans crept up to the Hampshires' position and shouted "Retreat!" in English. It was all still a public-school game. British snipers tried to pick off the machine-gun crews and officers, distinguishable by their swords. Heavy fire was exchanged, and then, inexplicably, the guns on both sides fell quiet. "The stillness was remarkable; even the birds were silent, as if overawed." Just as suddenly, the battle resumed with deafening violence. Grey troops rushed across the clover, and it was "as if every gun and rifle in the German army had opened fire." Too late, the order was given for the Hampshires to withdraw. Seizing rifle and pack, Digby joined the throng fleeing down the narrow lanes. As dusk gathered, the chaos spread. "We marvellously escaped annihilation," Private Frank Pattenden wrote in his diary. "It was nearly wholesale rout and slaughter." Lurching south, the regiment began to dissolve, mixing with other fragments of the disintegrating rump of the British army. At nightfall, a small contingent of three hundred Hampshires briefly held on in the village of Ligny, but then fell back once more, leaving behind dozens of injured men in a temporary dressing station. The walking wounded made their way into the woods, and the remainder waited in the darkness.

The Hampshires tramped on through the night across fields. Two hours' sleep was snatched beneath a hedgerow. In the morning they stumbled into the village of Villers-Outréaux, where a German battery awaited them, having leapfrogged the retreating British in the dark. It opened up when the men were a hundred yards away. A force of fifty men under Colonel Jackson was left to provide cover, and fought dismounted German cavalry and cyclists with rifle and bayonet, as the main body of troops again scrambled away. Jackson was shot in the legs and carried into the home of the local *curé*, where he was captured a few hours later. Private Pattenden, trudging south on bleeding feet, noted the gaps in the ranks and the many missing men: "I am too full for words or speech and feel paralysed as this affair is now turning into a horrible slaughter . . . My God it is heart breaking . . . We have no good officers left, our NCOs are useless as women, our nerves are all shattered and we don't know what the end will be. Death is on every side."

The tall figure of Private Robert Digby was last seen by his comrades clutching a bloodied arm in the temporary dressing station in Ligny. A German bullet had passed through his left forearm, narrowly missing the bone, the sort of debilitating but survivable "Blighty wound," serious enough to warrant a passage home to the land they called Blighty, that men would later long for in the trenches.

When Digby re-emerged from the surgeon's tent, his arm hastily bandaged and held in a rough sling, he was no longer part of a moving mass of men, but alone. I "lost my army," he would later observe ruefully. He had also lost his Lee Enfield rifle, his bayonet, 120 rounds of ammunition, his peaked cap, his knapsack, and his bearings.

Captain Williams, the surgeon of the Hampshire Regiment, was still tending the wounded when the Germans stormed into Ligny. But by then Digby had taken solitary flight. A final, brief, and unemotional entry in British military records concludes his official contribution to World War I: "Private Robert Digby, Wounded: 26th August, 1914."

The previous day, William Thorpe, a tubby and genial soldier of the King's Own Lancaster Regiment, had been sitting down to breakfast in the corn stubble above Haucourt when his war started. Thorpe and the other men were tired, having marched for three days to meet the advancing German forces, but their spirits were high. "The weather was perfect," noted one of Willie's officers, and even the spectacle of Belgian refugees fleeing south, as "dense as the crowd from a race meeting but absolutely silent," had not much dampened the mood as the King's Own marched from the railhead. The soldiers whooped at a reconnaissance plane flying overhead, which came under ragged fire from somewhere in the rear, although Captain Higgins declared the aircraft to be British.

Lieutenant Colonel Dykes had led the column of 26 officers and 974 other ranks past a tiny church north of Haucourt, down a gentle slope to a little stream, and then up a steep hill to a plateau, on the extreme right of the British line, before he gave the order to rest. "A full 7 to 10 minutes was spent admonishing the troops when it was found that some had piled their weapons out of alignment." The time might have been better spent looking at the horizon. An hour earlier, the troops had been "greatly reassured," although amazed, by the spectacle of a French cavalry unit, clad in their remarkable plumes, breastplates, and helmets: handsome and conspicuous imperial anachronisms. Since the French advance guard was supposed to be out ahead of the British troops, an officer declared that the enemy "could not possibly worry us for at least three hours." This was, therefore, an excellent moment to eat breakfast. As they waited for the mess cart to arrive, the officers observed another group of uniformed horsemen some five hundred yards away, which paused to watch the relaxing troops before trotting away. One of the younger officers quietly suggested that the cavalrymen might not be French, and was sharply told "not to talk nonsense." The men were lounging and talking in groups in the quiet cornfield; the sun was growing warm when the mess cart finally rumbled up. Atop the wagon perched the regimental mascot, a small white fox terrier clad in a patriotic Union Jack coat, which had been adopted before leaving Southampton. "New life came to the men," who leapt to their feet, mess tins at the ready.

At that moment the German Maxim guns opened fire. Colonel Dykes was killed in the first burst, shot daintily through the eye, his groom making "a valiant attempt to hold his horse until it also was killed." "Some tried to reach the valley behind," but the older and cannier soldiers lay flat on their faces and hugged the earth, as the bullets flicked the tops of the cut cornstalks. "Of those who got up, most were hit." After two minutes of uninterrupted firing, the German gunners paused to reload and the survivors scrambled for cover below the crest of the hill. For the next five hours, what remained of the unit was pounded with shells. Through field glasses, the future Field Marshal Montgomery observed the "terrible sight" and then followed orders to try to help the trapped Lancasters. "There was no reconnaissance, no plan, no covering fire. We rushed up the hill." With predictable results. This was "terrible work as we had to advance through a hail of bullets from rifles and machine-guns and through a perfect storm of shrapnel fire. Our men . . . were knocked down like ninepins."

Many of the wounded were too badly injured to be moved, and by late afternoon, when the order came to fall back, the King's Own Lancasters had been ripped to shreds, dispersed like leaves in a hurricane. The Haucourt church was packed with bleeding and dying men, while dazed pockets of survivors, separated in the panic, wandered in search of their commanding officers and orders. A day that had started in perfect calm ended in utter confusion, as the remains of the King's Own joined the great retreat. "There was nothing to do for it but to leave the wounded and hope that any stragglers would rejoin," one officer said. When the battalion was finally able to draw breath, the losses seemed barely believable: 14 officers and 431 other ranks killed, wounded, or missing, along with the mess cart, commanding officer, two machine guns, and the fox terrier. (The distraught driver of the mess wagon was found to be carrying the dead dog under his shirt the next day, and was sharply ordered to bury it.) In three hours of battle, the King's Own Lancaster Regiment had lost half its strength and much of its morale. It had also lost Private William Thorpe.

David Martin, Thomas Donohoe, and the rest of the Royal Irish Fusiliers had arrived in France in typically jovial fashion, "singing and cheering and chanting the regiment's motto, *Faugh-a-Ballagh*, 'Clear the Way.'" The local French civilians found the Irishmen intriguingly odd, and the curiosity was mutual. During a reconnoitre to the east, one officer from the Irish regiment was taken prisoner by an overenthusiastic French commander who evidently suspected that he had come across a German spy posing as an Allied soldier. He also seems to have had some peculiar notions about the distinguishing anatomical features of a British officer, for he told his astonished captive: "Although I am sure you are what you say you are, still these are unusual times and perhaps you would not mind undressing, and giving me some proof that you are English." The officer huffily refused to demonstrate his nationality thus, and unfortunately we will never know what the Frenchman hoped to find that would have convinced him.

Like the King's Own Lancaster and the Hampshire Regiment, the Irish Fusiliers were positioned close to Haucourt, just south of the village, and by mid-morning on August 27, the regiment was locked in a ferocious artillery duel. "Outnumbered and outranged," the Irish troops fell back shortly before nightfall, and by the early hours of the next day, the battalion, one of the last regiments to quit the position, was in headlong retreat, but still displaying a jollity that astonished the regimental interpreter: "I do not understand you Irish," he said. "We Frenchmen are glad when we go forward but sad when we come back; you Irish are always the same, you always laugh and all you want is bully beef."

The laughter swiftly subsided as the withdrawal turned into a continuous forced march, often under attack from the rear. The day grew hot and humid, but there was no pause. Slogging along grimly, "as if in a trance," the men stripped off their packs and threw them by the roadside. As the twenty-fourth hour of nonstop marching approached, some were left "with only the remains of boots." Others collapsed, "physically unable to march further without rest," but there was no time to wait for them to recover, nor the means to move them. The brigade commander pressed on, noting, "To our rear the lurid glare of burning farms and haystacks shed a fitful light on the scene." On the evening of August 28, the exhausted Irish troops crossed the Somme River, just before the bridge was blown up, and rejoined the British rear-guard. When the muster roll was called, 136 men and officers were found to be missing, including Privates Thomas Donohoe and David Martin.

CHAPTER TWO

Villeret, 1914

❧

To the south of the cornfield-battlefields where the baptismal blood of the Western Front began to soak into the land, lay Villeret, a small village of simple brick houses with roofs of slate, tile, and thatch, tucked into the folds of the Picardy countryside. A wanderer stumbling upon Villeret by chance in 1914—and few strangers ever came through save by accident, since Villeret was not on the way to anywhere—might have paused to take in the picturesque view from the hill above the village, for, as one traveller observed, "nature is beautiful around Villeret, and the poet or painter might stop here to depict the scene, one in the harmonious language of verse, the other by fixing the scene on his canvas." The wayfarer might have stopped for a restorative drink, perhaps a glass of *genièvre*, the ferocious local gin, in the café on the corner: an establishment called Aux Deux Entêtés, the two hard-heads, with a sign showing two asses pulling stubbornly in opposite directions. Or he might have halted to observe the modest tombs in the undistinguished church, or to admire the well-kept rose garden in front of the girls' school, the pride of the young schoolmistress, Antoinette Foulon. He might have inquired what great personage lived in the ornate, still-new château on the hill. But since he would most likely have been lost, he would probably have tarried just long enough to obtain directions before hurrying on to the larger settlement of Hargicourt, just across the valley, or to the ruined fortress at Le Câtelet, the most important town in the canton, five miles to the north on the road between Cambrai and Saint-Quentin.

Villeret moved to a rhythm and pattern as immutable and familiar as the motifs in the cloth woven down the centuries by its villagers. Here Léon Lelong baked his bread to a recipe bequeathed by the ancients, women in wooden clogs drew water from a pump in the cobbled square, and looms rattled in every cellar, reaching a crescendo at dusk and then slowly fading into the night, the steady clanking heartbeat of a Picardy village.

That August, on its homely surface, Villeret appeared to be following its regular ambling course, as contented as the pig lounging in the shade of butcher Cardon's house. But a glance inside the door of the *mairie*, a grand two-story structure with the unmistakable pomposity of most French municipal architecture, might have offered a rather different impression, for in the summer of 1914 Villeret was on a war footing, and its elders were in a state of unprecedented anxiety. Of the approaching German army, and the carnage it had already wrought, Villeret knew almost nothing. Yet the war had already knocked the plodding pace of village life out of kilter, and Camille "Parfait" Marié, the acting mayor of Villeret, was having to put his mind to a problem not encountered by the village since the Prussians had marched into northern France forty-four years previously: with so many men already summoned into uniform, there would be barely enough hands to bring in the harvest, which was late this year as it was. (At the same moment, across the Channel, the populace was equally piqued at the way conflict in Europe was intruding on normal existence. On August 4, the *Catford Journal* reported: "What with the war and the rain, last Saturday was a most depressing day for the Catford Cricket Club.")

War had officially begun in Villeret at exactly five o'clock in the afternoon on the first of August, when the *garde champêtre* or municipal policeman from Le Câtelet marched portentously up rue d'En-Bas, clanging his bell to announce mobilisation. Some of the boys had been so anxious to get into battle they had dropped their tools in the fields. In a few hours of hasty farewells, the village population of roughly six hundred had shrunk by more than a third. Even the mayor, Edouard Séverin, rushed off to war, leaving his deputy in charge. Suddenly thrust into a position of uninvited responsibility, Marié, a charcoal-maker with drooping moustaches, thick spectacles, and a permanently unhappy mien, was finding the weight of office burdensome. The acting mayor was universally known as Parfait, which happened to be his middle name, but which also reflected his cast of mind: he was a perfectionist, albeit a constantly frustrated one, and missives from the *préfecture* at Saint-Quentin had begun arriving on his desk in swift and baffling succession.

On August 5, the *sous-préfet* demanded: "How many workers are needed to bring in the harvest? Please reply as soon as possible and before midday tomorrow." Then someone calling himself the "President of the Food Commission" wanted to know exactly how much wheat, dry and ground, was immediately available. Next, with powerful oddness, it was decreed that all street advertising for Bouillon Kub, a variety of powdered broth, should be torn down. German spies were suspected of leaving a trail of messages on such hoardings for the use of advancing troops, but since Marié could not possibly have known this, the request must have seemed, to say the least, eccentric.

A little over a week later, another impossible order landed on Marié's desk—"Extend help to all needy English, Belgian, Russian, or Serb families."

There were no such families in Villeret, for, even by the standards of rural northern France, the community was an isolated and self-contained one. The inhabitants of Hargicourt, just one-quarter of a mile away, were considered "foreigners" by the Villeret folk, and regarded with abiding distrust. In turn, the people of Villeret were often dismissed by neighbouring communities as a collection of "gypsies," backward peasants who kept to themselves. There was a local saying: "The rich folk of Hargicourt, the clever folk of Nauroy, and the savages of Villeret." Like that of many villages in Picardy, the social structure of Villeret was founded on an interrelated network of clans, families linked by blood, marriage, and feuds. For as long as anyone could remember, Villeret had been home to the Mariés, the Cornailles, the Morels, the Dessennes, the Foulons, and the Lelongs—united by a common distrust of the world beyond the village boundary. Few Villeret villagers spent much time in Hargicourt or Le Câtelet, and only rarely would they travel the eight miles to the market town of Saint-Quentin, for the rest of France was a fickle place, important as a market for beets, wheat, and brightly coloured cloth, but otherwise to be avoided. Villeret was not unique in this philosophy. One of the region's historians described his fellow Picards as "frank and united, rarely keen to leave their land, living on little, sincere, loyal, free, brusque, attached to their opinions, firm in their resolution." An old Picardy saying aptly captures the Villeret attitude, lying somewhere between selfishness and self-reliance: *"Chacun s'n pen, chacun s'n erin"* (*Chacun à son pain, chacun à son hareng*), each has his own bread, each his own herring. In other words, mind your own business. Many of Villeret's inhabitants had multiple businesses: weaving, seasonal farming, occasional manual labour, perhaps a little tobacco-dealing or a café on the side. Alphonse Morelle, for example, called himself a weaver by trade, but explained, "Before the war I had a café and sold some tobacco, but in between times, at home, I did some weaving, and in the summer I hoed the beets and helped with the harvest."

Some of the Villeret men worked in the Templeux-le-Guérard phosphate mine, beyond Hargicourt, and although this brought in extra money, it coincidentally tended to compound the village reputation for antisocial behaviour. Inhaled phosphate dust had left many mine-workers with damaged lungs, which were often treated only with copious quantities of *blanche*, a white liqueur similar to absinthe. The drink dulled the pain but, like absinthe, it also destroyed the mind, and there were at least forty people in Villeret with brain damage resulting from addiction to this poisonous brew. The village contained no fewer than thirty "cafés" in 1914. Some of these were little more than cellars with a single barrel; others were almost luxurious. The Aux Deux Entêtés offered a billiards table, wind-up gramophone with sixty records, and an archery gallery, as well as a multitude of different drinks, from fine champagne to the throat-roasting *genièvre*.

Outsiders, particularly those with claims to cultural sophistication, were inclined to see the village as a rustic throwback. A new schoolteacher, Monsieur Duchange, had arrived in 1907 to find what he called a "thoroughly mediocre intellectual and moral standard," a community populated by thieves and drunks, riven by internal bickering, and run by a mayor who was corrupt, oppressive, and violent. Duchange left after three years, declaring he "would not want to stay a moment longer in such a place." What the scandalised schoolteacher failed to appreciate was the other side of the Villeret character: a streak of hardy independence that could easily be taken for ignorant belligerence, until it was on your side. Villeret was an easy place to miss, an easy place to disdain, but as the Kaiser was about to discover, it was not an easy place to subdue.

As the armies massed, the first gusts of fear, gossip, information, and disinformation began to blow through the region, reaching even the isolated enclave of Villeret. Rumour insisted that German spies were in the area, posing as Swiss mechanics repairing the looms. Two optimistic volunteers with a single gun and two cartridges set up a guard post on the road into Le Câtelet, and hung a chain across the road to hold back the German army. Some of the better-informed inhabitants made preparations to leave.

On August 16, four days after the first troops of the BEF crossed the English Channel, the locals had their first glimpse of an Englishman in uniform, an affable fellow on a motorcycle. With the schoolmistress of Le Câtelet translating, he managed to explain that he had been following an air squadron and was trying to get to Brussels. The villagers pointed to the north. Before heading off, the jovial motorcyclist surveyed the rolling fields, as if he were a carefree tourist and not the harbinger of a war that would turn the land to charnel-mud. His words were carefully recorded: "Oh, France, beautifully."

German troops marched into Brussels four days later, but a week went by before another English soldier appeared in Villeret, this time demanding the whereabouts of the largest shop. He was duly directed to the establishment of Alexis Morel, who was a part-time grocer, haberdasher, café proprietor, liquor salesman, and sometime chairman of Villeret's archery club. He also sold bread. The soldier instructed Morel to supply every loaf he had in stock to feed the advancing British army, and to prepare another batch for the following day. Morel complied without demur, but assiduously noted the cost of the requisitioned bread: "295 francs."

It would be more than six years before Morel saw a crumb of reimbursement, for it swiftly became apparent that the British army, fuelled on his bread, was no longer advancing, but retreating. The first sign of the calamity was the spectacle of Belgian refugees, initially a trickle, but soon a torrent, trudging into Le Câtelet, heading south. "They had the unspeakable in their eyes; they carried their belongings and their gestures were despairing." The guns were now clearly audible. Achille Poëtte, the cadaverous, indefatigable postman of Villeret and chief local gossip, suddenly found himself unemployed when the postal service was abruptly terminated. That evening, an exhausted squadron of French cavalry passed through Le Câtelet, their stumbling mounts, drawn faces, and evident lack of *élan* offering the first clear sign that victory had not materialised. The officer gamely insisted the retreat was merely strategic, a prelude to the flanking movement that would drive the Germans back. The people chose to believe him and when a passing refugee claimed that Walincourt, ten miles north, was already occupied, he was threatened with jail for spreading alarming news. But then came incontrovertible proof: long lines of horse-drawn ambulances carrying the British wounded, and behind them columns of soldiers, their faces pallid from fatigue and fear. Ninety-five injured soldiers were treated at the makeshift hospital set up in Mademoiselle Fournier d'Alincourt's château at Le Câtelet, while the baker's ovens churned out extra loaves for the retreating men.

In her diary, the schoolteacher who had helped the lone English motorcyclist watched the British in retreat: "They had only one desire, to go faster, ever faster, to escape the enemy who, their desperate gestures seemed to say, was snapping at their heels." Cavalrymen slept slumped in their saddles, and infantrymen collapsed in the Le Câtelet square and slept as they fell. Now the civilian exodus began. From Hargicourt some three hundred people headed south, on foot or in wagons, and others began to seep out of Le Câtelet. "It is very sad to see the poor villagers flying south as we retire," wrote one British officer. "Those who, as we came north a fortnight ago, looked on us as their deliverers, are now thinking we are broken reeds. They are crying and asking us to save them and their homes . . . A ghastly business. Poor creatures."

Out-of-the-way Villeret did not witness the British retreat, but the tales of what was happening in Le Câtelet, spread graphically by Poëtte, set the exodus in motion. Cardon loaded up his horse and cart with his possessions and family, and it creaked off down the road to Saint-Quentin, watched by the rest of the population, and the anxious butcher himself. A handful of others trickled away in the ensuing hours, but most chose to stay. The tales of German atrocities were only rumour, after all.

From the top of his monumental château on the hill above Villeret, monumental François Theillier trained his telescope to the north and saw rumour made fact. A thick column of smoke, invisible to those in the valley, was rising from the town of Caudry, just twenty miles to the northeast. Theillier was the nearest thing in Villeret to a feudal lord: many of the villagers worked his land, he owned an automobile with a radio in it, and he was so much wealthier than anyone else for miles around that a man who had won at cards or sold his crop well was said to be "as rich as a Theillier." The family fortune had been dug from the mines of Anzin, and François's father, Colonel Edouard Theillier, had naturally set about building himself a château commensurate with the family's social standing. Completed in the 1880s in a style intended to echo that of the early seventeenth century, the Château de Grand Priel dominated the skyline, a statement of unlimited cash and limited taste, boasting pink granite columns, lordly turrets, and exactly ninety-nine windows, since one more would have meant a higher rate of tax. The colonel's wife, in the great tradition of the châtelaine, dabbled in the most fashionable forms of agriculture, installing her prize herd of Swiss cattle in stalls adorned with "polished brass balls." A semaphore relay manned by retainers was set up on the roads leading up to the château, as a sort of primitive traffic-light system to ensure that when any member of the Theillier family wished to be on the road nobody else was in the way. The old colonel had died in 1900, leaving one son, Pierre, to manage the estate, and the other, François, to indulge his twin passions of hunting and food. The only occupation François Theillier liked more than killing animals was eating them. Large concrete drinking troughs were imported from Paris and placed at strategic points around the château to lure deer, wild boar, and other game within range of Theillier's guns. Rabbits were left to breed unmolested to produce a sufficient supply for the master's bag, even though they chewed the Theillier fields to shreds. Bred pheasants were added to the wild partridges that furnished his groaning table, and imported snails from Burgundy were farmed in vast cages, fattened to the correct size and succulence by an estate employee whose sole task was the provision of limitless gastropods for the gastronome.

François Theillier was, inevitably, enormous. Even as a child, he had been portly, and the locals joked (in an undertone) of the measures taken to try to combat his ballooning bulk: his parents were said to dangle rattles out of his reach, just to try to make him move, and the colonel was rumoured to have locked the teenage glutton in the cowshed to keep him out of the pantry, whereupon he was said to have eaten the cattle fodder. By the outbreak of war, Theillier had reached his full, majestic corpulence, with a weight variously estimated at somewhere between 28 and 37 stone, or 390 and 500 pounds. "He had to sit on three chairs side by side," it was said, and while out hunting he was pulled in a large cart with a revolving seat on top and a loader stationed behind, thus enabling François to slaughter the local fauna in droves while expending a minimal amount of energy. The landowner's preferred method was to hunt with a rifle in each hand. "He waited until the birds crossed in flight, and with four cartridges he could kill eight birds." One day, a stranger to Villeret came across François Theillier asleep under a tree at the gates to his château. The man did not stop running until he was safely back in the village. "I've just seen God the Father," he reported.

For such an immense man, Theillier could move fast, and what he now saw from the château roof sent him bounding into his car, whose doors had been widened to admit him. The chauffeur was instructed to drive to Saint-Quentin as quickly as possible. The local seigneur did not trouble to stop and warn the people of Villeret about what was so dramatically bearing down on them from the horizon.

Field Marshal Sir John French, the commander of the British Expeditionary Force, had made his headquarters in Theillier's grand house on rue Antoine Lécuyer, where a Swiss chef was the only staff member remaining. French arrived there just a few hours before Theillier, having been rousted out of his bath in Nauroy Château before his dinner, to be told that the Germans were at Estrées, just over a mile away. Theillier knocked on his own door, and informed the Scottish guardsman who opened it that he had important information for the field marshal, only to be told that the British commander-in-chief was packing and preparing to leave Saint-Quentin. Twenty minutes later, French and his staff had gone, heading south with the rest of the BEF. Wandering into his dining room, Theillier found a package of papers "bearing the inscription 'Secret Service' . . . Then, moving on to the kitchen, he noticed a large pot full of freshly chopped leeks for the dinner of the field marshal, who once again had been forced to miss his meal. The chef had a sour expression on his face."

The secret-service papers would eventually find their way back into the hands of British intelligence; the fate of the leeks, given Theillier's fabled appetite, is less mysterious. Having finished a supper intended, literally, for an army, Theillier heaved himself back into his car and followed the exodus south. He would never see his château again.

The evening that Theillier motored away into comfortable exile in Paris, the first squad of German cavalry, the very tip of the enemy's advance guard, entered Hargicourt, in pursuit of English stragglers. Not recognising the German uniforms and believing he was welcoming English hussars, the mayor came out to offer the horsemen champagne. But the patrol of eight German dragoons led by a lieutenant did not stop, for they had spotted two men in khaki uniforms struggling on foot up the slope to Villeret. One of these was John Sligo, a thirty-year-old Welshman from the Rhondda Valley. His regiment, the Somerset Light Infantry, had come under heavy fire at Ligny, and in the retreat, Sligo, like many others, had been wounded and left behind. The other man was Robert Digby.

In the three days since he had become separated from the Hampshire Regiment, Digby had wandered along empty country roads, moving at night and hiding by day. At the village of Gouy, which adjoins Le Câtelet, he had sought the help of the local priest, the Abbé Morelle, who rebandaged his arm. There he found Sligo, who had also been tended by the priest, and the two fugitives had trudged on together. They rested a few hours in "an abandoned factory," before setting out again. Dusk was gathering as Digby entered Villeret for the first time.

The German dragoons spurred their horses. Hearing the clatter of hooves and turning to see the German patrol less than half a mile behind them, the Englishmen ran. Through the town square, past the town hall and the butcher's, they ducked right, out into the open again, sprinting towards a dense copse some two hundred yards from the edge of the village. Seconds later, the German dragoons entered Villeret at a gallop, revolvers drawn. Digby was younger than Sligo and a keen rugby player. The Welshman may also have been more seriously wounded, for Digby reached the woods well ahead of his companion and plunged into the thick undergrowth, just as the leading horseman caught up with Sligo, and shot him dead.

The wood was impenetrable on horseback and night was closing in. The German dragoons paused briefly at the edge of the copse to peer into the vegetation before they "swung around in the direction they had come" and trotted away. As one villager later remarked: "It was the last pointed helmet we would see for some time." When it was quite dark, a handful of village men warily emerged from their homes and retrieved the body of the dead soldier from beside the place they called "Les Peupliers de la Haute-Bruyère" (The Poplars on the High Heath), a romantic name for a grim little death-scene. Parfait Marié filled out his first death certificate, copying the Welshman's strange-sounding name from his identity tags in immaculate curling script. That night, John Archibald Sligo was buried in an unmarked grave, the first foreign resident of Villeret's tiny graveyard.

Robert Digby was not the only fugitive in the woods around Villeret that night. Over in the forest below the Château de Grand Priel, where François Theillier was wont to carry out his daily depredations on the local wildlife, Arthur-Daniel Bastien, a dashing young *maréchal des logis*, or sergeant in the French cavalry, was perched glumly on a log, still wearing his magnificent crested helmet with horsehair plume, *cuirasse*, and spurs, and wondering why he had been ordered into a twentieth-century battle with equipment and tactics designed for the Napoleonic era. Bastien had been trained, as he put it, in "hand-to-hand combat with a sabre handled at full gallop, a long lance for charging the enemy, a carbine with three cartridges, and, for noncommissioned officers, a revolver." He believed he had been "sent to war with methods practically the same as those employed under the Second Empire," and, like every French cavalryman "schooled in the arts of war on horseback," he had considered it his patriotic duty to charge the German army with drawn sabre at the first opportunity and drive it out of France and Belgium. Only the first part of Bastien's plan had come to pass. Unlike the French, German cavalry units were usually accompanied by infantry with machine guns, and though the breastplate looked wonderful on parade, it was visible from miles away. And it was not bulletproof.

On August 27, Bastien's 9th Regiment of Dragoons, part of General Sordet's cavalry corps, had found itself at Péronne, about ten miles due west of Villeret, on what would soon be the line of the Western Front, attempting to protect the left flank of the British force against the advancing Germans, and getting utterly disorientated in the process. "With the Germans on our heels, and constant contact between our patrols and those of the enemy, to physical exhaustion was added the permanent nervous tension of knowing the enemy was right behind us," recalled Bastien. Reaching the crest of a hill east of Péronne, Bastien and his troop realised that they had strayed into the very midst of the enemy army: the infantry division directly ahead was composed not of retreating British soldiers, as they had blithely assumed, but of advancing Germans. Here was an opportunity to display the *élan* around which French military leaders had built an entire philosophy. Years of training obscured any vestige of common sense, and the commanding officer, one Captain de la Baume, did not hesitate. The cavalry troop must fight its way back to the rest of the French army, he ordered, and "charge, without hesitation, anyone who got in the way."

"The dragoons made a beautiful sight as we advanced across the plain, helmets on, plumes blowing in the breeze, blue-black jackets, and red trousers, arms glinting in the sun." The German machine-gunners had plenty of time to line up their sights. "The lieutenant ordered the charge. Lances were lowered, the riders leaned forward and spurred into full gallop." Bastien's troop broke through eight successive lines of German infantry, pausing before each fresh charge.

Here was heroism, but here, too, was mounted suicide in full-dress costume. "The infantry scattered before us every time, but their fire decimated the squadron and the bullets whistled around my ears," wrote Bastien, who was positioned at the extreme right of the rapidly thinning line of horsemen. Suddenly Bastien found himself galloping down a steep incline which brought him onto a road. No more than twenty feet away was a stationary German convoy. Bastien lowered his lance and charged once again. "The convoy of soldiers was kneeling and firing, and I could hear the bullets wailing around me. Thanks to God and the speed of my mount, neither I nor my horse was hit. No German cavalryman dared to confront me, and the last bullets came from behind me. The countryside ahead was empty, but the rest of the squadron had gone."

Bastien was one of the few survivors of one of the last great cavalry charges in history. In less than an hour, the 1st Squadron of the 9th Dragoons had been all but wiped out.

Still looking for someone to skewer, Bastien galloped on for a mile, his "nerves at full stretch." Then, when the adrenalin had subsided, the Frenchman hid in a small wood, which happened to belong to François Theillier, and wondered what to do next. "Having thanked Providence, I tied up my sweat-soaked mount and checked I was not being followed. The wood seemed to be empty of people, with a château on one side, and on the other a forester's cottage which appeared to be unoccupied." Bastien broke in through a window, took what food he could find, and left an apologetic note to the owner for this "forced loan."

"As night fell, I stretched out in the ferns, beside my horse. My sleep was agitated, the night was cold, and I woke up time and again, my teeth chattering. The next morning, I tried to analyse the situation calmly." After pondering long and hard, Bastien concluded that his best option was to head south and try to catch up with the retreating French or British armies. "The Germans don't take isolated prisoners," he reflected, wrongly. "They execute, on the spot, any straggling soldiers they catch . . . I decided to keep my weapons and fight to the death, if necessary." Returning to the forester's house, he raided the rabbit hutches behind the building and dined on "raw rabbit for the first time," declaring it to be "quite acceptable for a starving man." While Bastien was chewing his *lapin tartare,* he caught sight of "three new occupants coming into the wood, who turned out to be three British infantrymen, utterly disoriented."

Willie Thorpe of the Kings Own Lancaster Regiment had linked up with Donohoe and Martin of the Royal Irish Fusiliers, and all three were in an advanced state of distress, mortally scared, and famished. As befits a French cavalry officer, Bastien, who spoke a little English, did not forget his manners and courteously offered to share his unappetising meal: "I gave them a gift of the remains of the rabbit, and pointed out the general direction of the Allied troops." The Frenchman then bid farewell to the British soldiers: "I remounted, lance in hand and revolver in pocket, my sabre clipped to my saddle, and set out in a southwesterly direction."

Four months later, Bastien finally rejoined the French army, after disguising himself as a civilian, walking over a hundred miles to

his home town on the Belgian border, and finally returning to unoccupied France via Holland, Folkestone, and Calais. "I will never
forget those months in 1914, the last great days of the French cavalry," he wrote in his memoirs. Fifty years later, Arthur-Daniel
Bastien still wondered about the fate of the soldiers he had met in
the woods of Château de Grand Priel by the village of Villeret,
where the quarry bred for a rich man's sport had now been joined
by human game.

CHAPTER THREE

Born to the Smell of Gunpowder

Villeret sits on a small plateau at the edge of the European flatlands where English, French, Austrian, Spanish, Prussian, and Russian armies have marched and fought for centuries. Memories of warfare run through the land like the rivers and thick chalk seams. To the north of the village flows the River Cologne, to the south is the Omignon, and to the east the Saint-Quentin canal, fed by the River Escaut, all tributaries of the great Somme. Long before that name became a synonym for slaughter, war was part of the very earth. The village young were weaned on tales of the brutal Russian soldiers, the dreaded Tartars and Kalmucks, who marched in after the Battle of Waterloo, and the older folk remembered well the Prussian siege and occupation of Saint-Quentin in 1870; the painter Henri Matisse, a boy growing up in the nearby weaving town of Bohain, was fourteen months old when the occupation of his home came to an end, but at every meal his mother bitterly recalled how an invading soldiery had gorged itself on France: "Here's another one the Germans won't lay their hands on." The schoolchildren of the region sang the songs of war:

> Children of a frontier town,
> Born to the smell of gunpowder.

Villeret: the very name was the legacy of a Roman invader. For this was the spot chosen as the site for his summer villa by some unnamed but "powerful personage" from the Roman camp at nearby Cologna: his villa became Villaris in the tenth century, Villarel by the thirteenth, and finally Villeret. Le Câtelet had once marked the northern frontier of France, and here François I built a great fortress starting in 1520, a massive, moated declaration of military muscle in brick and stone, 175 metres long, 27 metres high. The Spanish had laid ferocious siege to the citadel, and Louis XIV finally ordered the fortress abandoned, but the great edifice still stood, the village clustered around its base, its chalky face pockmarked by cannon shot and studded with flint. Beneath the Villeret church, a local archaeologist uncovered the burial place of even earlier warriors, Merovingian damascene plates, belt buckles of steel inlaid with bronze, left by the knights of Clovis and then Charlemagne; a crumbling document in Saint-Quentin attests to the martial piety of "Jean, seigneur de Villeret, son of Evrard of Fonsommes," who dutifully set off for Jerusalem in the year 1193 to slay the infidel in Holy Crusade.

War, invasion, and occupation forged a robustly pessimistic people "rude and rough, scoured by the winds from the North," in the words of one local historian: "The Middle Ages lived on in our midst." Over the years, Villeret had come to look with practiced mistrust on any soldier, friend or foe. In 1576, the village even sent a letter to the French king requesting that he cease to employ foreign mercenaries to defend his realm, since "foreigners, notably the Germans, have come through Picardy in the past, with their wagons and ravenous horses, stealing anything they can find, laying siege to the mansions and forts, raping women and girls, killing gentlemen and others in their own homes."

Villeret, Le Câtelet, and the surrounding villages had seen soldiers come and go before, but nothing to compare with the military Titan that tramped down from the north. The curé of nearby Aubencheul gazed on the massed ranks of German soldiery with a mixture of terror and admiration:

What an unforgettable spectacle! The artillery filed through: light guns, heavy cannon shining and clean, pulled by superb horses bursting with vigour, as fresh as if they had just come from the stables. On and on they came. Infantry buoyed up by their first victory, immune to fatigue. These men were like giants, their dominating stares seemed to penetrate everywhere. They sang, and cried out, *"Nach Paris! Paris dans trois jours!"* Oh, such beautiful men, robust, drunk with pride. We shall never see their like again.

But at the same time, fear coursed through the veins of the land, pumped by stories of German brutality, murder, looting, and arson. The villagers watched the invaders come, and later told tales of horror: In Vendhuile, to the north, Oscar Dupuis stood by as a group of German infantrymen pillaged his home, and then fetched his revolver; he wounded two of the looters before he was shot dead. At Bellicourt, a young British soldier had been discovered hiding in a cellar by rampaging Germans in search of drink; he was tortured, it was said, by being doused in boiling water, then shot, and thrown in the canal. The people of Gouy stared as the columns of German infantry marched through the town, chanting and singing. At Beaurevoir, they shouted *"Où sont les Anglais?"* and "looted every house, drinking wine straight from the bottles and then smashing them in the street."

The body of Pierre Doumoutier, Villeret's carpenter, was brought back to the village the same night, and buried alongside that of John Sligo. Doumoutier had been guarding a bridge at Joncourt as the first enemy patrols came into view, and he had rapidly, and sensibly, concluded that his ancient shotgun was no match for the German army. Attempting to make their way back to Villeret, he and two other villagers had stumbled into a German patrol, which immediately opened fire. Doumoutier was killed, but "the other two managed to escape." Some said the carpenter had been a fool to resist in the first place.

In the German military mentality, the *francs-tireurs* of the Franco-Prussian War, irregular partisans waiting to put their bullets in German backs, were still lurking behind every tree and building. Any hint of armed defiance was to be met with extreme, salutary violence.

Le Câtelet, a key strategic point on the route south to Saint-Quentin and Paris, bore the full brunt of the invasion and, when it attempted resistance, felt the furious metallic lash of *Schrecklichkeit*. On the evening of August 27, the last significant body of British troops moved out of the town, leaving behind a small rear-guard of seven men to try to slow the German advance. These were, by co-incidence, men of the King's Own Lancasters, William Thorpe's regiment, who "sat playing cards in the estaminet, with great sang-froid," and then ranged themselves across the main street as the en-emy cavalry came into view. A small troop of hussars gingerly advanced. "Only two cavalrymen continued to come forward right to the bridge, where they dismounted, about one hundred metres from the six or seven Englishmen, who just watched them, without moving, impassable." The tense stand-off might have continued in-definitely had not a troop of German dragoons burst into view at a canter from the direction of Villeret, unaware that Le Câtelet was still effectively held by the enemy. "The English opened fire and the German officer—an Alsatian aristocrat, we later learned, who was headed for a brilliant career—was shot dead along with his horse di-rectly in front of the presbytery." The other riders dashed for cover, but noticed as they fled that gunfire was coming from another di-rection. In an upper-floor window stood a man in civilian clothes, an abandoned British-army cap jammed on his head, firing as fast as he could at the fleeing Germans. This was Guy Lourdel, the tax of-ficial and town clerk, who had been unable to resist joining the fray. The English soldiers, along with a handful of walking wounded who had been treated by the *curé* Ledieu, now scattered into the surrounding fields, leaving behind some forty men too badly in-jured to move. Half an hour later, the German hussars returned, ac-companied in force by the 66th Infantry Regiment, to flush out the murderous *franc-tireur* and teach Le Câtelet a lesson. "Hundreds of soldiers, unleashed like wild beasts by their officers, ran every-where, brandishing revolvers, shouting, beating down with their ri-fle butts doors that did not open fast enough, ransacking the church and the bell tower in search of English and French soldiers who they claimed were being hidden by the inhabitants."

Joseph Cabaret, the distinguished old schoolteacher, was

dragged into the street by his white goatee and told to identify which perfidious Frenchman had killed the hussar, whose dead horse still lay in the street, abuzz with flies. "Hand over the guilty man or it is death for you and the village goes up in flames." The *curé* Ledieu was struck in the face by an Uhlan, a German cavalry-man. Delabranche, the elderly pharmacist, was dragged away, beaten up, tied to a tree, and then locked in the town cells with his hands "so tightly bound, they bled." Henri Godé, the mild and diminutive deputy mayor of Le Câtelet, was also "arrested" and hog-tied, along with the town notary, Léon Legé. In terror, several villagers took refuge in the undergrowth of the moat surrounding the medieval castle. A bullet retrieved from the body of the cavalry officer was found to be of English manufacture, but the German of-ficer in command continued to insist that even if a Frenchman had not fired the fatal shot this was a measure of incompetence rather than innocence: "Bring us the sniper or else, at 7:00 a.m., you will be shot and this place will be burned to the ground."

Lourdel was a wildly eccentric man, with a patriotism verging on mania and a commitment to his government and country that was excessive even for a tax inspector. At the age of thirteen, he had joined a band of partisans in the Franco-Prussian War, and on the first day of mobilisation he had dispatched his three sons to war. He attempted to join up himself but, at fifty-seven, he had been re-jected as too old.

At dawn, Lourdel presented himself to the German officers now lodged in Mademoiselle d'Alincourt's château, proudly acknowl-edging that he had opened fire on the German troops but also pre-tending to be even more peculiar than he was. "He knew he had to take whatever was coming to him, for the sake of the village, which was in such deadly peril on account of his bravura, but also for the sake of his self-respect," a neighbour later wrote. "He put on a good performance as a blood-thirsty killer, and, standing amid the Ger-mans, as if blind to their presence, he kept shouting, 'Kill the lot of them!' " Lourdel's captors became convinced they were in the pres-ence of a genuine madman, and locked him up instead of killing him.

During the night, a jumpy German sentry had heard a rustling in the bushes around the moat and opened fire, shooting through the throat Madame Lemaire-Liénard, who had hidden there with her husband and daughter. "The German officers, after the death of a woman, began to calm down. They had wanted innocent blood, and they got it."

After twenty-four hours, the invaders finally released the hostages, and the main body of troops moved on. A handful of guards remained behind to keep order as the people of Le Câtelet "cleaned out and disinfected their homes" in the wake of their first, traumatic experience of German occupation. "The body of the horse, which had been covered in religious ornaments by the passing German troops, was dragged away," and so was tax inspector Lourdel, under guard and still raving for German blood, to Reims. That city, and Lourdel, were duly liberated a few weeks later, in the Allied counterattack, and Le Câtelet's eccentric patriot finally succeeded in persuading the French army to allow him to join the ranks. He survived the battles of Verdun and the Somme, was wounded twice, and lived on into old age boasting of how he had resisted the German army single-handed. Lourdel's actions ensured that he never had to submit to living under German occupation, but this was not the moral drawn by the more cautious folk of the region, who years later still referred to Lourdel as "that imbecile who shot at the German hussar and nearly had the lot of us killed." There were other ways to defy the Germans than by shooting at them, they said. The German occupation was only a few hours old, but already some had concluded that accommodation rather than confrontation was the best approach.

The most immediate manifestation of that moral dilemma, which would trouble the occupied people of northern France for the next four years, was the continued presence of scores of British soldiers left behind in the retreat. At Vendhuile, just hours before the Germans arrived, the mayor spotted a group of British soldiers drinking in a bar and could not suppress the suspicion that "they wanted to be caught." In Hargicourt, the deputy mayor reported, an English soldier who had hidden in woods by the road into the village "had the audacity to open fire, as a despairing gesture," when the enemy columns arrived, and then ran to hide in the nearest barn. When German troops began bayonetting the straw, he emerged and surrendered.

Suddenly deprived of orders and a clear line of command, the lost soldiers reacted in different ways. Since the British military command had not anticipated any such eventuality, the rules governing what a soldier should do if trapped behind the lines simply did not exist. Some gave themselves up. Others wandered blindly around the countryside, avoiding every human being and hoping for miraculous deliverance. Some literally went to ground, like Private Patrick Fowler of No. 1 Troop, A Squadron, of the 11th Hussars, who "rode about aimlessly" for several days before abandoning his horse and concealing himself in a wood near Bertry. He would spend the entire winter there, living off whatever he could kill or uproot, as the war continued to the south. Nineteen-year-old David Cruikshank of the 1st Scottish Rifles resorted to transvestitism, with the help of Julie-Célestine Baudhuin, a local woman in Le Cateau, who procured for him a wig and clothes. Cruikshank was fresh-faced enough to pass for a woman, but his Highlander's stride was a giveaway. He solved the problem by tying his ankles together with a short piece of string.

Yet others chose to throw themselves on the mercy and charity of strangers. Some were turned away, but most were hidden in cellars, attics, haylofts, and outhouses.

The earth of the Villeret graveyard was beginning to settle over John Sligo when Florency Dessenne, village mason and professional tobacco-smuggler, opened his back door to find a dishevelled creature on the doorstep, with four days' growth of beard, a bloody bandage around his arm, and surprisingly good French. Holding the hand of the bedraggled British soldier was Florency's seven-year-old daughter, Marthe, who explained that she had found him under a bush while she was out collecting dandelion leaves from the fields by the Hargicourt road.

"My God," said Marie-Thérèse, Florency's pregnant wife, as she joined her husband to gawp at the stranger. "Marthe, what have you brought upon us? This is going to mean trouble."

Robert Digby was swiftly ushered inside, and into the presence of the widow Dessenne, universally known as Marie Coulette, and probably the most formidable being in Villeret. A compact, bullet-eyed woman with a personality as sharp as a hatchet, Marie Coulette was sixty-five years old and the undisputed power in the Dessenne household—or, rather, households, for the family was an extended and chaotic one, occupying two adjacent buildings on rue d'En Bas, with granary and outhouses, and a third single-story brick building on the opposite side of the road. This was Marie Coulette's tiny empire, where she ruled, with extreme vigour and periodic explosions of violence, over three generations of the family: her son Florency and daughter-in-law Marie-Thérèse; her brother Léon Recolet and his wife, Berthe, her daughter-in-law Eugénie (whose husband, Jules, was away at the front); at least eight grandchildren; and a large German-shepherd dog. The smaller members of the tribe took pains to stay as far as possible from Marie Coulette, whose sudden outbursts of affection could be as disconcerting as her temper. "I always tried to avoid being embraced by my grandmother," one of the brood recalled. "She had a moustache, which was very prickly." In the words of another relative: "Marie Coulette was the matriarch, the clan chief, with a temperament to match. Everyone liked her, and everyone was scared of her. She was always willing to lend a hand, but you did what she said. One word from Marie Coulette was enough."

One word was what she now issued, and the exhausted, trembling Englishman was immediately brought inside and seated beside the stove. The grandchildren clustered and stared at the wild-looking figure, while Marie Coulette prepared food and Marie-Thérèse dressed his wound. Florency insisted that the Englishman stay, at least until his injured arm had properly healed, but Digby declined. Restored by the food and warmth, he thanked Marie Coulette and the others in barely accented French, before striking out again into the countryside at dusk, heading northwest, perhaps in the hope of slipping past the right flank of the advancing Germans and eventually reaching the Channel coast. A dozen pairs of Dessenne eyes watched him head off across the field, and among them was a particularly large and arresting pair belonging to Claire Dessenne, the nineteen-year-old granddaughter of Marie Coulette, the daughter of Eugénie, and by common agreement (and historical acclamation) the prettiest maid in Villeret. It is quite possible that Digby, exhausted and on the run, did not fully register Claire's presence during his first, dramatic appearance in the Dessenne homestead; but equally, it is impossible to imagine that if he had seen her, he would quickly have forgotten her.

CHAPTER FOUR

Fugitives

৩১৫৯৯

Private Digby crept through a land on which a brittle peace had settled. A few German soldiers had been left behind to guard sites of strategic importance and maintain order in what was now occupied territory, and fresh troops continued to stream down the main roads heading towards the battlefront. But bands of German cavalry no longer roamed the lanes, and a queasy tranquillity reigned. Digby's actions over the next few days followed no discernible pattern. He might sensibly have turned south, to follow his retreating comrades, or struck out towards the coast, or gone north into Belgium and Holland, as others had done, but instead he seems to have gone to earth, and waited. The rolling land, dotted with copses and latticed with rivers and streams, offered ideal cover, and the locals later commented on how well Digby seemed to understand the obscure sustenance and contours of the countryside. During the day, he slept and hid in the thickets; only at night did he venture charily into the open, avoiding the villages and larger roads, darting under cover at the first sign of danger. When the food the Dessennes had given him ran out, he began gathering wild fruit and raw vegetables from the fields. The hedgerows teemed with raucous life: robins, larks, and nightingales sang as if the battle had never been, and would never return. Moving from one concealing grove to another, Digby shared his hiding places with deer, rabbits, and wild boar. And creatures like himself.

In the Grand Priel woods beyond Villeret, Digby came across Privates Thorpe, Donohoe, and Martin, waiting precisely where the French cavalryman Bastien had left them, too terrified to quit the protecting shelter of Theillier's trees. Perhaps men who had spent so long in uniform felt, wrongly, greater safety in numbers. The woods were so close to Villeret that even lighting a fire would invite notice, and so, like some unlikely Pied Piper, Digby urged the trio to follow him. That night they slipped out of the copse and pushed north, in precisely the wrong direction. For three days, anxiety steadily rising, they moved from one patch of woods to the next, avoiding every human being and praying for deliverance. Starving and filthy, expecting at any moment to be captured or killed, they adopted a near-feral existence.

Near Walincourt, a farm hand and his dog found the men in the undergrowth, and led them to a safer patch of thick woodland outside the village. The ease with which the man had recognised the fugitive soldiers only added to Digby's fears. Their uniforms were a serious liability: without their khaki, they ran the risk of being treated as spies if they were captured; but in battle dress they were instantly identifiable, not just to enemy troops, but also to overinquisitive locals. The farm hand agreed to hide their uniforms and returned with civilian clothing, but he also seems to have spread word of their whereabouts, for more stragglers from the Mons retreat began to emerge from hiding to join Digby's little band in the woods, directed there by nearby residents anxious to help, or possibly eager to move such human liabilities off their hands. The first to arrive were Harry May, a fellow private from the Hampshire Regiment, and an Irishman named William O'Sullivan. Then Jack Hardy, a raw-boned Lancashire boy, presented himself in the Walincourt woods accompanied by another young soldier whose age, eighteen, became preserved in local memory, but not his name. A few days later, another Frenchman appeared in the copse, delivering to the band one Corporal John Edwards, a little food, and some encouraging news: the Germans had been pushed back from Péronne, and the town was again in French hands, offering a break in the German line and the possibility of escape. After a brief conference, the soldiers, now numbering nine in all, struggled to their feet and "set off to try to reach the gap." Once again they were in the open, a desolate troop of uniformed refugees searching for the battle line.

The opposing armies, having locked in a wrestler's clinch across the River Marne, were now staggering back towards Villeret. The German army that had marched through Le Câtelet chanting "*Nach Paris*," whose soldiers had been promised they would be "home before the leaves fall," was now itself in retreat. Above the River Aisne, the German army dug in and fought back. Duelling artillery could be heard again, south of Le Câtelet. "The French are here," the children shouted. "Those are French guns." Léon Lège, the town notary who had suffered the indignity of being held hostage just days before, now "wept with joy" when an advance party of French troops arrived in the village and the German sentries melted away. "It's over," the French officer told him. "You won't see those Germans again, except for stragglers, and all you have to do is give them a kick in the ass."

The military situation became all but unreadable as the front line lurched back and forth. This was warfare as fluid and erratic as the coming trench battle would be static and predictable. When news spread that Péronne had been retaken by French troops, scores of Frenchmen of fighting age and some army stragglers moved swiftly to cross the lines and link up with the Allied armies—exactly what Digby and the others were now attempting to do without the benefit of local knowledge. But with victory and liberation apparently imminent, most of the civilian population and the concealed remnants of the British army hunkered down, assuming the battle would pass through and on, as it had done before. Few expected a world war to be waged in their back gardens.

On September 16, as the village mayor later reported, "Villeret became French once again," and a French "cavalry division composed of chasseurs, cuirassiers, dragoons, cyclists, and machine-gunners" surged up the hill from Hargicourt into the village. "It was a day of celebration." Had Robert Digby chosen to remain in Villeret, enjoying Marie Coulette's hospitality and her grand-daughter's gaze, he would have been able to rejoin the Allied forces and this story would be very different. Indeed, it would not exist at all.

Villeret's moment of elation was short-lived, for the battle line that had flexed northwards in a precarious arc was now bending in the opposite direction; the momentum that had brought the French troops back to Villeret and Le Câtelet slowed, stopped, and then abruptly reversed, as a flood of German soldiers poured down from the north, turning the tide once more. The French horsemen vanished from Villeret as suddenly as they had arrived. On September 21, a French machine-gun troop dug in at the Cologne farm, on the ridge above the village, and opened up briefly at a squadron of mounted Uhlans. But an hour later, they, too, had packed up and retreated. As the French gunners sped down the mill road, "there was an exchange of fire with the German horsemen who were following from a distance. Two animals were left dead on the ground." And then the fickle war evaporated once more. The people of Villeret would not see their compatriots in uniform again for four years.

On the same day, Digby and the others found themselves on the banks of the River Escaut, a tributary of the Somme, with the sounds of battle clearly audible. They stared at the river, swollen by overnight rain, too wide and fast to cross. Their situation was by now becoming desperate. Thorpe was so weak he could hardly walk, and a wound to Hardy's arm showed signs of infection; they were all soaked, terrified, and beginning to suffer from malnutrition. There was no way to cross the Escaut until the river subsided, Digby concluded. "We were trapped, and took refuge in a wood, in the quarry at Hargival, a little way north of the river." Surrender must, at some point, have entered their minds, offering at least the chance to eat and then sleep without fear of being woken by a bayonet in the stomach. For days they had eaten nothing but wild fruit and raw field-crops, sleeping in ditches and under briars. Digby had now been on the run for more than three weeks, yet he was back almost to the point where he had started, with Villeret to the south, the British and French armies just a few miles beyond that, and the German army massing in between.

A few hundred yards from where Digby's exhausted band lurked in a dank quarry, the mistress of Hargival was, if the rest of her existence is anything to go by, attending to her horses. Jeanne Magniez loved her husband, Georges; she loved her Afghan hound, Baddy; she loved her home, the charming Hargival estate, lying some four miles north of Villeret (and not to be confused with neighbouring Hargicourt), with its forests and lush fields grazed by Flemish cattle and Georges's herd of prize sheep; she loved the warm walled garden and the orchards sweeping down to the river. But most of all, Jeanne Magniez loved horses. To say that she was horse-mad would be to seriously underestimate her condition. "For her, human beings were divided into people who rode and people who did not; horses were sacred," and she treated people as she treated her horses, with gentle firmness, secure in the knowledge that there was not one, of either species, she could not render docile. Her vast photograph album was a precise index of her affections: there were several photographs of her moustachioed husband, scores showing the various dogs she had known, and horse pictures by the hundred. From earliest childhood, she had spent at least a part of every day on horseback, and her closest human friendships had been made in the saddle, with Georges, and with her friend and confidante Anne de Becquevort, whose father ran the brasserie in Vendhuile. Anne had been born with a displaced hip, and when the child reached the age of fifteen, her father was advised by a local doctor that she must ride side-saddle to rectify the problem. It was arranged that Anne would ride out with Jeanne. The exercise did nothing for Mademoiselle de Becquevort's hip, but made the two young women into the closest of friends. They became a familiar sight of the locality, trotting down the wooded lanes around Hargival, hacking across the plateau above Villeret, or watering their horses at the village trough in Le Câtelet.

Jeanne Delacourt was twenty-eight years old when she married

Georges Magniez in 1909, a match of love but also of dynastic logic, for the Delacourts of Gouy and the Magniez family of Hargival were joint pillars of the rural gentry, nothing like as rich as François Theillier with his industrial money and flashy tastes, but in an indefinable way grander. After five years of marriage, there was still no sign of any children in the Magniez household, but if Jeanne minded, she was so busy with her dogs, home, husband, and horses that nobody noticed. She was not quite beautiful in the conventional sense, being heavy-boned and masculine in dress, but many were left dazed by the force of her personality. Local gossips said that Jeanne was a "racy" type, who smoked cigarettes, drove an automobile without gloves on, and treated everybody with exactly the same direct, penetrating, and faintly lofty manner, usually from the saddle. Jeanne was tall and striking, whereas Georges was small and shy, with a diffident manner that belied a passionately romantic soul. There were many who said that Jeanne was the real squire of Hargival.

Georges enlisted as an officer in the 41st Artillery Regiment on the eve of war, and left Hargival for the front within hours of mobilisation. It was a most painful parting. Georges pledged to write, and Jeanne promised to exercise Flirt, his magnificent Thoroughbred, whom they had nicknamed Son of Steel. As the names of their favourite animals suggest, Jeanne and her husband were enthusiastic Anglophiles.

Jeanne had heard the gunfire over at Le Câtelet as the first German troops arrived; she had watched the bedraggled refugees fleeing south, and the weary columns of retreating British infantry, the wagons loaded with wounded men. From Vendhuile, the nearest village to the Hargival estate, the servants brought horrific tales of German brutality, the shooting of Oscar Dupuis and Madame Lemaire-Liénard, and the way the "notables" of Le Câtelet had been taken hostage, beaten, and mistreated. The equinomaniac Jeanne was particularly outraged to learn that horses requisitioned by the French government at the outbreak of war and gathered at Le Câtelet, including several from the stables of Hargival, had since been appropriated by the enemy. Capricious and undefined, the war was everywhere in this corner of Picardy, and yet nowhere. On September 17, on the road passing by the Hargival estate, a German staff car had been ambushed by a squad of French cavalrymen, led by one Lieutenant Bourbon-Chalus, and four Germans had been killed. On the plateau where the Magniez sheep grazed above Hargival, German gunners exchanged fire with a patrol of French chasseurs in the valley. But even as the war raged, a semblance of normal life continued. A woman from Vendhuile trudged up the hill with drinks for the French soldiers, as if at a sporting event. Nearby, a lone farm worker, "taking advantage of the fine weather," continued his rhythmic scything to the echo of heavy gunfire: "The battle and the harvest carried on side by side."

Anyone on horseback ran the risk of being mistaken for a soldier and shot by one side or the other, and the more cautious inhabitants barred their doors. Not so Jeanne Magniez, who was out taking her daily ride on Flirt when she came across the British soldiers huddled miserably in the woods on her property. "It couldn't really be called a hiding place, for the quarry was virtually open to the sky," she later recorded. She cantered back to the mansion and returned within an hour, bringing blankets and food. Not for the last time, the men hailed Jeanne as their "guardian angel."

"For several days I brought them provisions, since they had not a scrap to eat, as I tried to work out how to get them to Péronne. I searched in vain for a way through," Jeanne wrote. On September 23, Péronne was finally retaken by German troops. "The door was slammed shut."

That night, Villeret, east of the solidifying line, saw its first massive influx of German soldiery, in the formidable shape of the 8th Hussars Cavalry Regiment and a squad of Imperial Guards. The soldiers stayed only one night, before marching on to the west, but it must have seemed as if another horde had descended. On Emile Foulon's property alone, seven officers moved into the tidy, well-appointed bedrooms, while 280 soldiers stretched out in his barns and sixty horses were turned loose in his fields. Before they marched away, the Germans inspected every cellar, ostensibly in search of enemy soldiers, but in reality to pilfer whatever they could find. The 8th Hussars had a long history of fighting the French, having done so with enthusiasm in both 1815 and 1870, so they knew the rules: three carts were piled high with Villeret cloth, and the valuable plunder rumbled east, towards Germany. "Pillage took precedence over everything else," the villagers observed grimly.

As the opposing armies fought one another to a stalemate and the contours of a more permanent front took shape, they spread out from the main arteries and began to mass in ever greater numbers in the smaller villages. Le Câtelet found itself firmly under the boot once again. Hostages were crammed into the village prison at gunpoint, and the inhabitants were told to stay in their houses "on pain of death."

The German troops that now set about digging in across the region were not the proud Teutons of a few weeks earlier, but angry and in some cases increasingly disillusioned men who had tasted defeat in their turn. Henriette Legé, the daughter of the town notary, crouched in her father's cellar, listening in terror as the German army occupied Le Câtelet for the second time in three weeks. "We heard a loud hammering on the door and my father opened it. There stood a tall German officer with a long moustache. 'The Barbarians have arrived,' he said, and then he laughed."

The ever-practical Jeanne Magniez, faced with the reality that her home was now in enemy-occupied territory and likely to remain so for some time, set about finding more comfortable long-term accommodation for the nine British soldiers she now considered her guests. In the woods west of the Hargival estate, less than half a mile from the mansion, down a narrow track, stood a pretty little thatched building known as the Pêcherie, or Fishing Lodge. Here monks had once fished the River Escaut to provide Friday fare for the abbey, and here Jeanne Delacourt and Georges Magniez had courted, in the saddle and out of it. "I decided to move them to this isolated building, which, to all appearances, was empty and boarded up," she wrote. "With the aid of Mademoiselle de Becquevort and a young servant aged sixteen, I managed to provide the fugitives with everything they needed to survive." The Pêcherie must have seemed the height of luxury to men who had now spent a month living rough and in constant fear, but Digby was deputed to ask their redoubtable saviour for another service. "With only civilian clothes, they were afraid that if they were caught by the enemy out of uniform they would be shot as spies." Jeanne immediately had a message sent to the mayor of Walincourt, asking him to find the uniforms hidden by the farm hand and have them sent over to Hargival. "The mayor of this commune was very worried about the possible consequences" of aiding the fugitives, wrote Jeanne, with disdain. So, typically, and "despite the mayor's protestations," she did the job herself, riding over to the town, ignoring the German sentries, and retrieving the uniforms. "The men were delighted."

At night, the soldiers would occasionally steal out from their hiding place to walk in the woods, but by day they remained behind its barred shutters, sealed off from the war outside. In the early part of this strange captivity, only the arrival of Anne de Becquevort, Jeanne, or her servant interrupted the monotony. "They lived a quiet life," Jeanne remarked, with fine-tuned irony. "If a little cramped." Over the next month, as the Western Front took shape and hopes of escape dwindled, to fear was added boredom. The men had little to do but talk about themselves, their families, and their previous lives, knowing well that they might be outlining their own epitaphs. They were an odd assortment, this tiny lost army behind enemy lines.

Willie Thorpe, the oldest of the band at thirty-six, was a Liverpudlian, a short, stocky individual with a kindly disposition and a garrulous streak. Like many professional soldiers, he was nostalgic by inclination, given to singing sentimental songs, drinking too much whenever possible, and reminiscing about home. Thorpe had three children back in Liverpool, and they were his pride and obsession. He carried a family photograph in his wallet, which he would pull out, unbidden, to discuss the virtues of his offspring at length with anyone who would listen. Willie had come to soldiering comparatively late in life, having joined up in 1910, on pay of fivepence a day. A year later, he had obtained his third-class certificate of education, but there is no evidence he had any ambition to rise through the ranks. Willie Thorpe wanted to earn a bit of money for the family he doted on, and spend as much time with them as he could. Before August 1914, he had never set foot outside his native land. When he joined the King's Own Lancaster Regiment, the last thing on his mind, one suspects, was the possibility that he might someday have to go to war.

The three Irishmen in the group, Thomas Donohoe, David Martin, and Willie O'Sullivan, were a study in contrasts. Martin was a Protestant from the streets of East Belfast, Donohoe a Catholic from the little village of Killybandrick in County Cavan, and O'Sullivan was a Cork man, from the village of Barrackton. Donohoe, thirty-two, a farmer's son, had joined up in Glasgow in 1905, and later wed Maggie "Bridie" Young from Drumliff. When the time was right, he planned to leave soldiering, return to Killybandrick, and take over the family farm from his father. Thomas and Bridie Donohoe had been married four years, and were looking to start a family when his unit was sent to France. Burly and ruddy, with huge hands, Donohoe might have the looks of a bruiser, but his was a gentle and sensitive soul. Martin had been born in County Down, but brought up in the Castlereagh area of Belfast. Some four years younger than Donohoe, and fully a head taller than any of the other soldiers, Martin was also a married man, who had worked as a cook before deciding to join the army. Both the men of the Royal Irish Fusiliers were steady professionals with little taste for danger, but O'Sullivan, the third and youngest of the Irish trio, was made of more boisterous stuff: one of eight siblings, with three brothers also in the army, O'Sullivan was a wild youth, much given to horseplay, drink, and practical jokes. At least one of his enforced companions had marked him down as a liability from the outset.

Harry May and John Edwards were quiet, cautious men who kept largely to themselves. The two youngest members of the band remain almost entirely shadowy figures: Jack Hardy is known only by a signed photograph he later gave to Jeanne Magniez, showing a handsome youngster with a jutting chin and neatly combed hair.

In this assortment of regular soldiers, Robert Digby seemed oddly out of place. He had joined the army just the previous year, enlisting in Winchester, and completed his training nine months before the outbreak of war, at the age of twenty-eight. Digby's father, also named Robert, was a crusty former colonel in the Indian army whose career in various imperial outposts was brought to a premature end when he was shot in the head and seriously injured during a hunting accident. Surgeons had tried, and failed, to remove the bullet from Colonel Digby's skull. Robert Digby had been born on home leave, in Northwich, Cheshire. A second son, Thomas, was born two years later, while Colonel Digby was serving in Roorkee, Bengal, and a sister, Florence, appeared three years later. Ellen Digby, their mother, was the daughter of a fishmonger from Northwich, but marriage to Colonel Robert Digby ("soldier" and son of a "gentleman" on his marriage certificate) and the years she spent lording it over servants in the colonies had thoroughly imbued her with the snobbery to which the British middle class is sometimes prone. The family was comfortably off, if less than wealthy, and Robert and Thomas had both received a sound education, complete with Latin and Greek, at Bedford Grammar School. Robert, in particular, had proved an able student, a natural sportsman with a gift for languages, but also a rebel. One of his contemporaries remembers the elder Digby boy as "clever, and wild as hell."

The two brothers were quite different but very close. Whereas Robert was extroverted and liable to get into trouble, his younger brother, Thomas, was cautious, meek, and deeply serious. Tall, athletic, and charming, with fair hair and a cavalier's moustache, Robert Digby had a powerful effect on women, and eight decades after the war, his good looks are still recalled with something close to awe, mostly by people who could not possibly have laid eyes on him. Thomas, on the other hand, found women rather terrifying. As a child, Robert had often argued with his father, an irascible martinet whose naturally bad temper was worsened by his injury. An engaging and cheerful youngster, Robert tended to get away with murder; Thomas, however, did what he was told. When the boys were growing up, it was often noted that Robert was the leader and Thomas the follower in every game, and the roles were never reversed. Robert was protective of his younger sibling;

Thomas looked on his older brother "as a God." Ellen Digby also openly doted on her elder son, and made no secret of her favouritism.

Robert Digby was a strange mixture of parts: a little spoiled, sometimes deliberately wayward, he possessed an instinctive resistance to regulations, which enraged his father and baffled his officers. It was not insubordination exactly, more the impression he gave of fulfilling orders without engaging in them, as if his mind were fixed on a distant place. Years later, his distinctive manner was recalled in "an odd sort of smile, like he was laughing at a joke he didn't want to share." But he could also be deeply conventional, trotting out the accepted patriotic formulae about king and country embedded in every classical Victorian English education. Weaned on Kipling and tales of British valour, he liked to drill his younger siblings in the back garden, barking orders and marching them up and down until they were exhausted. From his parents, he had inherited a formal, ingrained notion of duty, which sat uneasily alongside a natural exuberance and a thick streak of devilry. "He was a *gallus* one," recalled a cousin, using the northern slang term meaning "outgoing" or "bold." At the age of fourteen, Robert had led his brother on an illicit underage expedition to the local pub in Northwich. The older boy swaggered up to the bar and demanded a beer; Thomas quailed at the last moment, and ordered tea. Robert mocked him: "If you want tea, why don't you go and see Mother?" As with his father, anger came quickly to Robert Digby—his temper had swept him into more than one fight in schoolyard and barracks—but it was equally swift to vanish. "He was quite highly strung, energetic, and very talkative," recalled a relative. When he became excited, he would gesticulate emphatically. But there was also a "natural gentleness" about him, which emerged most particularly in his dealings with children, people his mother considered her social inferiors, and animals. Ellen Digby's relatives in the north of England bred racing pigeons, and Robert had discovered a natural affinity for the birds. "He was never happier than when he was inside a coop, stroking and cooing to the pigeons." Ellen Digby considered this hobby to be "very common," which doubtless only stoked her elder son's enthusiasm.

In 1908, Colonel Digby, his mind deteriorating rapidly, was invalided out of the army, and the family settled in the Hampshire village of Totton. Robert was restless in the Home Counties. He tried a series of jobs—including a brief stint as a horse trainer and another teaching in a preparatory school—but could not settle. One summer he took the steamer to Boulogne, and then the train to Paris, where he spent several months improving his French, working as a barman in a café, and wandering along the Seine. On returning to Hampshire, he announced that he was going to move to Paris, a notion that was swiftly and definitively crushed by an appalled Ellen Digby, who held a low opinion of foreigners in general, and of the French in particular. By 1911, Digby was living in the north of England again, and hatching what was referred to afterwards as the Chicken Plan. With considerable difficulty, he convinced his younger brother that the future, and their fortunes, lay in poultry farming, organised on modern European production principles. Robert and Thomas Digby went into partnership, with money borrowed from their parents. The Digby chicken farm, just outside Northwich, limped along for a few years, and then went spectacularly bust. Thomas privately blamed the failure on his brother, who had no head for business and much preferred racing pigeons to raising chickens. Yet, when Robert announced he was joining the army and signed up with the Hampshire Regiment, Thomas once again followed in his footsteps. Thus it was that, while Robert Digby was hunkered down in the Pêcherie on the Hargival estate, Thomas Digby was on the other side of the solidifying front line with the rest of the British Expeditionary Force, helping to fight the German army to a standstill. Thomas Digby knew that his brother had been wounded in the first days of the war and had then vanished, but he clung to the belief that Robert was still alive.

Of the two brothers, it was Robert who seemed destined for a more distinguished military career than that of a mere private. With a senior-ranking soldier as a father, a socially aspirant mother, a good education, and a top-notch talent with a rugby ball, Robert Digby would seem to have been ideal officer material, and yet he had joined up at the lowest rank, initially earning a meagre sevenpence a day. There are several possible explanations for this apparent lack of ambition. Digby may have had girl trouble, since enlisting in the army was a well-known route for wayward middle-class men to escape the wrath of an angry father with a pregnant daughter. Another explanation may have been the financial fallout from the failed poultry farm, for the army was equally good at hiding bad debtors. Then again, he may have joined up as a humble private to prove something to his father, with whom his relations, always tense, had degenerated rapidly after the stuffing came out of the chicken business. Even members of his family, years later, conceded that there was something surprising in Digby's decision to remain in the ranks rather than take the officer's commission to which his birth and education seemed to entitle him.

The nine fugitives were all still part of, although thoroughly disengaged from, the British army, which theoretically made Corporal John Edwards the officer in command. But as the weeks dragged on, the authority of rank slowly eroded. Although the rest of the British army might have been only a few miles away, it grew more impossibly distant day by day, as an entire German administrative structure, along with hundreds of thousands of troops, set about occupying the region behind the lines. The Pêcherie became a prison, and soon a new pecking-order emerged within the group, with Robert Digby—failed chicken farmer, overqualified private soldier, and enigma—at the top.

CHAPTER FIVE

Behind the Trenches

᭡ᔥᔤᭊ

From the heights above the River Aisne, where the Germans had entrenched, the battle line spooled east to the Swiss border, west in stalemate, and then north, as the armies sought to outflank one another in the overlapping battles known as "The Race to the Sea" that more resembled a bloody game of leapfrog through Picardy and Artois. At Flanders, in October, the race came to an end, and another sort of war began. The battle line scored swiftly and arbitrarily across the landscape was gradually dug into a deep, disfiguring gash of trenches hedged with barbed wire and punctuated by machine-gun nests, running 480 miles from Switzerland to the North Sea. On opposite sides of the muddying gulch, the forces massed. Le Câtelet saw eighty-nine artillery pieces pass through in a single day, accompanied by column after column of German troops heading towards the front. From the air, it seemed as if two vast teams of uniformed navvies were labouring to build some enormous and pointless ditch across northern France. From Nieuport in Belgium it ran south past Ypres, Arras, and Albert, before turning east above the Aisne. In the crook of that wheeling line lay Villeret, less than ten miles from the front line just west of Péronne. In time, the point where the River Ancre crossed the front, west of Péronne, would mark the division between the French and British armies: for ninety miles to the north, the trenches were manned by the British; to the south, the line was held by the French.

The British force simultaneously expanded and shrank. At the end of October, Kitchener would call for three hundred thousand volunteers, but these were smaller men. The soldiers of the original BEF had all been over the regulation height of five feet eight inches. Henceforth anyone over five feet three was deemed an acceptable warrior. The war of movement staggered into stasis, and for the people of Picardy, what had been an invasion now became a vast, minutely organised, and thoroughly repressive occupation, the methodical pillage of a strip of industrial and agricultural land containing about 2.5 million people.

The villagers listened and wondered, while "the cannons grumbled away to the west, and the occupation covered everything, like a cloak of lead." The war seemed impossibly, terrifyingly near. Ernst Rosenhainer, the tender-hearted young German infantry officer who had recoiled from the cruelty of the initial invasion, was struck by the way the landscape suddenly changed from bucolic idyll to pitted wasteland as he marched with his regiment to the trenches southwest of Villeret, between Péronne and Noyon. "We came through the lovely valley of the Oise River," he wrote. "At times through the most beautiful beech forests." But just a few miles farther on, "a veritable labyrinth of trenches is opening up before us . . . There is nothing but death and devastation, and now a solemn silence under the autumn sun."

In the village of Aubencheul, a friendly French-speaking German army captain from Alsace paused to chat with the *curé* and told him: "A mighty blow is being prepared. If it succeeds, the war is over. If it fails, the struggle may continue for five years, perhaps seven, for the English are tenacious and their resources are immense. They are our real enemies, an infernal race. Oh, if only we could overcome them."

Through the rest of October and for most of November, the remains of the BEF and units of the Indian army slugged it out with the Germans across a strip of Belgian Flanders: seventy-five thousand died before the First Battle of Ypres ground to an inconclusive halt by winter. Farther south, the German occupiers settled in for a battle of attrition, and the region behind the front lines east of the Somme River, including the villages of Villeret, Hargicourt, Hargival, Vendhuile, and Bellenglise, now became a single administrative unit. Under the new German military government, the *Etappe*, or rear zone, was ruled by the *Etappen-Kommandant* headquartered in Le Câtelet, who in turn came under the command of an *Etappen-Inspekteur* at the German military HQ, now established in Saint-Quentin. To the north and east, the German occupation was more fluid, allowing rural and industrial life to continue much as before, but here, immediately behind the front line, the German yoke was at its heaviest. Every inhabitant, from well-to-do Jeanne Magniez in her mansion at Hargival to the Dessennes in their tiny home in Villeret, was now a part of the German war machine—to be kept in order, carefully controlled, and gradually bled of any available resources and luxuries that might contribute to the effectiveness and enjoyment of the German occupiers. As the soldiers burrowed down along both sides of the Western Front, so the German forces entrenched themselves into the lives and homes of the local inhabitants. Sandwiched between the front lines and the occupied areas behind, this strip of territory became a strange no-man's-land for those who remained there, deprived of all rights and information, pinned down by the crushing weight of occupation. No aspect of daily life was left untouched, unregulated, or unmolested; the troops came on in numberless waves, and so did the rules. Within a few months, Germany succeeded in transforming occupied France into what the future U.S. President Herbert Hoover described as "a vast concentration camp." Survival was increasingly difficult, and escape nearly impossible.

Major Karl Evers—or Etappen-Kommandant 8/X of the 2nd Etappen-Inspektion, to give him his full title—had been a wholly undistinguished magistrate before the war in the town of Celle, near Hanover. The administration of this small but important area of occupied France was a job precisely suited to his limited imagination, casual cruelty, and obsession with bureaucratic minutiae. His tasks were to ensure that the civilian population did not impede the German war effort, to weed out spies, to provide adequate billets in the scattered villages for the thousands of troops heading back and forth to the front, and to extract from the land and its people whatever could be of use, value, or pleasure. A minor functionary who now found himself the seigneur of Le Câtelet and the area around it, Evers plunged into the job with relish.

In Le Câtelet, the villagers watched with foreboding as the German imperial flag rose above the police station, now the headquarters of the military police, "telling everyone that there were, henceforth, no rights and no liberties." A command post was officially established on October 19, "when soldiers requisitioned furniture to set up their offices." Here Evers called together all the mayors of the region, including Parfait Marié of Villeret, and "delivered a lecture in a language that was almost French, describing the various duties that were now incumbent on them, on pain of death. He played the tyrant. Every morning officials of each commune were required to come, whatever the distance, to the dictator's office to . . . be told of his decisions, receive instructions and particularly orders for requisitions, with the required quantities, of horses, livestock, carts, wine, food, bed linen, money, and so on."

Over the coming months and years, hundreds of thousands of German soldiers would pass through the villages behind the lines, staying at most a week or two to rest and recuperate before returning to battle. But Major Evers and his men were a constant presence, investigating, regulating, punishing, and plundering. In the journal he would keep throughout the war, Joseph Cabaret, the schoolteacher, described the new German ruler of the region: "Of medium height, he looked well over 50 years old but liked to pose as a bit of a dandy. He was a Lutheran, but there was nothing very religious about him and he displayed a particular loathing for priests." Evers could be charming when the occasion suited. "Initially, he displayed a certain affability, but this was soon stripped away to reveal his profound mendacity, and when drunk he became excessively brutal, arrogant, and insufferable. Low of height and low of morals, he was less slovenly than others, but dryly ruthless, in the Prussian manner." Another elderly resident of Le Câtelet was pithier in her assessment: "He was wicked."

Under the command of Evers came an array of lesser military officials—"little people thrown into authority by the war," in Cabaret's words. Even taking into account the locals' understandable tendency to caricature them, the German occupiers appear to have been a rum bunch: a second-in-command from Münster named Flemming, "a young squirt, fatuous, pretentious, and pedantic"; a judicial clerk named Bode, considered "a ferocious troublemaker," and Captain Deutsche, the organiser of forced labour, who was "responsible for overseeing agriculture, stables, granaries, barns, timber-cutting, and open-air inspections of horses, mules, and asses." Variously nicknamed "the Pig" and "the Bulldog," Deutsche swiftly made himself one of the most hated of the occupying officials by meddling with every aspect of village life, and drinking all day. "He was a fantastic drunk, who could absorb ten litres of beer at one sitting." To their number would be added the peculiar military vet, Lieutenant Fischer, a former café pianist who, when not tending sick animals, "liked to creep up on cats sleeping in the sun, and shoot them." Perhaps the most intriguing, and certainly the oddest, of the German administrators was the military judge Hans Grumme. Lanky and awkward, with a tuft of reddish hair that refused to lie down, Grumme was nicknamed "the Big Red Turkey," though he was regarded as almost human by some of the locals. "His attitude was less detestable, and he sometimes showed respect for the French people, even when passing sentence on them." A lawyer from Wennigsen, outside Hanover, he had an offbeat, dark sense of humour. It was Grumme who had knocked on Léon Legé's door and announced the arrival of the "Barbarians."

Carrying out Evers's commands, and permanently stationed in Le Câtelet, was a brigade of military police and a squad of sentries which together "terrorised the population: their principal role consisted of confiscating food for the *Kommandant* and his men, and keeping the best bits for themselves. They seemed to enjoy great freedom of action and arbitrary power." Evers liked to claim that every rule and order came directly to him from the German High Command, but in reality he was a power unto himself, basing his decisions and regulations on little more than whim. All along the front line, the various *Kommandanten* of the different zones made up the laws as they went along, issuing varying proclamations on the same subject at different times, often contradicting one another and sometimes themselves. Orders were issued irrespective of whether they were enforceable, let alone logical or, still less, fair. Evers was, in many ways, a classic bureaucrat, treating the trivial and the vital with the same leaden seriousness, and insisting that obedience to the rules was the single guiding principle, except when applied to himself. The bulk of the officers installed themselves in the château at Le Câtelet, unaware that the owner, the elderly spinster Mademoiselle Fournier d'Alincourt, was secretly hosting another guest in the attic, one Emmanuel Le Hérissé, a French cavalry officer who had been shot in the foot during the retreat and taken in, tended, and hidden by the châtelaine.

Evers himself decided to take up residence in the substantial home of Legé, the town notary. "The windows looked out over the *gendarmerie*, and the view made it easier for him to keep an eye on everything." The owner of the house did his best to make this unwelcome and demanding resident as uncomfortable as possible. "Every time Evers walked into a room where he was, Legé would walk out of the other door." But his daughter, Henriette, recalled a more "genial" side to Major Evers: "He used to give me chocolate bars."

The locals got their first taste of Evers-style administration on September 29, when posters were pasted outside every *mairie* under his control: "All eggs are for German officers," it declared, and then added, by way of clarification, "Civilians are forbidden to eat eggs." A week later, demonstrating Evers's uncanny knack for juxtaposing the absurd and the severe, it was announced that the canton of Le Câtelet would be required to pay eighty-six hundred francs in "war contributions," with the explanation that, since they were no longer paying any tax to the French government, the inhabitants had nothing to complain about. Over the next few months, Evers and his minions unleashed volley after volley of prohibitions, sequestrations, and petty orders. Gradually, the German machine also took over the local industry: Monsieur de Becquevort's brewery in Vendhuile was dismantled; the phosphate from the mines around Hargi-court was diverted to Germany, and within weeks the woods around Hargival, where Jeanne Magniez had loved to ride, began to be cut down to line the trenches. Brass was confiscated for shell casings, and iron was requisitioned to make barbed wire. The demands began slowly, and became steadily more repacious as the war dragged on and Germany's needs grew acute. In Villeret, it was Parfait Marié's unhappy task to sign the paperwork for every item taken by the Germans, his once-perfect copperplate becoming more slapdash and forlorn with each fresh requisition order he signed. The Germans even seemed to view the people with a utilitarian eye; one villager later recalled the arrival of an administrative officer whose notions of physical purity foreshadowed those of the Nazis a generation later: "He saw all the mentally sick people in Villeret, the mine-workers addicted to the drink *blanche*, and said he was going to have them all shot because they were no use to the German soldiers and were extra mouths to feed. He was only persuaded not to do so by the mayor."

Evers and his fellow *Kommandanten* were convinced from the outset—and entirely correctly—that enemy soldiers and others with the potential to damage the German war effort were lurking in what was now occupied France. A similar attitude prevailed briefly on the other side of the line, where some German stragglers had also been left behind when the German army retreated from the Marne. Unlike the British or French fugitives in German-occupied France, the Germans trapped on the wrong side of the line could not hope for local aid. Most were swiftly rounded up, and although proclamations were issued in German and French warning that "all enemy soldiers not surrendering at once would be treated as spies and shot if found with weapons in their hands," there is no evidence that this threat ever needed to be carried out.

Evers had been installed for only a few weeks when, in mid-October 1914, "the manhunt for soldiers who had been left behind began in earnest . . . From the outset, an exact inventory of the male population was the *Kommandant*'s main preoccupation, for he was most concerned about hidden soldiers." On October 22, the mayors were summoned to Le Câtelet and handed the following proclamation, a masterpiece of administrative gibberish:

> 1. All mayors are required to present, at once, a register of all men living in their community: (a) men liable to military service, (b) men not liable to military service, (c) men belonging to the French army (deserters etc.). 2. All mayors will forfeit their lives, and the community its property, if any man enrolled in the army is allowed to leave the community; any inhabitant found without the correct authorisation will be shot as a spy. 3. All cars, bicycles, arms, ammunition, and carrier pigeons must be handed in to the *Kommandant*'s office by October 25. Anyone who is found after that time in possession of any of the above will be shot. 4. All mayors are required to arrest or disarm English, French, or Belgian soldiers. Mayors who conceal the presence of such soldiers will be shot. Inhabitants who hide them will be hanged. A very large fine will be levied on the community, or else the entire village will be burned down.

This was vintage Evers: he knew that it was impossible to round up, in three days, every revolver and bullet in such a vast area, and the *ad hoc* nature of his threats is betrayed by his evident indecision over whether it would be more useful to burn or fine offending villages. In this rural community, every household had at least one gun, and most had several. Emile Foulon of Villeret, a retired cavalry officer, possessed a veritable arsenal, comprising three shotguns, one revolver, three antique pistols, three sabres, one rapier, one sword stick, and a dagger. Much of what Evers decreed was completely unenforceable, yet there was also a sinister psychology underpinning his orders: if the threatened punishment was sufficiently dire, and the demands were sufficiently extravagant, then someone, eventually, would come forward and reveal the whereabouts of a fugitive soldier. Once an example had been set and punishment meted out with due severity, others would follow. The swaggering *Kommandant* of Le Câtelet saw enemy agents everywhere, and weeding them out became his obsession. An intelligence officer, working in conjunction with members of the Secret Military Police disguised as civilians, was made responsible not only for debriefing German spies when these succeeded in crossing back over the lines, but for counterintelligence operations across the entire rear zone. This was no easy task, for the officer had a staff of only six, of whom three spoke not a word of French.

Major Evers was a hunter, and not just of men. Like many officers on both sides in the conflict, he viewed the war not only as a sort of jolly blood sport, but also as an opportunity to enjoy the hunt in a land teeming with game. The woods around the Hargival estate were overflowing with rabbit, partridge, deer, pheasant, and woodcock, and so it was there, every afternoon, that the German officers repaired to enjoy some sport. Digby and his band found themselves under fire once again. "The officers from the Command Post in Le Câtelet came to hunt every day around their hiding place," Jeanne Magniez wrote. "The Germans even used the walls of the Pêcherie for target practice with their revolvers, without for one moment imagining that eight [actually, nine] Englishmen were behind the walls, their ears out on stalks."

The soldiers might remain invisible beneath the noses of the German officers, but the comings and goings at the Magniez Fishing Lodge did not escape notice in the locality, where Evers's threats were beginning to have the desired effect. "An inhabitant of Vendhuile, having solved the living mystery of the Pêcherie, tipped off the mayor, who became deeply alarmed." Monsieur Luquet, the mayor of Vendhuile, had every reason to fear German reprisals. Just weeks earlier, he had found himself begging a German officer not to burn the village after Oscar Dupuis had shot and wounded two German soldiers. The mayor had finally dissuaded the officer, General Thaddeus von Jarowski, from carrying out his punitive orders by giving a personal commitment that there would be no further acts of resistance. "I have strongly recommended that all people under my administration retain the utmost calm," he told the general, who finally agreed to spare the village on condition that every person in the parish gave "a promise of passivity."

The formidable Madame Magniez was only marginally less intimidating than a German general, but Luquet finally screwed up his courage to intervene, although he still did not dare to confront the mistress of Hargival in person. As she would recall: "On November 1, he sent me a formal order to evacuate the fugitives from the place. For eight days I refused, but then I had to give in, faced with the anger of my compatriots who knew what was going on and who were appalled by what they called my imprudence and the peril to which they said I was exposing the village." Jeanne was not the sort to pay much attention to her faint-hearted neighbours, but she was aware that, if gossip about the residents of the Pêcherie was already spreading through Vendhuile, then it was only a matter of time before it reached the ears of the *Kommandant*. There was another, equally practical reason, why the men would be safer elsewhere. Digging in for a long war, the German military authorities had begun taking over all the substantial houses in the area as officers' billets. (In Le Câtelet, Mademoiselle Fournier d'Alincourt was becoming increasingly concerned about the wounded French officer in her rafters, for her "château was infested with Germans and decidedly unsafe." The *chevalier* Le Hérissé, following a long tradition of evasion, was "lent some female clothes, and dressed himself up as a young woman of good family." Bundled into a cart belonging to one of the Le Câtelet shopkeepers, who pretended that the passenger was his sick daughter, the Breton officer was successfully driven to Saint-Quentin, where, showing rather less gumption than his protectors, he immediately surrendered to the Germans.) The vast Château de Grand Priel, above Villeret, which had been so swiftly vacated by François Theillier on the first night of the invasion, was also transformed into sumptuous quarters for German officers, who marvelled at the rich furnishings as they tucked into Theillier's extensive selection of game and deep cellar. Jeanne Magniez knew that her spacious home, and possibly even the Pêcherie itself, would shortly lose what remained of its "tranquillity."

"On horseback with Mlle de Becquevort, I rode around all the deserted farms and houses in the area searching for a refuge for my protégés, but with no success. I could see no alternative, for the moment, other than hiding them in a small hunting lodge belonging to my brother-in-law [Victor] Carlier, deep in the woods next to Villeret."

After six weeks in the Pêcherie, Digby and his companions were on the move again, but this time through a region inundated with German troops. Weeks of enforced inertia suddenly gave way to a burst of activity, and renewed fear. In the middle of the night of November 8, wrote Jeanne Magniez, "I sent the poor fellows on their way." Laying a long ladder provided by their patroness across the narrowest point of the fast-flowing river, the men crossed the Escaut near the Pêcherie and then headed south towards the mouth of the Riqueval tunnel.

The *souterrain* at Riqueval is a remarkable feat of Napoleonic engineering, a tunnel carved through the hill that runs for four miles, taking the Saint-Quentin canal from just west of Le Câtelet, underneath the village of Bony, to a point two kilometres east of Villeret. In time, the Germans would convert this into a huge underground barracks capable of holding three thousand men—by laying planks across the canal, they converted the tunnel into a cavern, damp and eerie with the water running below, but virtually impregnable to attack and protected at either end by machine guns. In the early days of the war, the place was deserted. Above it ran a long line of trees.

Using the trees as cover, the men followed Jeanne's detailed directions, and by dawn they had reached the Trocmé wood near Villeret and the comparative safety of the hunting cabin. Jeanne Magniez, who was not going to see her wards go hungry in their new accommodation, appeared on horseback a few hours later, accompanied by Anne de Becquevort and her teenage servant driving a small cart: "I brought them some food, and a barrel of beer," she recorded. David Martin, the former cook, set about making a meal, while the others warily began exploring their new hiding place. It was Robert Digby's second sojourn in the woods outside Villeret. At night, he could slip out to the spot just beyond the treeline where John Sligo had been killed weeks earlier and look down on the little village that had first taken him in.

The easy pace of life in Villeret had been shattered in the preceding weeks, as Evers's reign plunged the village into a new world of edicts, threats, and fear. A place that had lived by its own rules for centuries was now under regulation of an intensity few had imagined possible. The butcher Cardon was turned out of his home on the crossroads, the largest in the village, to make way for the offices of a German *Orstkommandant* named Scholl, one of Deutsche's underlings, who set about "organising" the local agriculture, or, more accurately, plundering it. Before the war, Emile Foulon had been one of the most prosperous men in Villeret, with his military pension, more than four hectares of land, three horses, four cows, a hundred chickens, and twenty ducks. Suddenly his possessions were no longer his own: within a month, Scholl had deprived him of one horse, two cows, his prize bull, "chickens on various occasions," the entire crop of clover, and what few beets he had been able to harvest before the troops arrived. The old soldier watched as his four-hundred-bottle wine cellar was loaded into one of his mule wagons and confiscated.

Parfait Marié trudged to Le Câtelet every day, returning with fresh orders, threats, and demands from the *Kommandant*. Volley after volley of rules were fired from Evers's limitless arsenal, and in the space of just a few months the people of Villeret and their neighbours found they were no longer permitted to light fires in the fields, look at aircraft, leave home after seven o'clock at night, gather in groups of more than three people, hang laundry on washing lines, display a light visible in the window at night, gather fallen wood more than six centimetres in diameter, or travel to the next village without a pass. Hunting was also banned, but the villagers had been taking game from François Theillier's acres and the woods around Hargival for as long as anyone could remember, and as yet the Germans were not in a position to stop them.

Arthur Tordeux and Désiré Dubuis were poaching rabbits on November 15 when they discovered Digby and his eight companions in the Trocmé wood. After a week in the tiny cabin, the men's nerves were already horribly frayed, "because the local inhabitants were continually in the copse, gathering wood for their fires." For several days, Dubuis and Tordeux brought food to the fugitives, but swiftly they concluded that "their situation was becoming impossible": the men were too numerous and too close to Villeret, and the hunting cabin was too small to serve as a long-term hiding place. Jeanne Magniez called a meeting with the village elders. The British soldiers were now a shared problem, she declared, and the time had come "to change methods" to ensure they were not captured by the enemy. No one raised an objection, or pointed out that by merely discussing how to conceal the soldiers they were courting death. "Why should they undertake the risk?" a British general later wondered, as he recorded the instinctive French actions in defence of British soldiers. "Yet they did . . . A long drawn-out martyrdom of suspense, the daily risking of their lives for another, was [now] their existence." Among those present at the meeting were Tordeux, Dubuis, and Florency Dessenne, the mason who had found Digby on his doorstep three months earlier, along with his mother, the redoubtable Marie Coulette. Parfait Marié was also brought into the secret, since, as acting mayor, he had the most to lose if the men were discovered. Léon Lelong, the baker, was also there, along with several other senior village figures, including Emile Foulon.

Lelong, a balding, habitually plaintive man with disappointed eyes, swiftly pointed out the obvious: the nine fugitives amounted to "a veritable garrison" in their midst. Together, they were immediately identifiable, but separated, they might just be made to blend into the scenery, at least until they could be moved elsewhere. It was therefore agreed that the group should be split up and lodged in different houses around the village. That way, if one was discovered, the others might still escape detection. The second part of the plan was more ambitious. After prolonged discussion, it was decided that "it would be more sensible, and less trying for the men, to be mixed in with the population as fully as possible." The people of Villeret would act as human camouflage, if the soldiers could be taught to "live as country people, without trying to hide."

Some of the new arrivals would be easier to conceal than others: Robert Digby, as a French-speaker, could already pass for a native, except to a native. Thorpe, with his darker looks and squat build, was quite similar to the Villeret physical type. The tall Irishman

David Martin, on the other hand, towered over everyone else in the village and would stick out "like a poplar in a pond." Rosy-cheeked Thomas Donohoe, Irish to the roots of his reddish hair, also had a telltale habit of whistling Irish songs, out of tune. The most obviously conspicuous members of the group, however, were the two youngest soldiers. Jack Hardy and his friend were still teenagers; every German sentry would wonder why two healthy men of evidently mobilisable age and too young to be heads of households were not at the front. They would be questioned constantly, and since neither spoke more than a smattering of French, they were serious liabilities. Jeanne Magniez stepped in: "It was feared that the two youngest would never pass undetected, so they returned with me to Hargival. In defiance of both the military and civilian rules laid down by the Germans, I installed them, in strictest secrecy, in my own house. None of my servants, with the exception of my serving maid, had a clue they were there."

The remaining men emerged from the Trocmé wood that night and took up residence in the village. "They were each given civilian clothes and their uniforms were buried," as their new hosts set about the courageous but daunting task of turning these English and Irish soldiers into northern-French peasants.

CHAPTER SIX

Battle Lines

❧

The Englishmen came to Villeret at the same time as the hunger. The village had never been as rich as Le Câtelet or Hargicourt, but it had not experienced real want since the war of 1871. With the demand for grain in the run-up to war and now a spate of requisitioning from the new German authorities, food stocks were running perilously low before the onset of winter. What remained had to be strictly accounted for and was liable to summary confiscation. In Villeret, "as everywhere else, mattresses, linen covers, gold, copper, food of all sorts, animals, and so on were requisitioned, and numerous searches were carried out by the enemy to get their hands on what they wanted." Evers and his minions developed an increasingly Byzantine regulatory system to ensure that not a single chicken, egg, or bushel of wheat went unnoted: in the German ledgers there were entries for pigs of over a hundred kilos and pigs under a hundred kilos; sows; suckling pigs; pigs aged from four weeks to six months; and so on. All hens were required to lay one egg and then two eggs per day to be handed over to the German authorities; all female rabbits must be listed; even the domestic cats and dogs had to be numbered and then kept inside, or they would face summary execution, apparently to ensure they did not run in front of German vehicles.

Evers considered himself to be an expert on matters agricultural, although his grasp of animal husbandry seemed a little shaky. Orders that every cockerel must produce an egg, every wild rabbit must be counted, and all molehills flattened met with astonishment, and then discreet hilarity. "You got the feeling they would demand that hens to do the goose step and marshal the swallows into regiments," one local remarked, as the avalanche of restrictions and rules smothered the area.

Dwindling food stocks, the ban on hunting, tight monitoring of existing supplies, and the mounting demands of the German invaders meant that, by November 1914, there was barely enough to go around in Villeret when seven more adult male mouths were added to the community. "Lelong agreed to provide the bread" that was needed to keep the men alive, and Marie Coulette declared that she would arrange the rest: if Evers could resort to arbitrary measures to fill the stomachs of his army, so could she. "They had to be fed, even though there was nothing to eat and food had to be sent off with those who were working in the phosphate mine. Marie Coulette couldn't feed them on her own, so it had to be properly organised." It was a brave neighbour who dared to argue with Marie Coulette, for, as her granddaughter observed, "She was a hard one. *Elle n'avait pas la langue dans sa poche*" (she didn't keep her tongue in her pocket). The old woman had very few teeth left, but her bite was fearsome. As a child, Florency Dessenne had only once defied his mother: he swore at her. "She picked up a hatchet, and threw it at him. Florency dodged the axe, but it stuck in the door of the barn. It stayed there a long time." Thereafter, for the rest of his life, Florency did exactly what his mother told him.

While their hiding places were being prepared, the men were hidden first in an empty building on the farm known as the Petit Priel, and then in the granary behind the Dessenne household, where "they slept in the straw." Many would later claim credit for sheltering the British soldiers, but their presence was initially known only to a few. Even the priest, who came every other week to preach in the church on the rise beside the village, remained in ignorance of his new parishioners.

The conspirators threw themselves into the task with an energy all the more remarkable for being, as yet, unquestioning. Marie Coulette collected civilian clothes from women whose husbands were away at the war. Emile Foulon and his schoolteacher daughter, Antoinette, concealed extra supplies of wheat and dried vegetables in their barn. Léon Lelong surreptitiously baked extra loaves, which his half-sister-in-law, Suzanne Boitelle, delivered to the men in a covered basket. The refugee soldiers started to grow their moustaches long, in the Villeret manner, and the distinctions between the fighting men of one land and the peasants of another slowly began to blur.

Like most small rural communities, the village was riven with feuds so ancient no one could quite remember how they had started. The sprawling Marié clan, with the parsonical Parfait at the head, cordially disdained the Lelongs, and neither family had a good word to say of the Foulons, believing they had ideas above their station just because he had a bit of money and Antoinette wore a crêpe hat to church; the Bochards gossiped about the Morels, who bad-mouthed the Marié family as a clutch of scheming liars. In peacetime, Marie Coulette had maintained a permanent, low-level conflict with most of her neighbours. "Our house was a house of God and anyone was welcome there, except the people of Villeret," recalled her granddaughter. "In the village, everyone kept an eye on everyone else all the time." Villeret was famous for the complexity and venom of its internecine vendettas, which were sometimes taken to comic lengths. "Once Florency and Marie Coulette happened to drop in on Clara Bochard and smelled something cooking. They asked Clara what she was making. 'Nothing,' she replied. So Florency and Marie Coulette stayed there, talking, until whatever was in the oven had burned to a cinder. She was too mean to share the dish she had made, so she preferred to let it burn rather than surrender any of it."

Relations between Marie Coulette and Elise Lelong, matriarch of the Lelong clan, were particularly arctic. Elise had always considered herself a cut above the uncouth and boisterous Marie Coulette. Tubby and short, with salt-and-pepper hair and a moustache that somehow added to her grandeur, Elise had a "strong character and a fine spirit." She was not only the baker's wife, and thus a woman of some standing, but also a former schoolmistress with firm opinions on everything. Her cousin ran Villeret's only industrial concern, a tiny factory employing three workers and two young women to produce a fine hessian cloth (burlap) with a large and loud machine that had been built in England. The cloth was then shipped from Hargicourt by rail to Paris to make patterned wallpaper for smart bourgeois homes, a fact which Elise considered an additional boost to her social status, even though the machine had been silent since the start of war. Elise Lelong doted on her daughter, Clothilde, a somewhat podgy but vivacious teenager whom she dolled up in velvet dresses with lace cuffs and collars. The Lelongs regarded the Dessennes as common smugglers, who did not go to church; the Dessennes thought the Lelongs gave themselves airs and ought to mind their own business. "Their curtains were always twitching, they were forever spying on us from behind their windows," recalled one of the Dessenne clan.

These traditional animosities, stoked by Achille Poëtte, the postman, who gossiped to and about everyone, were as much a part of the glue that held the village together as the belief that Hargicourt, half a mile down the valley, was another country populated by Huguenot bandits. The arrival of the British soldiers, however, unified the village as never before, and the old rivalries were temporarily suppressed in the effort to shield the men from a common enemy.

It would be months before the military gait of the fugitives could be adapted to the clog-clad Villeret shuffle, and even longer before they had absorbed enough of the Picardy patois to fool a German sentry. In the meantime, they were concealed, scattered among the homes of the conspirators. Initially, social relations were severely strained by the language barrier. "The Englishmen were very polite, but they said absolutely nothing at all. None of us knew how to speak English, and they only spoke a little French," Louise Dessenne, Florency's younger daughter, recalled. The families took turns feeding the men, and slowly, with sign language and goodwill on both sides, they settled into a routine.

One of the most sought-after dining spots was in the Foulon
household, where the men would sit at a large oak table beneath
a grand brass chandelier with nine candles. Emile Foulon was a
wealthy man by Villeret standards, almost a squire, and also a culti-
vated one, with a library of fifty volumes ranging from treatises on
botany and horse-breeding to the novels of Victor Hugo and works
of history. He and his daughter could also speak some English, and
their home was among the most comfortable and well appointed in
the village, with fine furniture and possessions, including Oriental
silhouettes by Alfred d'Ancre, a Réaumur barometer, and a stuffed
fox in a glass case. Emile even owned a bowler hat, and twelve pairs
of shoes in a village where most people clopped around in wooden
sabots. It was a relief for the men to be able to converse in their own
tongue, and a positive pleasure to be able to look across the dinner
table at twenty-one-year-old Antoinette, who was not only clever,
vivacious, and a fine cook, but remarkably pretty to boot. After dinner, if the coast was clear, the men could sit in Foulon's garden beneath the great elm tree, two and a half metres across the base,
or wander his orchard among cherry, apple, and Duchesse d'An-
goulême pear trees neatly trained into espaliers against the garden
wall. Robert Digby struck up a firm friendship with the Foulon
spaniel.

The luxuries of the Foulon home stood in contrast to the more
modest accommodation in the Dessenne establishment. Louise
Dessenne, Florency's daughter, described her wartime childhood in
this typical Picard home: "We all lived in four rooms, the children
sleeping together on wooden beds, and the adults in the kitchen.
The floor was of red tiles, and the walls were hung with cloth.
There were no decorations, no pictures, and no books. Every room
had a single window, and the kitchen had a charcoal stove. At table
we mostly ate beans and potatoes. In the morning, it was coffee
with milk or chicory, and some bread; in the evening, it was soup, a
little cheese—Marolles, now, there was a cheese! There was no running water, the toilet was outside the back door, and we washed in
a big tub on the stove. There was always a pot of coffee on the hob.
In the evening, we lit an oil lamp, or candles. But my father said we
had to make economies, so we did not keep the lamps lit for long.

We would stay around the fire. Every evening a German guard would walk down the street, bellowing, when the curfew went into force. As he went back up the road, *maman* would open the curtain a chink and say: 'Look, there goes a rabid dog.' "

Long before curfew, the fugitives would have thanked their hosts and slipped off to their various hideouts around the village: the cellar of the Dessenne house, Parfait Marié's woodshed, and, most ingenious of all, the space behind Léon Lelong's wood-fired oven. "The bread oven was built towards the middle of the largest room in the house, with a concealed area between the partition and the exterior. The Germans never even suspected there was this gap. Lelong put in a mattress, and two of the Englishmen slept here. They were hot, but invisible."

Robert Digby moved gratefully into the attic of the house occu-pied by Suzanne Boitelle and her two-year-old son, Guy. This was not the most commodious of sanctuaries, or the safest, being rather too close to the building occupied by Orstkommandant Scholl, but it was among the most welcoming.

Marie-Suzanne Laurence had married Paul Boitelle two years before the war, when she was nineteen. Suzanne's mother, Céline, had been widely considered the most immoral woman in Villeret—a significant distinction, according to village moralists. Céline bore several children within marriage, one of whom was Elise Lelong, the wife of Léon Lelong, the baker. But after her husband's death, Céline had enjoyed a series of romantic liaisons and produced at least two more illegitimate children by different fathers, each of whom was given her maiden name, Laurence. Suzanne never knew who her own father was, and it is entirely possible that the sporting Céline had only a vague notion herself. Suzanne had dark eyes "like two pistols" and black hair. Some said she was the product of Cé-line's lightning dalliance with a passing Gypsy peddler. Years later, two of her descendants were found to carry a minor genetic mal-ady peculiar to Southern Europe. Céline had died, possibly from overexertion and drink, when Suzanne was still a child, and the or-phan had been brought up by Elise Lelong, her older half-sister. Suzanne was closer in age to the Lelong children, Lucien and Clothilde, and Elise's sense of her own position in Villeret society was disturbed by the presence of Suzanne, an illegitimate half-sister, eighteen years her junior and living proof of her mother's wild ways. Suzanne appears to have been treated as little better than a servant in the Lelong household. When she married Paul Boitelle and moved out to live in his house, barely forty yards away, Suzanne was probably as relieved as Elise, although she continued to work for the Lelong family, delivering the bread. The baker's wife never ceased to look down on her bastard half-sister: when the latter gave birth to Guy, Elise Lelong insisted on calling the child Etienne, since "she considered 'Guy' to be a very pagan name."

Guy had been born in May 1913, and a second son, Roger, appeared the following June, but Suzanne's taste of domestic happiness was brief. In August 1914, Paul Boitelle was mobilised and sent to the front, and barely a month later, the infant Roger was also gone, carried off by Spanish influenza. It was a sadly depleted household that Robert Digby secretly moved into in November 1914, and Suzanne was grateful for the distraction of her secret lodger. Digby told her stories of his family and his childhood in imperial India; for both of them, this was a chance to wander far from Villeret, the battlefields, and the perpetual fear of discovery.

The war, it was generally agreed, could not last very much longer, but the growl of guns from the front swelled, as did the flood of new orders and demands from Le Câtelet. There was no news of any sort, merely rumour, some good, some bad, none accurate. In the waning months of 1914, the grip of winter and the German military machine tightened around Villeret. In December, any young men in the locality aged between eighteen and twenty who had not been mobilised before the invasion, including a dozen from Villeret, were rounded up and marched off in forced-labour gangs. "They were harshly treated," the mayor reported, tuberculosis was rife, and more than half never returned. That same month, rationing was imposed, with cards to show how much bread and meat each inhabitant was permitted. Every household was ordered to post on its door a complete list of all occupants. All French citizens, the orders read, must carry a formal identity card.

The fugitives had been installed less than a month when, as the mayor later recalled, "the occupation of Villeret began in earnest" with the arrival of the 15th Campaign Artillery Regiment and the 81st Infantry Regiment. Suddenly the population was outnumbered by German soldiery, haggard from the front line, with pallid complexions and wide eyes. They were billeted on every house, including those in which the Englishmen were hiding, and they took whatever they wanted. German quartermasters scrawled the number of men and officers to be allotted to each house on the door lintels, the first rash of official military graffiti. Alexis Morel, once one of the richest men in the village, watched gloomily as his stock of food was gradually devoured by the German troops, noting every fresh depredation: "December 16, one black cow; December 21, 6 × 450-kilo bags of flour and 100 litres of peas . . ."

For weeks, the British soldiers were imprisoned in their funkholes, silent, still, and scared, surviving on whatever could be smuggled to them under cover of darkness without alerting the Germans. Poëtte, still acting as a sort of village postman even though there was no mail to deliver, ferried messages between the soldiers. Digby passed the time by reading books smuggled to him from Emile Foulon's library: he pored over leatherbound histories of ancient Greece and Rome recalling his classical education, the novels of Balzac, and, appropriately enough given his current circumstances, Maquet's *History of the Dungeon at Vincennes*. But the volume with the most obvious practical use for a man contemplating escape through enemy-held territory was Foulon's *Guide to Northern France and the Low Countries*, complete with detailed maps and landmarks. Digby had enough time on his hands to memorise every tiny town and back road between Villeret and the Dutch coast.

If the Englishmen of Villeret found themselves in cramped and trying circumstances, their situation was at least more comfortable than that of Private Patrick Fowler, the British hussar who had spent the autumn "in dread of every living soul," living off whatever he could scavenge from the woods around Bertry—a town to the northeast of Le Câtelet, on the very edge of the territory under the control of Major Evers. Fowler had eventually been discovered hiding in the woods by Louis Basquin, a woodcutter rejected by the French army on account of his tubercular condition who was in search of a heroic deed. Basquin led the fugitive to the small cottage belonging to his mother-in-law, Marie Belmont-Gobert, and her twenty-year-old daughter, Angèle. Although Bertry was some distance from the front line, the town was an important staging-area for German troops. Indeed, some twenty soldiers were already billeted in the upstairs rooms of the cottage. Madame Belmont-Gobert therefore acted swiftly, taking a decision that is unique in the annals of warfare. She put the soldier in her cupboard. The widow was poor, but the cupboard was her finest possession, a bulky oak armoire, five and a half feet high, twenty inches deep, with shelves on one side, and on the other, a space to hang clothes or conceal a fairly small cavalryman. It was, nonetheless, a cupboard, and Patrick Fowler's home for the rest of his war.

For the fugitives and their protectors in occupied France, expecting discovery and possible death at any moment, the permanent presence of so many German troops was a nerve-shredding ordeal. Even those French citizens without British soldiers hidden behind ovens, in cupboards, or in attics recoiled at the way every protected corner of their old lives was now invaded, liable to desecration and seizure:

> The most private rooms were violated, the best were taken by the officers, the kitchens were commandeered. There was no longer even the simple satisfaction of being master of one's own home, of enjoying family life in peace . . . Either it was men stationed in the rear or on prolonged rest, or else the continual coming and going of regiments heading to or, worse, coming back from the battlefront, nerves in shreds, their hair standing on end, desperate for rest and recreation. Soldiers covered in mud poured into the houses by the dozen, sometimes even kicking the proprietor out of his own bed.

Longing for the brief amnesia that alcohol could bring, the Germans accused the French of hiding their wine stocks, and cellars were searched time and again. Some complained that the occupying troops fouled the bedrooms, lewdly eyed the village girls, and lit such extravagant fires in the grates that the floorboards ignited.

And yet a few households, including some in Villeret, offered the Germans a cautious, curious welcome. The infantrymen of the 81st Regiment, from a corps of hardened warriors which had participated in no fewer than eight wars against France since 1690, were particularly polite. "At this time, the enemy did not cause any problems; indeed, quite the opposite. Because the soldiers had their meals in the people's homes, many families profited greatly from the leftovers." The Germans were not too bad, some said, and since they were clearly going to eat every scrap of food in the place anyway, it made sense to try to eat it with them.

The war was not yet six months old, but the land was already adapting to its new rhythm. There were those who found the German occupation surprisingly tolerable, even occasionally pleasant. Despite their gruesome reputation, some of the German soldiers turned out be unexpectedly human. In the Château de Grand Priel, the domestics found serving the German officers not much different from serving François Theillier, except that the Germans hunted and ate rather less. One German officer was so impressed by his luxurious surroundings that he photographed the rooms in the occupied château to send to his friends and family back home, showing off the great table beneath chandeliers, bottles of champagne chilled and opened, the bedrooms with their ornate coverings, and a pretty French serving girl—pictured smiling in the kitchen and apparently not at all put out to be included in the photograph album of an enemy invader.

As she had anticipated, Jeanne Magniez also found herself playing unwilling hostess to numerous German officers, who never imagined that hiding directly overhead in the Hargival mansion were two teenage British soldiers. "They were confined to a room from which they could scramble into the attic through a trap door at the first sign of danger. They could only move about at night, or when the house was not full of billeted soldiers, which was rarely." To Jeanne's disgust, a German officer appeared one morning and

informed her that every horse in her stables had been comman-
deered by the German army, leaving only enough animals to continue the farm work. She had just enough time to remove Georges's
Thoroughbred, Flirt, from his stall before German stable-hands arrived to carry out the order. On the rare occasions that Jack Hardy
and his fellow refugee dared to venture outside, "they walked
around the garden, where my husband's horse kept them company,
for he, too, was a fugitive, hidden from German eyes by means of a
large haystack." It is a moot point whether Jeanne Magniez would
rather have surrendered her beloved horse, or her two young
guests.

CHAPTER SEVEN

Rendezvous

❦

Early in 1915, the German troops that had been billeted in Villeret
since December finally headed east, and Digby and the others cau-
tiously re-emerged from their hiding places. A precarious air of
normality returned to Villeret. The village men still worked the
phosphate mine, but now under German supervision. In addition
to the *Orstkommandant* and his staff, too busy counting eggs to pay
much attention to the villagers' faces, "our garrison now consisted
of a corporal and four dragoons, who remained in place and whose
role was that of policemen." They installed themselves in Emile
Foulon's home, moving the farmer and his daughter into an out-
house. Candlelit dinner *chez* Foulon was now a thing of the past.

There were sporadic moments of tension between these "police"
and the villagers, and on one occasion "an old man of 82 was
thrown to the ground by one of the soldiers." But the Germans stationed permanently in Villeret were not looking for trouble, and
gradually the fugitives felt confident enough to spend more time
out in the daylight. During the intervening weeks of semi-captivity,
there had been an opportunity to learn a smattering of the local
tongue, rehearse their stories, and adopt their new identities. The
men's protectors were impressed by how swiftly the soldiers had
picked up French, and Foulon's English-French dictionary was on

hand to help them surmount any serious linguistic hurdles. Robert Digby had spent much of the winter crafting fake identity papers, and each of the men could now pass for a Villeret peasant, at least to the eyes of an incurious German dragoon.

As for the villagers not directly involved in the conspiracy, Marie-Thérèse Dessenne observed: "It's nothing to do with anyone else who we have in our home." But in a village where gossip was the traditional communal pastime, the sudden appearance of these rather odd-looking and taciturn strangers cannot have passed unnoticed; the people of Villeret might be "savages" in the view of some, but they were not blind or deaf. Martin's height and Digby's fair colouring, not to mention their accents, immediately marked them out as strangers. Unfairly, it was later charged that the British soldiers had not made sufficient efforts to blend in: "They never altered their physical appearance, which was playing with fire." Nothing short of cosmetic surgery could have achieved that.

The previous November, the village elders had agreed that, once Digby and his companions had been sufficiently "Villeretised," they would be safer (and certainly more comfortable) living in the open. The drawback to the plan was an obvious one, since it was only a question of time, and loose talk, before the entire village became aware of their identities. The people of Villeret had already displayed courage in abundance, but what had been the conspiracy of a handful would now become a secret shared by the entire village, which any member of the community could betray at any moment, by design or accident. In the meantime, the soldiers could only hope that the war would end, the line would break, or some other way might be found to cross over into Allied-held territory.

There were only two potential escape routes. The first was to head north, cross into Belgium, and try then to get through to Holland across the electrically wired frontier. This had been hard enough for fugitive soldiers to achieve in the first, confused days of the war, but now, with the German military structure in place, with roadblocks and sentries demanding identity papers and travel permits at every crossroads, it seemed barely possible. The alternative was, if anything, even more daunting. The Allied armies might be just a few miles away to the west and south, but between them and Villeret were ranged countless enemy troops, fields of barbed wire, and the hostile subterranean labyrinth of the trenches. Even if, by some miracle, the men managed to sneak past those obstacles and into no-man's-land, they risked being shot dead by their own side as they approached the Allied lines. Had not cunning Germans been heard to shout, "Don't shoot! English!" before launching an attack? Almost completely cut off from news of the war, Digby and the others cannot have known quite how hard it would be to rejoin their armies, and, plainly, they did not care to find out. Only fools or heroes would have attempted such a feat, and there is no evidence that these men fell into either category. A particularly steely British court-martial might have looked on the fugitives as men who had abandoned the flag, and had them shot. Perhaps they were, in a sense, deserters, but they were clearly not cowards. At any time they could have surrendered, resigning themselves to imprisonment but at least escaping the threat of death; instead, they waited.

The Englishmen reacted in different ways to their strange captive circumstances. Taciturn Corporal John Edwards seemed to draw into himself and seldom went outside. Some thought the strain was slowly driving him mad. Willie Thorpe, by contrast, had never been much of a soldier, and seemed almost happy to be out of uniform. "He would play with the village children for hours, doing conjuring tricks," the people recalled. Donohoe and Martin—a Catholic from County Cavan and an Ulster Protestant—had never been great pals when they were in the ranks of the Irish Fusiliers, but as the weeks went by they became inseparable. When the younger man came down with what appeared to be chronic and life-threatening pneumonia, Donohoe nursed him through the illness and delirium with the tenderness of a mother, feeding him the best morsels of his own meagre portion of food. Martin emerged from the sweat-soaked straw of his bed emaciated, and more attached than ever to his fellow countryman.

Of all the soldiers, Robert Digby seemed most in tune with his new home. Villeret may have offered him the freedom that his strict British military upbringing had denied him. He had always craved adventure and chafed at convention; here were excitement and abnormality in excess. Digby absorbed, and was absorbed into, Villeret in a way unlike any of the other fugitives. The Parisian accent he had picked up in the bars of Montparnasse was now overlaid with the guttural twang of Picardy. He learned the slang terms for the local crops, the best method for snaring a rabbit in the Trocmé wood, and, with the help of Marie Coulette's gnarled fingers, the way to thread a Villeret loom. From Suzanne Boitelle, he learned who was related to whom, whose children belonged in which house, and which families had sons and husbands at the war. "It's almost like he was running for mayor," one latter-day villager remarked wryly. Digby's had been a wandering life so far: shifting from one colonial post to another as a child, a failed business, a dominating father and a smothering mother, a stab at soldiering. But in Villeret, an inhospitable terrain of fear and deprivation, he began to put out roots, while hourly hoping for escape.

Conditions at the battlefront were evident from the state of the German troops as they trudged in to rest, and the fugitives must have grasped at least an inkling of the horror they were missing. Somewhere to the west, Digby's younger brother, Thomas, was fighting a more familiar battle, the obscene war of mud, lice, and noise, of human excreta everywhere and sudden death in verminous holes and stagnant ditches, of meaningless sorties and courageous, long-forgotten raids, pointless offensives and counterattacks across a land no longer recognisable. While the Englishmen of Villeret learned French and the rustic village ways, their former comrades were learning to die in numbers too grotesque to comprehend. In March, the British kicked off the spring offensive with the attack on Neuve-Chapelle, in the Artois sector, twenty miles south of Ypres and forty miles north of Péronne. The initial onslaught was a success, but then halted in confusion. By the time the advance resumed, the Germans had reinforced. There were about twelve thousand British killed or wounded and some eight thousand German; most of the ground captured was immediately retaken. Neuve-Chapelle was, nonetheless, considered a success. A month earlier, the French attacked in Champagne: fifty thousand dead, for a mere mile of territory, barely a bend in the line. Even when the generals were not organising major offensives, the French army alone lost soldiers at the rate of a hundred thousand a month. In the less active Picardy sector, the boom of the howitzers could still be heard back in Saint-Quentin, a fresh flood of death with every report, blowing men into pieces so small that often they simply vanished. Thomas Digby did not trouble his family, already distraught over the disappearance of the beloved elder son, with letters detailing his life in the trenches; his war records, like so many others, have been destroyed, burned when the German bombers of a later war blitzed London. But in one rare flash of anger, he let slip to a cousin how much he had hated the "pure hell of it." Thomas would never have laid down his gun or spoken out against the war, yet even he found himself wishfully wondering whether, given his father's accelerating mental illness and his brother's uncertain fate, the king might let him go home. No doubt he believed Robert to be dead, or at best captured. Hunkered in trench and dugout, a sodden world infested by vermin and terror, with rotting duck-board underfoot and a mud-wall horizon of sandbags overhead, Private Thomas Digby thought he was the lucky one.

"The landscape in front of us was similar in character to the one behind us, but mysterious with its unknown quality of being 'behind the Boche line,' " wrote Siegfried Sassoon. As he gazed across the battle line, Thomas Digby prayed, often and fervently, that his brother had survived somewhere in that other world. "I still had hope," he later wrote. Their circumstances could hardly have been more different, yet in some strange way the brothers were both suspended in the limbo of war, with the line of the trenches a distorting mirror between them: stuck in the Picardy earth, fearful to go forward, unable to go back, imagining deliverance on good days, expecting to die on the others.

When the guns fell silent, the Aisne Valley in the spring of 1915 seemed almost unruffled by the conflict. One British reconnaissance pilot flew over the lines into the occupied region, and wondered where the war had gone: "Far behind, in enemy territory, I saw factories with smoking chimneys and pleasantly normal villages. I counted six plumes of steam from equally normal trains."

In Villeret, the frogs rasped in the ponds down by the crossroads, and the priest came every second Sunday to say Mass. In the past, "the three pretty bells pealed happily in the tower, calling the faithful to sacred prayer," but no longer, for, like all church bells in the occupied region, they had been taken away to be melted down in aid of the German war effort. The congregation had swelled with war, and if the British soldiers discreetly joined the choir to add their devotions to those of their protectors, the *curé* Véron did not seem to notice. The people worked the fields, and the steady clack of the shuttles rattled up from the cellars. Antoinette Foulon continued to teach her thirty pupils in the little school and tend the roses of Picardy that grew outside it, and in her schoolroom the hungry children sang patriotic marching songs that the German authorities would doubtless have silenced had they understood the meaning of the words:

> Où t'en vas-tu, soldat de France,
> Tout équipé, prêt au combat?
> Où t'en vas-tu, petit soldat?
> C'est comme il plaît à la Patrie,
> Je n'ai qu'à suivre les tambours.
> Gloire au drapeau,
> Gloire au drapeau.
> J'aimerais bien revoir la France,
> Mais bravement mourir est beau.

> Where are you going, soldier of France,
> Kitted out, ready for battle?
> Where are you going, little soldier?
> Wherever the Fatherland orders,
> I have only to follow the drums.
> Glory to the flag,
> Glory to the flag.
> I would love to see France again,
> But a brave death is beautiful.

Overlaying the ancient sounds of Villeret came newer, but increasingly familiar ones. The crump of high explosive from the front was absorbed into the daily rhythms, a part of the tonal landscape accepted and for the most part ignored by occupier and occupied alike. Ernst Jünger, the celebrated German writer, war hero, nihilist, and militarist, recalled hearing from behind the lines the "slow pulsation of the machinery of the front, a tune to which long years were to accustom us." Very occasionally, stray shells, fired by accident or wildly off course, would provide sanguinary reminders of the war's proximity. Marie-Thérèse Dessenne described to her daughter how she was returning from Lelong's bakery one morning when "a shell landed on a German who was walking ahead of her. She saw his head land first, and then the body."

François Theillier would have fumed at the way the six German reconnaissance planes, stationed at the new military aerodrome on the plateau opposite the Château de Grand Priel, sent the game running for cover with their noisy manoeuvres. In the village it was said that among the German officers enjoying the comforts of Theillier's château was a handsome German flying ace who had shot down scores of French and British planes. That a certain romance was beginning to attach to some of the occupiers was only one reflection of a time knocked out of alignment, in which the old certainties were reversing. The fertile land was tended in the way it always had been, but now under the orders, and for the benefit, of the foreign invaders. As Henri Lelong recorded: "The Germans made everyone in the village work for them. The crops of potatoes, wheat, and beet were grown in the fields, but then sent off to Germany." By command of Major Evers, everyone in Villeret was required to aid the German war effort, "under the surveillance of the corporal and his four sentries."

With their own (albeit forged) identity papers, Digby and the other soldiers were now officially part of the Villeret community, and since their faces were as familiar to the German sentries as those of any other villager, they, too, were marched out to the fields. "They left the village and went to work, joining the columns of civilian labourers, under the very noses of the enemy soldiers, who, for a long time, never suspected a thing." Perhaps the sight of the British men digging undetected alongside them in the fields gave renewed hope to the people of Villeret, who now lived in a world of ever weightier repression and privation. But for the fugitives, the days spent in the spring sunshine must have come as a relief, after a winter of captivity and anxiety, crushed into attic and cellar or sweltering behind the village bread oven. Tom Donohoe had spent his childhood extracting potatoes from the fields around Killybandrick, so it was no hardship to do the same in Villeret. Martin, still pasty from pneumonia but regaining strength, worked alongside him in the fields.

Early in 1915, the people of Le Câtelet had found themselves mulling over the most bizarre command yet to emanate from the indefatigable Major Evers: "The officers have heard a cock crowing in the village. These are evidently concealed chickens. The owners must come forward and surrender them, or they will be severely punished." Nothing edible or of value should be hidden, under the occupiers' philosophy, and any attempt to do so was tantamount to armed resistance. It was, remarked one inhabitant, "a return to the cruelty and morality of the Dark Ages." The keeping of gold louis pieces was forbidden; passes to visit other villages were henceforth to be issued only in "cases of extreme seriousness." No tree could be felled. "With the cellars pillaged and exhausted, they desperately sought possible hiding places for wine," and any house thought to be concealing supplies of alcohol was liable to sudden search.

Nothing was too insignificant to escape the grasping reach of Evers and his men. A typical requisition order, to a bourgeois family in nearby Vendhuile, read: "You are required to provide, as soon as possible, potato plates, vegetable plates, cups, coffee bowls with matching saucers, flat plates, curved plates, sauceboats, coffeemakers, tablecloths in good condition, white napkins, toiletry table, a night table, a toiletry service, a chamber pot, tables, armchairs, dining chairs . . ." For the humbler folk of Villeret, the demands were more simple, and more devastating: pots, pans, lamps, mattresses, axes, scythes, nails, brushes, cooking oil, leather, grease, geese, and paper all poured into the gaping maw of the German invader. Emile Foulon's great elm was felled and planked. Then the walnut trees lining the graveyard were cut down and dragged away, to make German rifle butts.

By mid-1915, white bread could not be found anywhere in the locality, other than on the German officers' tables, and in Villeret, Lelong's oven went cold for lack of flour and fuel, forcing the villagers to seek other forms of nourishment. "The continual surveillance could not prevent the inhabitants from venturing out at night and gathering whatever grain they could find in sacks. This was then ground in coffee grinders and used to create a sort of coarse bread . . . Some of the scavengers were caught by the German dragoons, and beaten up." Evers heard about the use of coffee grinders and immediately ordered, with towering pettiness, that all such machines be confiscated. This removal of "a tool by which a starving people kept itself alive" was noted down as "a particularly cruel method of deprivation." When Evers was told that requisitioning and rationing had reduced some communities to near-starvation, his reply (no doubt intentionally, for he had spent part of his education in Paris) recalled the apocryphal remark attributed to Marie-Antoinette: "Let them eat salad and potatoes," he said.

The mayor of Villeret noted that the food situation improved slightly "in June 1915, when we began to receive some meagre American rations," thanks to Herbert Hoover. The businessman who would eventually become the United States' thirty-first president played an important role in keeping Villeret alive through his Commission for Relief in Belgium—the international civilian relief effort which collected food and cash from local committees in neutral countries, principally the United States, and then distributed vital supplies to Belgium and the occupied regions of northern France. Hoover's "miracle of scientific organisation," as Lord Curzon called it, became markedly less scientific as its network approached the battle zones. Often the supplies did not get through, despite German promises to let the convoys pass. Villeret had once taken pride in its self-sufficiency; now the irregular occasions when the trucks arrived offering a few packets of donated food were enough to bring the village inhabitants pouring into the street, hands outstretched.

As the soldiers found in the trenches, even terror can become routine. The British fugitives, and their protectors, lived under permanent threat of exposure, arrest, and summary death, and yet, as the months passed, the fear began to recede. The men could never relax, but they could at least begin to breathe. Initially the village people had openly stared at them and refused to understand when they spoke, but gradually the French came not merely to accept their presence but to regard them, in some way, as trophies of resistance: "Our Englishmen." Curiosity and mistrust gave way to familiarity, and then to guarded affection. The refugees were at once exotic and vulnerable, and in a village now composed largely of women, they brought out a variety of instincts: maternal, patriotic, adoptive, romantic, and complex. William Thorpe, the Liverpudlian with the atrocious French accent and gentle manner, became a special favourite. Some of the younger Englishmen threw themselves into the task of becoming Frenchmen, but Thorpe literally carried his past around with him, certain that he would eventually retrieve it. "He had a photograph of his three children, which he showed to everyone. He was very proud of those children." In the Villeret code of values, family was of paramount importance: the village gave him the nickname Papa. "He was a serious fellow," one recalled with approval.

The young Irishmen were also popular. Willie O'Sullivan's horseplay made the village girls giggle, although older heads shook and called him *hardi*, reckless and impudent. Thomas Donohoe might eat like a horse, but he also worked like one; David Martin, the onetime cook, often lent a hand in Villeret's kitchens. "He was particularly good at making hot chocolate," and so, whenever anyone in the village happened to obtain some of that precious commodity, the Irish cook was called in.

But it was Robert Digby who provided the village with the most food for thought, and gossip. Digby had a different poise that set him apart from the others. Back in barracks in England, the Digby brothers had often joked of being related to the aristocratic Digby family of Dorset, although there was no link whatever. As the focus of so much flattering attention in Villeret, Digby appears to have brought that harmless lie with him, forging his own mythology and boosting his rank, socially and militarily: "He was a nobleman, an aristocrat related to the king of England." He awarded himself the rank of sergeant, and eight decades later, the mythology has refused to die: "He was an officer, from a great military family." In this remote peasant village, stripped of its natural defences and most of its native men, Robert Digby must have seemed like an alien deity, and he evidently played up to the part. "He was so handsome. The women thought a lot of him." When Marie-Thérèse Dessenne gave birth to her fourth child, in the spring of 1915, she named the boy Robert. "She loved Digby. She thought of him almost as a grown-up son," said her daughter. While Digby easily charmed the women of Villeret, young and old, some of the men were rather less smitten.

It is possible that Claire Dessenne first caught Digby's eye when he staggered, wounded, into her family's home in August 1914, but most sources agree that the affair began in Marie Coulette's kitchen early in 1915. It was an unlikely place for love to bloom. Digby and the other men were crammed around the table alongside the Dessennes, who usually spoke nothing but Villeret patois (as distinct from Saint-Quentin patois, or even Hargicourt patois), at high volume. The noise was deafening, for Marie Coulette "was always laughing and shouting." She and Marie-Thérèse doled out from a vast pot whatever had been hoarded, cadged, or filched during the day. "It usually wasn't much, just potatoes in a soup," and her twenty-year-old granddaughter passed the bowls around.

Vivacious, slender, and alluring, Claire Dessenne was almost as out of place in dowdy Villeret as Robert Digby. Before the war, she had been employed in the cloth factory at Hargicourt, but now, like all the women in the village, she was forced to work in the fields under the surveillance of German soldiers. She gave them a hard time: "Germany *kaput*!" she shouted at the sentries. "*La France va gagner la guerre!*" (France is going to win the war!) Under the repressive Evers regime, such insolence was liable to dire punishment, but no German sentry would report a girl so pretty. Claire loved to dance, and she was proud of her looks and her auburn locks. "Her hair was very long, chestnut-coloured, and she wore it twisted into a *chignon*, a looping bun known as a 'double eight.'" Like the other women, she clattered around in wooden clogs or galoshes, but even in her long peasant dress "reaching to the floor" and ragged shawl, she was the belle of Villeret society. Achille Poëtte was said to be among those smitten with Claire, and the lugubrious postman was often to be found lingering at the Dessenne front door. "You could hear him coming, shouting: '*Ma p'ti' Tiot*,' 'my darling' in patois." Claire barely gave Achille the time of day, which may only have made him more ardent.

Digby still lodged at night with Suzanne Boitelle, but spent more and more of his time at the Dessenne household, a place of fierce arguments, loud noises, and pungent smells far removed from his own genteel upbringing in the British colonies. The other Englishmen moved from one family to another, depending on who had the resources to feed them, but Digby no longer went with them, preferring, for reasons that were fast becoming plain, to dine at the Dessenne table.

The Dessenne women were, in almost every case, made of sterner stuff than their menfolk: Marie Coulette ruled the roost from her tiny lair in the eaves, smoking her pipe and bellowing merrily. Next in the line of authority was Marie-Thérèse, Florency's wife, a gentler creature than her mother-in-law, but with a similar resilience. "Even when she was carrying tiny children, she went out to pull beets from the frozen fields." At the age of forty, Marie-Thérèse had already worked hard enough for two lives, but she looked half her age, as a result of an accident that is tempting to see as apocryphal and symbolic of the remarkable goodness of her soul. She had been just eleven years old, working as a scullery maid for a wealthy lawyer in Péronne, when her face and arms had been horribly burned in a kitchen fire. After six months in a hospital, she had emerged with a face still blackened and disfigured. Her daughter recalled: "One day several months later, she was eating a piece of chicken and the bone stuck in her lip. She pulled, and the skin from her entire face peeled off in one go. She was terrified. But underneath she had the most beautiful complexion, perfectly pink, perfectly soft. As she grew older, her skin was always lovely, with barely a wrinkle."

Claire's mother, Eugénie, was also a formidable power in the Dessenne ménage, with beetling brows and strong views, an odd contrast to Claire's father, Jules, now fighting somewhere in Alsace. Jules was a burly, happy man, with an enormous appetite and grotesque table manners which had earned him the nickname Le Boeuf (The Bull). "When he sat down at the table, they closed the shutters to stop anyone from seeing the spectacle," his nephew recalled. Claire had inherited her mother's forthright manner and her father's hunger for life, and the combination did not always sit well with her neighbours: "She had a mouth on her, that one, and she wasn't afraid of anyone. She was a liability."

The Dessenne men were, by contrast, a pallid lot. Léon Recolet, Marie Coulette's brother, ought by rights to have been head of the household, but was more than happy to yield authority to his sister, spending most of his time in the village cafés or gossiping in the square. Some dismissed him as a simpleton.

Tall, cadaverous Florency had a stout heart, but the rest of him was distinctly passive. His record book for military service in 1902 offered this assessment of his talents: "Can't read, can't write, can't swim." But there was one job at which Florency excelled. Although he called himself a mason, he was, as everyone in Villeret knew, really a professional tobacco-smuggler. His methods were rudimentary, but effective. "My father would leave at night and travel by cart up to the Belgian border," his daughter Louise remembered. The most direct route to Belgium was still the ancient Roman road. At a prearranged spot on the frontier, "they would send the dog across, carrying two bags strapped to its sides. My father and another man would wait, in hiding. When the dog came back across the border, the bags were filled with tobacco." Working with a Belgian accomplice, Florency had "imported" contraband for years, which he then sold for a substantial profit. Everyone in Villeret bought from him, since Florency's tobacco was cheaper than the legal stuff and good-quality. His daughters were sent off to distribute the haul to various customers around the village, and Florency's clientele extended as far as Hargicourt and Le Câtelet. Marie Coulette took a cut of the profits. "My father really enjoyed the smuggling," Florency's daugh-

ter said. "He was like a big child, playing cops and robbers. He even
sold to the *gendarmes*, when they weren't chasing him." Before the
war, Florency had enjoyed a happy and profitable existence: potter-
ing around the village by day, smuggling by night, and practicing
archery every Sunday afternoon behind the café.

In spite of his pivotal role in the community as the supplier of illegal tobacco, even Florency's own family considered him "a weed,"
though an obliging one. He had once worked as a well-digger, and
"because he knew how to clean wells, the families were always getting him to come and clean out their toilets. Since he didn't really
know how to say no, he always did it . . . he was a kind man, too
kind." Florency had his uses, but friends and neighbours agreed that
"it was his wife, Marie-Thérèse, who wore the trousers."

Robert Digby had been welcomed into the Dessenne household
from the moment he had lurched through the back door in August 1914. Digby's natural ebullience chimed with that of Marie
Coulette, and a strangely strong bond had developed between the
fugitive Englishman and the rough peasant clan; this was now reinforced and complicated by the accident of passion.

The moment when Robert Digby and Claire Dessenne fell in
love has entered Dessenne family myth. It is recalled, appropriately,
as the sound of a cannon shot: "They fell for one another. Boum!
Just like that."

Love was a new experience for both. The village was agreed that
Claire, despite the strenuous efforts of several village Romeos, "had
never known a man before." And whatever girlfriends Digby may
have had before the war, none had been serious enough to warrant
introduction to his family. In accordance with the manners instilled
from his youth, Digby simply did not discuss his amatory past, although his easy manner around women suggests he was no stranger
to them. Falling in love was a different matter. Digby's earlier life
had been marked by tension between the dictates of his tight-laced
upbringing and his more romantic inclinations. Beneath the up-
right middle-class soldier who could trot out references to duty,
God, and honour as required, and mean them, there had always
been another man, a headstrong, "gallus" youth who wandered off

to Paris and got into fights and now found himself utterly infatu-
ated by a French maiden in the middle of a battle. Digby had been
taught and trained to do the right thing, but nothing in his Victorian education or experience told him what to do when faced with
love in circumstances of such overwhelming danger. So he followed
his heart. He must have been aware that a love affair with Claire
would substantially increase the risk to them both, to his fellow soldiers, and to the entire village; but he was unwilling and perhaps
unable to stop it. Claire, too, must have wondered whether her feel-
ings were leading her, and her family, towards destruction.

Robert Digby—or Robert Boitelle, as he was now described on
his faked identity pass—helped Claire carry in the wood for the fire,
and his portions of food seemed a little more generous than those
of the other men. He lingered after the frugal evening meal, waiting
until the hour of curfew before hurrying from the Dessenne house
in rue d'En Bas and returning to the attic in Suzanne Boitelle's tiny
home. Claire and Digby could be spotted chatting happily together
down by the frog ponds. He promised to teach her to speak English; she helped him master patois and laughed at his accent. For a
time, Robert Digby may have forgotten about the war as entirely as
it had forgotten about him. Willie Thorpe, who considered himself
an authority on the joys of love and marriage, was whole-hearted in
his support for the match, but some of the other men began to
question whether Digby's ardour was not to prove his undoing,
and theirs.

The village girls were quick to cotton on to what was afoot, and
so were Claire's older relatives. Marie Coulette merely shrugged.
Affairs outside marriage were hardly unknown in Villeret, and in
fact common in the Dessenne family. There was a village saying,
much repeated: "God said behave, but He didn't say how."

Claire's mother, Eugénie, was markedly less sanguine about the
attentions being paid to her pretty but rebellious daughter by this
handsome and exceptionally dangerous young Englishman. However, Marie Virginie, née Dupuis (universally known, for some reason, as Eugénie), was hardly in the strongest moral position in this
regard. Claire herself had been born out of wedlock when Eugénie

was twenty-three, and it was not until the girl was four years old that Jules "Le Boeuf" Dessenne had finally wed Eugénie.

Robert Digby was not in a position to marry her daughter, but Eugénie's objections were probably more practical than moral. A hunted fugitive in occupied territory, likely to be captured and executed at any moment, was hardly the ideal long-term marriage prospect. Mother and daughter had never been close, and Claire made no secret of her belief that her mother paid more attention to her younger sister and brother, Marie and Jules, a view that was backed up by others: "Claire was much more like her grandmother Marie Coulette. In contrast, Eugénie was an aggressive type, and dour. Of the three children, it was Claire who got least affection."

Claire modelled herself on her grandmother: "Marie Coulette was a tough old bird, but a woman with a grip on life. Claire took after her, particularly in her sense of humour. They both liked to laugh and joke; Eugénie was more serious, and more strict." The obvious mutual attraction between Robert Digby and Claire Dessenne now set mother and daughter on a collision course, with Eugénie loudly complaining that this lunatic flirtation could easily get them all killed. She stopped talking to Digby altogether, and did her best to put an end to the affair before it began. "Emile, Claire's sixteen-year-old cousin, was given strict instructions to act as a chaperon and not let her and Digby out of his sight." Julie, another Dessenne cousin, was also recruited to spy on the couple and report back to her aunt. "Claire did everything she could to shake them off," and Emile swiftly turned collaborator. Claire and Digby would quietly disappear into Florency Dessenne's hayloft, while Emile acted as a lookout below, to warn of the approach of any Germans, or Claire's angry mother.

Marie-Thérèse, though fond of Robert Digby, also disapproved, and wondered aloud why Claire was flinging herself at the Englishman. "She looked askance at the whole thing. Claire imposed herself; she would make the other men come down from the hayloft so she could be with her lover." But Suzanne Boitelle, also the product of illicit romance, appears to have supported the love affair, and may have acted as another willing accomplice. As a trysting place, her attic could not have been more convenient. Digby had already managed to evade the German army. Getting past Eugénie Dessenne was child's play.

On February 15, 1915, Kaiser Wilhelm II himself passed through Villeret and Hargicourt, on his way to Saint-Quentin, as part of a grand inspection of the German lines linked to the celebration of his fifty-sixth birthday. His motorcade swept by "without stopping," noted the mayor of Hargicourt, with regret. "There was no time to see him." Here was the most savoury of ironies: the all-powerful, all-feted Kaiser, displaying his military muscle and lifting a superior gloved hand to the awed Frenchmen and -women lining the roads of the land he now occupied, while, in the hay a few yards away, an enemy soldier made love to a beautiful French girl.

A year earlier, before the British Expeditionary Force set sail for France, Britain's secretary of state for war had issued a warning to the troops: "In this new experience you may find temptation in both wine and women. You must entirely resist both temptations, and, while treating all women with proper courtesy, you should avoid all intimacy." But Robert Digby and Claire Dessenne were now as entwined in love as the armies were locked in war, and there was nothing Lord Kitchener, the Kaiser, or Eugénie Dessenne could do to stop them.

The German sentry posted on the edge of the village would turn a blind eye, villagers recalled, when the couple slipped out into the fields and climbed to the rise to look down on the village. Shortly before the war, the view had inspired one traveller to lyricism, and even in 1915, when the sound of crickets eclipsed the groaning guns at dusk, Villeret must have seemed a charming place for lovers, "with its undulating folds of landscape, its little copses and woods, its gentle slopes, its crops of wheat, rye, and hay, dotted here and there with poppies, their red petals in June contrasting with the green of wheatfields and the oatfields speckled with little yellow flowers. It is such a picturesque vision of rural nature that you will be captivated, you will stop to contemplate, and admire."

In May, the Allies attacked the German lines to the north, the French at Vimy Ridge, the British at Aubers Ridge, with negligible military results apart from a hundred thousand French dead and sixty thousand British losses. As the blood tide rose, Robert Digby wooed Claire Dessenne with urgency, a doomed and importunate courtship in a condemned land. The novelist Frederic Manning, who fought on the Somme and the Ancre, wrote of the romantic passion unleashed by war: "In the shuddering revulsion from death, one turns instinctively to love as an act which seems to affirm the completeness of being." In the trenches and behind the lines, men and women struggled to hold or re-create fragments of an ordinary life—a letter from home, a pot of jam, a kiss—to remind them of their own humanity. It was this, the juxtaposition of the normal and the abominable, that gave this war its peculiar, horrific character, what one writer on the Great War has called the "ironic proximity of violence and disaster to safety, to meaning, and to love."

As one Villeret villager observed, "There was no dancing in Villeret at this time, during the war." But in the dusty Dessenne cow byre, Robert and Claire twirled around to her favourite dances, "the waltz, the polka, the mazurka," while Thorpe, Donohoe, and Martin clapped and stamped.

The June poppies were out, splashing arterial scarlet across the green fields, when a development that had been known to Claire and suspected by her mother for several weeks, became apparent to the villagers of Villeret: Claire Dessenne was carrying the Englishman's child.

CHAPTER EIGHT

Aren't Those Things Flowers?

❧

Both the Digby brothers, on either side of the line, caught the pungent whiff of mouldy hay that spring. While Robert Digby had been making love to Claire in the Dessenne hayloft, a distinctive odour was heading on the wind towards the Allied trenches. Germany launched the first successful chlorine-gas attack in April, north of Ypres, sending a ten-foot-high cloud of lethal lichen-green vapour into the opposite trenches. Thousands coughed themselves to death. The use of chlorine by the German *Stinkpioniere* units was followed by asphyxiating phosgene gas, carbon oxychloride, treacherously invisible and twenty times more deadly. Phosgene did not kill immediately. Death came painfully by drowning, after the victim had retched up several pints of yellow mucus, the much-praised phlegm of the British soldier turned lethally against him. The first warning of a gas attack, followed by a frantic scramble for gas masks, might be just the faintest tang on the breeze, murderous but beguilingly familiar: the smell, in Thomas Digby's words, of rotting straw.

In June, the British 3rd Army agreed to occupy parts of the line hitherto held by the French, and moved down to defend the line from north of the Somme, due west of Villeret. The fugitives were now closer to their own army than at any time since they had lost their units in August 1914. As Robert Digby looked to the west,

Thomas Digby clutched his gun and faced east. Thomas detested the war, but his few pronouncements on the subject suggest he never questioned it or doubted its moral purpose. He was a devout man, patriotic, romantic in the most conventional way, awed by God and king as only those born before the war could be, and as those who came after never could be again. He followed the rules laid down by parent, schoolmaster, officer, and Bible, and he never did less than whatever he was expected to do. He was the sort of Englishman extolled by Sir Henry Newbolt: steadfast, polite, incurious, and never doubting that it was his allotted role to "play up, and play the game," with a tot of rum to stiffen the dullard sinews. The armies of the Great War were filled with such unquestioning souls, as are the graveyards of northern France.

Not far from where Thomas Digby crouched, an American poet and French foreign legionnaire called Alan Seeger composed a poem that precisely caught the robust fatalism of the hour, the gung-ho, idealised acceptance of a date with death, expressed in simple rhymes. A Harvard graduate, classmate and friend of T. S. Eliot, and rising star in the bohemian poetic circles of Greenwich Village, Seeger had been among the first Americans to join up, marching off to battle in 1914 at the age of twenty-six.

> I have a rendezvous with Death
> At some disputed barricade,
> When Spring comes back with rustling shade
> And apple-blossoms fill the air . . .

Seeger would have envied but disdained the sort of rendezvous Robert Digby was enjoying.

> God knows 'twere better to be deep
> Pillowed in silk and scented down,
> Where love throbs out in blissful sleep,
> Pulse nigh to pulse, and breath to breath,
> Where hushed awakenings are dear . . .
> But I've a rendezvous with Death.

Thomas Digby's war was a squalid but simple affair. That of his older brother was turning out to be surprisingly pleasant—what his former comrades-in-arms would have termed a "cushy" billet—but increasingly complicated.

The moral absolutes that still steered the likes of Thomas Digby and Alan Seeger were fast disappearing behind the German lines, where relations between the British fugitives, their protectors, and the German invaders were undergoing subtle and complex evolution. The initial occupation, although harsh and terrifying, had been ethically unambiguous for those who suddenly found themselves under German rule. The Boche, *les Pruscots* (as the Prussians were dismissed in slang), were savages, objects of disdain as well as fear: protecting the fugitive soldiers was a patriotic duty; the war would be over soon; life would return to normal. But as another summer came and went, and the hunger gnawed more deeply, each of those comforting assumptions became fragile, indistinct, shifting, and treacherous. The Boche might be beasts collectively, but individually they were human, several were courteous, and some were even attractive. The British soldiers in Villeret had become obligations, and feeding them a chore that left other, French stomachs even emptier. Claire's swelling belly was only the most visible sign that new calculations and considerations would have to be made.

On either side of the trenches, the soldiers marvelled at the adaptability of the French, whose lives had been so invaded. "You'd think these Frenchies had lived in a war for years and years," remarks a character in Frederic Manning's novel of trench life. Those who had thought the battle could never come, now wondered if it would ever leave, as the normality of village life drained away, leaving a muted shell of the former life. Even the dogs were banned from barking, and then suddenly taxed, in some cases to death. Many dog-owners felt obliged to kill their animals, since they had no money to pay the tax. Florency Dessenne apparently concluded that his German-shepherd dog, his smuggling companion in earlier days, threatened to draw lethal attention to the house; a single bark could bring the Germans bursting in when the Englishmen were inside. One day, the dog disappeared. Foulon's spaniel also vanished.

Jeanne Magniez's home in the Hargival mansion had now become one of the most popular billets for German officers, thanks in part to its feisty and amusing proprietress. With her house permanently filled with Germans, Jeanne was increasingly concerned for the safety of the two young soldiers hidden above. One accidental footfall, one officer with particularly acute hearing, and these friendly German officers could put all of them in front of a firing squad. "They went through some horribly dangerous moments," she wrote. "As a last resort, I gave up my own bedroom to them." Surely no officer or search party would dare to break into the private quarters of a respectable and wealthy Frenchwoman. Inevitably, given Jeanne's somewhat risqué reputation, there were those who gossiped that at least one officer had already been welcomed into her bedroom. "Finally, the day arrived when my home and farm became, from cellar to attic, a veritable German barracks, and it was completely impossible to hide the two young men any longer . . . They would have to give themselves up. But who to?" Jeanne was not about to let her wards fall into the hands of Major Evers. "The *Kommandant* of Le Câtelet had a reputation as an evil man, but the one over at Ronssoy was said to be a good fellow, with a reasonable nature." Ronssoy was just five miles or so to the west, on the other side of the canal, but getting there without official passes or transport, and with two Englishmen in tow, was a daunting prospect even for Jeanne Magniez. "But it was to Ronssoy that Mademoiselle de Becquevort and I set out, once again leading our two protégés, having succeeded, in spite of the numerous sentries, in getting them across the bridge at Vendhuile." Leaving Jack Hardy and his companion in a wood, to surrender to the reputedly tender-hearted *Kommandant* of Ronssoy when they were well away from the area, Jeanne and Anne retraced their steps and arrived back at Hargival before dawn.

Finally, the British soldiers were off her hands, and Jeanne could relax for the first time in a year. Her relief lasted only a few hours. That night, Jeanne Magniez found herself wondering whether she had risked her life for a pair of ungrateful traitors. "The very same day, some officers from the German command post at Ronssoy came to pay a visit to their compatriots staying at Hargival. One that I had met before greeted me with the words: 'Your two Englishmen arrived safely.' " Jeanne was profoundly shocked, and briefly terrified. "It was only by God's good grace that I managed to prevent myself from raising my eyebrows." The two young men whom she had protected and fed for month after month had, it seemed, blithely told their story to the Germans as soon as they were in captivity. Was it possible? "Had my two young Englishmen, without a care, turned informers and given away their place of refuge?" she pondered. Nothing came of the officer's apparently nonchalant remark, yet for the first time, Jeanne began to wonder whether the British soldiers, for whom she had put herself in mortal danger, were worthy of the sacrifice. If her two special wards had put her head in a noose within hours of surrendering, what might the others, still lurking in Villeret, not do to protect their own skins?

If the appeal of the fugitive Englishmen was fading somewhat, then the Germans were also ceasing to be painted in lurid colours as murderers and looters. The strain was taking a toll on occupiers and occupied alike. Early in 1915, word went around the district that a young German officer, in despair at having to order his men back to the front, had burned himself to death. A few months later, the body of another German was found floating in the canal. Some could not bear the transformation in themselves, like the narrator of *All Quiet on the Western Front* who suddenly catches sight of his own brutalised soul:

> A little soldier and a kindly voice, and if anyone were to caress him, he probably wouldn't understand the gesture any more, that soldier with the big boots and a heart that has been buried alive, a soldier who marches because he is wearing marching boots and who has forgotten everything except marching. Aren't those things flowers, over there on the horizon, in a landscape so calm and quiet that the soldier could weep? Are those not images that he has not exactly lost, because he never had them to lose, confusing images, but nevertheless of things that can no longer be his? Are they not his twenty years of life?

To their own surprise, the French found there were different species of German. The Prussians were the worst, it was generally agreed, "imbued with the ancient spirit of race." The soldiers from the Bavarian Alps, with "gold earrings and knives in their boots," were given "to screaming like wild animals," but on the whole the Bavarians were more sympathetic and could sometimes be heard complaining that they were being deployed as cannon fodder, "human sacrifices . . . under Prussian hegemony." The ordinary German foot soldier, weary and homesick, was often more to be pitied than loathed. A few of the invaders would "offer around cigars, on occasion, or even food to the people in whose houses they were lodged," although the more patriotic types insisted they only accepted such gifts in order "to throw them in the fire" later. One or two of the more congenial German soldiers earned the gratitude of the French villagers by agreeing to pass on messages to relatives and friends in neighbouring communities. "It was hard to maintain an absolutely cold and distant attitude and a blanket refusal to speak to the invaders—although many managed to affect one—when they were involved in every aspect of our existence." As the perceptive Ernst Rosenhainer observed: "Under the circumstances, the people have little choice but to be friendly to us."

Faced with the prospect of returning to the trenches, the German soldiers were often loath to leave their French billets, however humble. "Some soldiers could not hide their anguish at leaving," recalled one inhabitant of Le Câtelet. "A horrible vision obsessed them: death, dreadful death, beneath the bullets, in a foreign land far from their families. The officers were no less upset than their men as they bid adieu to their hosts: some could not hold back tears." It was getting harder to hate all Germans. "After a time, a shared agony brought together the suffering soldiers and the suffering people."

France under occupation was a confused and confusing place. In April, the official German school-inspector, a rotund pedant by the name of Uppenkamp, waddled into the village school at Bellicourt and demanded to know why, at 8:00 a.m., the children were not working at their desks as they would be in a German school. From behind her own desk, the headmistress, Claire Hénin, replied sharply, "Under the rules issued by the French school-inspectorate, classes begin at nine."

"I am your inspector, you do not have another," spluttered Uppenkamp.

Mademoiselle Hénin rose to her feet, fixed him with a look that had reduced successive generations of schoolchildren to tears, and declared: "Monsieur, you forget that we are an occupied country, not a conquered one."

The schoolmistress, defiantly singing the "Marseillaise" at full volume, was immediately arrested, taken to Saint-Quentin, tried by the military court, and deported to Germany, where she spent the rest of the war.

Local opinion was divided over the matter. Some declared Mademoiselle Hénin a heroine who had made a "glorious and valiant" stand, but others thought that going to prison for the sake of an extra hour of school was ridiculous, and some pointed out that the school had been closed and the entire community punished because of the teacher's hopeless gesture of defiance. "She lacked the sense to control her indignation and anger in front of the enemy," one villager remarked; another argued that, since it was impossible to beat back the German horde, one should learn to live with them: "In her place, I would have kept my mouth shut and spent the night in my own bed."

For every voice urging accommodation, another urged resistance. All across the occupied region, small groups of men and women were meeting in secret, to undermine the invaders, organise acts of sabotage, and pass on information. But even the resisters urged prudence over defiance: "Under the regime of terror which we are undergoing," declared the secretly printed and wittily titled *Journal des Occupés . . . inoccupés* (literally, "Newspaper of the Occupied People . . . with nothing to do), "we must understand how to *dare*, but we must dare with *caution*, with *moderation*, without *rashness*."

While the French under occupation scrabbled to survive, wrestling with unpalatable choices, and the front-line soldiers lost their minds, their humanity, and their lives, those Germans who, like

Major Karl Evers, had the good fortune to have permanent post-
ings in the rear, were learning to live in France with no difficulty
whatever. This was hardly surprising: Evers was enjoying an existence close to that of the feudal prince who had ruled the area a mil-
lennium earlier, with every available comfort taken as his due. "I'm
paid 1,000 marks a month to hunt pheasants," he once remarked. "I
can't complain."

Unlike the fighting men, the administrative officials never ran
short of drink, for Evers was in a position to intercept stocks destined for officers in the line. Women of easy virtue were brought in
from Saint-Quentin and then "shipped back before dawn." When
one mayor dared to complain of such immoral behavior, Evers issued a characteristic riposte, and an order: "I forbid you to repri-
mand women who wish to be agreeable to the officers." While the
local inhabitants lived on grey bread, rotting potatoes, and thin
soup, the invaders appeared in French eyes to be pursuing a life of
leisure and stupendous Bacchanalian excess: "Country walks, hunting trips, orgies: everything took place amid copious quantities of
drink, toasting public holidays, their various birthdays, victories
cheered to the rafters, medals and promotions. Even their administrative work seemed like just another sport, since it consisted of
daily depredations and searches, without hindrance or limit." Emile
Foulon's piano was confiscated, shipped by cart to Le Câtelet, and
installed in the German officers' mess to provide nightly entertainment.

The administrators of Le Câtelet indulged not only their ap-
petites but also their foibles: Jeanne Magniez was astonished one
day when she looked out of her window to see the German Judge
Grumme, the "Big Red Turkey," floating down the River Escaut,
stark naked, with a fishing rod in his hand. As she later remarked to
her nephew, "Grumme was a very odd man, but rather fun."

Evers, too, had made himself entirely at home in the Legé
household; indeed, he was becoming so attached to the land and
his new way of life that he began, bizarrely, to wonder whether to
make a permanent home there when German victory finally materialised. "Evers himself dreamed of personally running Bellevue Farm

at Beaurevoir [just outside Le Câtelet]. 'This will be my farm,' he used to say." Considering himself an agricultural expert, for reasons that nobody else could divine, Evers decided early in 1915 that he would teach the local peasantry something about farming. "He organised the planting of real German potatoes, imported from Germany by cart. We would be shown what a real harvest of real potatoes was like, genuine Pomeranian potatoes." The crop was a disaster, and when the mayor of Beaurevoir pointed out that the harvest was only a fraction of what it had been the year before, he was fined, and then, when he protested again, locked in a cell for "an entire weekend and forced to eat German marmalade . . . a concoction that defied analysis and which even the German soldiers said was disgusting."

Evers was all-powerful, or believed he should be, and, as with many little dictators who exercise arbitrary control over others, his spreading corruption and self-indulgence came with a poisonous admixture of paranoia. The preening major was convinced that the people were concealing from him not only supplies of food but also fugitives, and he was correct on both counts. The *curé* of Nauroy, in one of the more impressive acts of smuggling, managed to keep twelve pigs undetected for nearly a year; others developed techniques for evading German efforts to keep track of every person, animal, and grain of wheat. "When a sheep died of illness, the *Kommandant* insisted that before it could be removed from the register the body had to be produced." To bypass the system, "every dead sheep would be presented successively by five different villages." Since Evers could not tell the difference between one dead sheep and another, each village could officially remove one sheep from its list, having butchered and shared out a healthy animal.

Evers's immediate response to rule evasion was to create more rules. "For four years, the *Kommandant* of Le Câtelet never for a single day ceased to demand declarations, accounts, lists of animals, people, crops, descriptions of everything in existence, or not in existence . . . Snowed under by statistics and lists of what had been requisitioned, Kommandant Evers himself eventually found that he had not a clue of the real picture." Still the Evers machine continued to scour under every hedgerow. In July 1915, the people of Villeret were informed that "every fruit, gooseberry, raspberry, and blackberry must be individually accounted for." Evers was so preoccupied with tallying up his lists of wild fruits and animals that he tended to overlook basic supplies. Finally, Jeanne Magniez decided she could tolerate no more demands to list her chinaware when the most important things in life were being ignored. She stormed into the *Kommandant*'s office to complain that the "working horses on the Delacourt family farm at Gouy were not getting enough to eat." Lickspittle Evers, aware that Jeanne was popular with some of the more senior army officers, immediately attended to the matter. "She terrified the Germans; Jeanne Magniez had a nerve."

Evers suffered from the instinctive and mounting fear that, despite all his efforts, fugitive soldiers, enemy spies, arms caches, and clandestine information networks were flourishing under his nose. In November 1915, German counterintelligence uncovered no fewer than three distinct spy networks in northern France and Belgium, including one operated by the wife of a French officer who had been trained in Paris and then secretly sent over the lines into the occupied zone. A series of attacks on military trains prompted yet another decree threatening the death penalty against anyone involved in sabotage.

All forms of communication, and even the keeping of diaries, was "treated, on principle, as evidence of espionage." Anyone found carrying a letter was liable to immediate arrest and imprisonment. For all Evers's determination to seal off every village from its neighbour, a trickle of news eventually seeped through, by word-of-mouth or more ingenious means. In mid-April, the Le Câtelet lawyer managed to get his hands on a copy of *Le Figaro,* already more than five weeks out of date, which had been floated over the lines from unoccupied France using a balloon; this was the first authentic news about the war to reach the canton since the start of the war.

Balloons and carrier pigeons were the best methods of passing information and propaganda across the lines, and as the war progressed, the Allies developed a method for using the two in

conjunction to gather information on conditions and troop movements in occupied France. Balloons from which a cage containing a
carrier pigeon was suspended would be floated high across the
front line when the wind was in the right direction. Attached to the
bird's leg was a note, in French, asking whoever found it either to
take it to a certain spot (where it could be picked up by an agent on
the ground) or else to fill in answers to a series of questions—about
troop movements in the area, the morale of soldiers, and so on—
and then reattach it and release the homing pigeon to fly back over
the line.

Pigeons brought out the most paranoid streak in Major Evers.
In July 1915, a farmer was dragged before Judge Grumme in Le
Câtelet and told that two carrier pigeons had been found on his
property. The dead birds were produced as evidence, and in vain
did the man point out that these were not carrier pigeons but birds
raised for food. "A German soldier who claimed to be a pigeon expert insisted that the birds had been crossbred with carrier pigeons
and could have been used to send messages . . . after which, for having raised two bastard pigeons, the man was condemned to two
years' imprisonment in Germany." Pigeons of whatever breed were
then banned, and anyone found to have been secretly keeping
pigeons would be arrested, and shot. (This rule nearly deprived
the world of a vaccination against tuberculosis: Albert Calmette,
founder of the Pasteur Institute and a distinguished scientist in occupied Lille, was arrested and sentenced to death for failing to surrender his "research team of pigeons." He was released only after a
German doctor interceded on his behalf. Calmette survived the war,
continued his research, and eventually won recognition as the middle initial of the BCG vaccine.)

Evers was ever vigilant for feathered spies, but what truly obsessed him was the belief that enemy soldiers, who might use this
or some other method to pass information back to their superiors,
were being hidden by French sympathisers. There was plenty of evidence to stoke his suspicions. In April, it was announced that a
couple in Joncourt had been arrested for hiding "a fugitive English
soldier wanted by the German authorities." The prisoner, it was re-

ported, "only escaped the firing squad because he betrayed the people who had hidden him." The woman was fined two thousand marks, and her husband was sentenced to two years' imprisonment in Germany.

Patrick Fowler remained securely hidden in his cupboard, with Germans sometimes billeted within feet of his hiding place in Madame Belmont-Gobert's cottage in Bertry, but the sartorial disguise of Private David Cruikshank proved less durable. The Scotsman, who had adopted women's clothing and now went by the name of Mademoiselle Louise, was also betrayed and captured, allegedly at the instigation of "a woman who had been rejected by the soldier and took revenge in the worst possible way." Cruikshank was thrown into the cellar of an abandoned convent, tried by a German military court, and condemned to death, a sentence that was commuted to twenty years in prison at the pleading of his protector, Julie-Célestine Baudhuin, who was herself sentenced to ten years in jail.

Others were less fortunate.

In February, two lorry-loads of German troops, accompanied by mounted police, arrived in the village of Iron, some fifteen miles to the west of Villeret, where they surrounded the mill and farm belonging to Auguste Chalandre. Inside were eleven British soldiers who had been hidden and fed by the Chalandre family for the previous six months. They emerged with their hands in the air, having been betrayed by a neighbour. The prisoners were led away to Guise, the German administrative centre adjacent to Le Câtelet, and the village inhabitants were lined up to watch as Chalandre's house was burned to the ground. On February 25, Auguste Chalandre and the British soldiers, the youngest just seventeen years old, were taken to the château at Guise, lined up beside a large pit, and shot by firing squad.

In the wake of such incidents, Evers peppered the district with threats, in both English and French, warning of the fate awaiting enemy soldiers and anyone who aided them. He made no distinction between soldiers left behind from the retreat, and military agents purposely sent across the lines by the enemy. All were spies.

"Any men who have worn military uniform and who do not come forward by 7:00 p.m. on June 5, 1915, will be shot"; "Soldiers who do not surrender as prisoners-of-war will suffer the death penalty, and their protectors and the mayor responsible will each be fined 15,000 marks." July 3, 1915: "Inhabitants, on pain of execution, must not give help or clothes to any English soldiers who may be in the region." And so on, without consistency, but with an insistence that gradually drummed itself into the mind of every French citizen.

Evers was a bully and an upstart, but he was not a fool. He knew that human frailty could be manipulated for political purposes, that time, fear, and want could erode the will to fight, and that today's hardy *résistant* might be fashioned into tomorrow's willing *collaborateur*. Such techniques would be put to horribly efficient use by the next generation of Germans to occupy France.

The changing political chemistry across the occupied region was particularly notable in Villeret, where Claire Dessenne's pregnancy had produced a subtle but increasingly unstable reaction. The British soldiers were no longer quite so simply viewed as symbols of defiance in the face of a nameless, faceless, and brutal German invader. The Germans had taken on human faces, some of them rather sympathetic ones; Robert Digby had become, more obviously with every day, Claire's sole property. "Everyone knew who the father was," recalled one villager. Digby's glamour had faded perceptibly. "He made himself a part of the village," it was observed and, as such, he was now exposed to its spite as well as its generosity. Eugénie Dessenne, the unhappy mother of the happy mother-to-be, was not the only person in Villeret to wish the English soldier had allowed his affections to alight elsewhere, or not at all. The old animosities festered again, and the whispering began.

CHAPTER NINE

Sparks of Life

❧❦❧

The baby growing inside Claire Dessenne was not the only sign that new life was coming to Villeret, defying the torrent of death in the trenches nearby.

From his nearby dugout, Lieutenant Rosenhainer marvelled at the fecundity of the Picardy countryside. "We felt Spring's arrival everywhere. With a magic hand it had produced the most luscious green, violets and spring flowers were already in bloom. We could literally feel buds swelling and leaves and blossoms bursting open."

The German troops billeted on the village through the winter had been welcomed by some for the extra food they brought, but in a few instances, evidently, the reception had been even warmer. At least two other women were pregnant, carrying the children of German soldiers. One of the expectant mothers was Marie Sauvage, Claire's cousin, contemporary, and friend, whose family lived just a hundred yards away down rue d'En Bas. Marie had married young, to Richard Sauvage, one of the first Villeret men to leave for the front. It was never clear whether the father of Marie's child was one of the Germans permanently stationed in Villeret, an officer from the château keen to exercise his borrowed *droit de seigneur,* one of the "birds of passage" relaxing after a stint at the front, or, the most likely possibility, a soldier of the artillery regiment stationed in

Villeret over Christmas 1914. No one in the village much cared to find out, and, as it had over the centuries, Villeret closed ranks around yet another natural child, while quietly wondering what Richard Sauvage would make of the infant bearing his name if he ever got home.

In the village, Claire's pregnancy was seen, by some, as a mark of honour. Conversely, there is no evidence to suggest that the women impregnated by Germans were considered traitors, at least not yet. Ernst Jünger, the German writer who would find himself carried into Villeret on a stretcher before long, believed that the weavers of northern France were a particularly dissolute breed. "It was agricultural, and yet there was a loom in nearly every house. The inhabitants did not appeal to me. They were dirty and of a very low moral development," he sniffed. "Our relations with the civil population were, to a great extent, of an undesirable familiarity. Venus deprived Mars of many servants." Yet the German philosopher understood the urge to seize a moment of comfort amid the surrealities of war: "The little pleasures that life offered, took on an unimagined enhancement from the increasing thunder of the guns and from the destiny whose oppression never left one's mind. The colours were more affecting. The wish to knit oneself with life in enjoyment was more urgent. For the thought crept into everyone's mind: 'Perhaps this is the last Spring you will see.' "

Villeret had a long and fairly broad-minded history of illegitimacy—indeed, the first archival document to mention the village records an inquiry by the mayor of Saint-Quentin in 1240 into a "question of parentage" concerning one "Rogier of Villier"—but there is no evidence to suggest that the village folk were markedly more promiscuous than those of any other rural community. In later years, what would be become known as *collaboration horizontale* was cited by those determined to paint the inhabitants of the occupied territories as "Les Boches du Nord," suggesting, quite unfairly, that they had been happy to welcome the invaders into their homes and beds. There was even a bizarre rumour that Adolf Hitler, a signals runner and volunteer with the 16th Bavarian Reserve Regiment, might have fathered a child in northern France, a suggestion for which there is not a scrap of evidence.

After the war, the official French historians of the occupation tied themselves in knots trying to explain the baby boom in a region where most husbands and fathers were fighting at the front. "Every case was different . . . No absolute judgement is possible," they concluded, for the "obscure magnetism of men for women . . . is a well-known, classic, and eternal form of weakness." Some offered the oddly modern, even feminist rationalisation that sleeping with the enemy could be seen as a patriotic act: in such liaisons, "both sexes were on the same footing, since there was no distinction between an offensive sex which takes and possesses and the defensive sex which is taken and possessed. The French women who had commerce with Germans could congratulate themselves for having dominated and subjugated them." A few observers took comfort in the reflection that, "indisputably, the very few women who abandoned themselves to the Germans would uniformly have preferred to give pleasure to a French man"; others maintained that women were victims, forced into sexual relations with the oppressor by the spectre of hunger and misery. "They took what they could get."

That last observation probably came closest to the general view in Villeret, at least while the war was still in progress, and it remains the view today, as expressed by a latter-day member of the Dessenne clan: "Almost all the young men had gone. There were only old men and the heads of families left. Five years without a man is a long time. Of course the women slept with Germans." As W. H. Auden once wrote: "In times of war even the crudest kind of positive affection between persons seems extraordinarily beautiful, a noble symbol of the peace and forgiveness of which the whole world stands so desperately in need." And love came in unexpected forms: between friend and foe, between soldier and civilian, and between comrades. Erich Maria Remarque depicted two German soldiers in gentle communion amid the violence. "We don't talk much, but we have a greater and more gentle consideration for each other than I should think even lovers do. We are just two human beings, two tiny sparks of life; outside there is just the night, and all around us, death." He might have been describing the war-deepened friendship of the Irishmen Thomas Donohoe and David Martin.

Both Claire and her cousin Marie had seized some love where they found it. The fathers of the Villeret babies might have been enemies at the moment when they were conceived, but the children spawned by rival armies would eventually grow into close friends.

Curé Crépaux of Aubencheul was troubled by the blurring of the battle lines. He had resolved to have nothing to do with the German officer billeted in his home, but the man had such an "open and intelligent face" that the priest felt he could not turn down his invitation to dinner. The German officers had been warm, intelligent, abstemious, and polite to the servants, while their commander, a fifty-year-old from Alsace, had been the "very model of moderation and German courtesy."

"He didn't hide his regard for the French people, but by contrast displayed a profound dislike for the English, whom he accused of starting the war out of pure greed and a desire to dominate the universe in order to enhance their commercial power."

The *curé* left dinner flattered and impressed, but confused.

At Hargival, Jeanne Magniez was also finding it harder to distinguish friend from foe as the war progressed. With the English soldiers and the threat of sudden exposure removed, Jeanne found the company of educated German officers perfectly tolerable—indeed, rather pleasant. Once they got over the initial surprise of being treated not as fearsome invaders but as equals if not inferiors, the German officers came to revel in Jeanne's sharp wit and charming conversation. She took photographs of them playing cards and listening to gramophone records in her elegant salon. Jeanne enjoyed conversations with the eccentric Grumme, but there was one German whose company she found particularly convivial, a cavalry officer by the name of Wilhelm Richter, an aristocratic farmer from Hünvingen who shared her equestrian passion and love of the land. She referred to him affectionately as "Mon Vieux," my dear old fellow. There is a photograph in Jeanne Magniez's collection, among those of the dogs and horses, taken in the back garden of Hargival in the summer of 1915, that shows Jeanne standing beside a plump and pleasant-faced German officer. The German is gazing at the camera, but Jeanne's head is averted, an unreadable expression on her face. Was she looking away out of embarrassment, was the sun in her eyes, or was she declining to look in the lens to dissociate herself from the man beside her? Whatever the answer, she kept the photograph for the rest of her life.

Although Jeanne had tried to get messages to Georges, on the other side of the line, she had received not a single word from her husband since he left for the war. Intensely religious, Georges Magniez wished away a part of his war by imagining a "daily communion" with his distant wife, and his diary written from the front line is that of a man concerned not just for the safety of his beloved, but also, perhaps, for her virtue. His grim experiences as an artillery officer could hardly have been further removed from the polite international conversation taking place in the drawing room at Hargival, but every time he escaped death, Georges wondered about his wife: "It is madness, another ten horses killed, torn to pieces, bits of skin and flesh scattered around for 100 metres . . . A terrible bombardment all day . . . Crossing over the station bridge, a shell whistled over me and landed two metres away, the entire platoon was enveloped in black smoke, and the horses bolted. The explosion was so close that we didn't even get hit by the debris from the crater, which flew overhead. A few more metres and we'd have got it. How to thank God and Notre Dame de Lourdes? It is truly miraculous. Oh yes, they continue to watch over me, and my Jeanne. They brought us together, let them not separate us now." On a few days' leave in Paris, he was forced to listen to the couple in the adjoining room making love with abandon. "A memorable night," he noted wryly. "I heard everything, from the preliminaries to the finale." That set him to thinking about Jeanne. "I had hoped to be here with her," he wrote in his notebook. "The next time I come to Paris it will be with her."

In May 1915, one of Jeanne's letters got through, smuggled out of the occupied zone through Belgium and Holland by an unnamed "intermediary," possibly one of Jeanne's new German friends. Georges immediately dispatched a letter back by the same route:

At last I have heard something from you, after nine months of silence. Now I can live again, I can see that the Lord is protecting you, and everything I hear leads me to believe that you are getting through this ordeal with all your honour intact. I got so angry with you, being left in absolute ignorance of what was happening to you, and you will never know how much I have suffered to be in such anguish, you are all my life to me, and I never lost hope . . . I know you are brave, as you promised to be when I left, and I want to find a Jeanne just as I left her. Your task is to get another note to me, just a single line, if only you knew how much I miss you. Say that we only live for one another. If only we had never parted. Courage, my beloved little woman, the thoughts and love of your Georges are always with you, every morning I commune with you, what joy it will be to be reunited. Do not let anyone forget Georges. I embrace you, my own dear Jeanne, with all my heart, with all my soul, how much I love you, if you only knew how much . . .

Perhaps this was just the anguished letter of an adoring husband in hourly danger of death, but there is something unsettling in the wording. What reason did Georges have to wonder about his wife's honour, to doubt that his "beloved little woman" would be the same when, or if, he returned? Jeanne hid Georges's pained love letter inside the knot of an oak beam in the granary at Hargival.

Just as the invisible barrier separating German from French began to crumble, so did the unspoken alliance that, in the first days of occupation, had united all French citizens against the German invader. A thin and vicious trickle of anonymous denunciations began to arrive on the desk of Major Evers. "Every enemy invasion, every revolution provides an opportunity for old grievances to bubble to the surface, compounded in modern times by envy and class hatred," the official local historian of the war reflected, noting that "the few instances of individual weakness were insignificant compared with the collective attitude of resistance and pride." At first, the unsigned letters were principally of an economic nature, aimed at shifting the weight of requisitioning onto other shoulders: "The looters were pushed towards other doors than one's own: Monsieur So-and-So has more wine than I; another person has good rooms and fresh sheets." The rich were another target, with many letter writers believing that the wealthy were not bearing their share of the burden of occupation. François Theillier, as the wealthiest man in the region, became a general focus of resentment. "In 1915, this rich landowner was the victim of some 20 anonymous denunciations on the subject of his car, which had apparently been concealed in a silo of beets, and which the public claimed was filled with gold." In Saint-Quentin, the *Kommandant* received "another pile of written accusations, aimed at the millionaire." Evers did not find the gold-filled car, because no such thing existed, but he was "all smiles at having found so many willing tattletales at his service."

In Villeret, the Englishmen who had once united the community were slowly, almost imperceptibly pulling it apart. There were still those, like Marie Coulette and Suzanne Boitelle (who had recently learned that her husband, Paul, was a prisoner-of-war in Germany), whose defence of the Englishmen never wavered, and who still regarded the German occupiers as barbarians, to be resisted by any and every means. That spirit was not confined to those directly involved in the conspiracy to hide the soldiers. In July, an elderly Villeret matron was arrested and sentenced to nine months' imprisonment for turning on a German officer as he rode through the town and calling him a "filthy Prussian and a snivelling pig . . . which was no less than the truth, for the nose of the 'Herr Doktor' never stopped running." But others were more inclined to caution, notably Parfait Marié, the acting mayor, who would be held directly responsible for any acts of resistance among his constituents. As Henri Lelong pointed out, "the invaders were not that brutal. Certainly, they handed out the odd blow here and there with their cudgels, but these really were the exception." Parfait Marié and others, including Claire's mother, Eugénie, argued that it was wiser to live with the Germans than to die trying to defy them. The baker and his wife, Léon and Elise Lelong, continued to provide food for the Englishmen, but their former warmth and concern were replaced by a marked chill. Elise made little effort to disguise her opinion that Claire Dessenne was a shameless trollop, and she forbade her daughter, Clothilde, to speak to her.

The population of the village was draining as fast as its resolve, for at the beginning of May it was announced that all *bouches inutiles*, useless mouths who could do little work and were a strain on resources, could be repatriated to unoccupied France. On May 8, eighty-two villagers, mostly women and children, assembled in the school courtyard at Villeret. That afternoon, they were loaded onto trains at Hargicourt station, and more than a week later, after an exhausting journey via Saint-Quentin, Mézières in the Ardennes, and Bern in Switzerland, they arrived in the Landes town of Mont-de-Marsan. They were finally free of German domination, but it would be another three years before any of them saw Villeret again. Claire Dessenne, now three months pregnant, could have joined the exodus, but she elected to stay. "She and the Englishman were besotted with each other, they would not be parted. There was a strange calm about Claire; when she made up her mind, that was that." Some thought Claire's decision to stay was foolish and irresponsible, and a further threat to the community, since as long as she was in the village the Englishmen and the danger they represented would remain, too. "It was all Claire's fault: they stayed because of her, putting everyone in peril, the mayor, her family, everyone." Others blamed Digby for taking advantage of a foolish virgin: "Claire was only twenty and you don't have much in your head at that age. You do things you might regret later." There is no evidence that Robert Digby and Claire Dessenne were aware that their love affair had become a wedge dividing friends, families, and neighbours, infecting old wounds, and if they knew they did not care, for with the blithe blindness of love they were focussed only on each other, and the coming baby.

In September, the Allied offensive was renewed in Artois and Champagne, with even larger armies, but no greater success than before. The Germans knew what was coming. Indeed, with a massive preliminary bombardment, the Allies told them. At Loos, to the north, the British choked on their own gas when it drifted backwards, and were then thrashed by machine-gun fire as they advanced. The German gunners were so appalled by their own butchery, they called a unilateral ceasefire to allow injured survivors to get back to their trenches. French casualties after the similarly fruitless offensive in Champagne numbered nearly 150,000.

As the crop from the "corpse fields" grew ever more abundant, Robert and Claire talked avidly about the life they would make together after the war. Digby said he planned to buy a small farm near Villeret, if his parents would loan him the money, and go back to raising chickens. Not without some trepidation, he wondered what Ellen Digby of Totton, Hampshire, would think if she knew she was about to become a grandmother in Villeret, Aisne. Now when he talked of escape, he spoke of fleeing as a family. Willie "Papa" Thorpe set about building a crib for the child. A few doors away, Marie Sauvage was also growing heavy: two women, two fathers, two enemies, and a strange alliance of motherhood.

Claire was ready to go into labour when the English bombs began falling on Villeret. During the summer of 1915, the villagers had stood in gaping wonder as a dogfight took place in the skies over their homes, ending when the German pilot shot down the British plane and then landed at the Grand Priel aerodrome. "The pilot jumped into a car, drove to where the English plane had crashed, and paid homage to its brave pilot." The people of Villeret discussed the aerial battle with the German soldiers stationed in the village, and all agreed that the downed English pilot had been "a brave man, who should be saluted with respect." October had seen another dogfight, over to the west, in which two British pilots had been shot down and taken prisoner.

Following these losses, the Royal Flying Corps concluded that the time had come to attack the aerodrome outside Villeret, and on November 11, 1915, three squadrons from the 3rd Wing, near Albert, dispatched "all available aircraft to attack the aerodrome simultaneously, each squadron providing its own escort." From the ground, the villagers counted twenty-three planes above Villeret. Half the attacking planes carried a reduced load of bombs and a passenger-gunner, while the remainder carried only the pilot and a full arsenal of bombs. The raid, from the British point of view, was an unmitigated disaster. "At reconnaissance height there was a very high wind and over the German lines the weather was thick and cloudy and navigation very difficult." Several of the planes and their escorts became lost in the confusion, some released their bombs over the village instead of the airfield, and enemy planes intercepted others. One British aircraft was shot down and its pilot captured. Another, flown by one Lieutenant Harvey, was on the point of returning to base when it had the misfortune to be picked up in the sights of Hauptmann Hans-Joachim Buddecke, who at twenty-six was already one of the most celebrated aces in the German air force. (Buddecke's aerial exploits, including the shooting down of Second Lieutenant W. Lawrence, the brother of T. E. Lawrence [of Arabia], earned him an Iron Cross, the nickname "The Hunting Falcon," an early death at the age of twenty-eight, and a grand funeral in Berlin in March 1918.) Lieutenant Harvey came down in a field outside Villeret and was captured. He died in an internment camp in Switzerland, just four days before the Armistice. The Flying Corps report was understandably gloomy: "Few planes found the objective, all machines had great difficulty in finding their way back. Very little damage was done." It did not look quite that way from Villeret.

Elise Lelong never forgot, or tired of telling, how her house had been bombed. "We were about to sit down to eat when the bomb landed and blew off the roof above the window in the dining room," she told her grandson. "There was glass everywhere. Nobody ate that day, and everyone rushed to hide in the woods. They stayed there for a while, with the rest of the population, and then returned to the house." Miraculously, none of the villagers was injured in the abortive bombing raid, and the damage was swiftly repaired, but it had brought the war a giant step closer to Villeret. Later, it was claimed that the Lelong house had been damaged by a wayward German bombardment, but in reality, as Elise well knew, these were British bombs, and their arrival did nothing to endear Digby and his companions to the baker's wife.

Two days later, Claire Dessenne's labour pains began. Her cries echoed down the empty village street and were heard by all, signalling new hope to some, and fresh danger to others. After three generations, the event still evokes the same conflicting emotions, in the same street in northern France, just behind the trench line. "We were very proud of that little girl, she belonged to the whole village," says one inhabitant of Villeret; another wonders, "What was an English soldier doing fathering bastards with French girls when he should have been fighting Germans?"

Clara Boitelle, Claire's aunt and the unofficial village midwife, was summoned to Marie Coulette's kitchen, and at two o'clock on the morning of November 14, exactly nine months after the Kaiser had passed through Villeret, came a new sound, not heard since the war began, of a baby girl born to the smell of gunpowder, a small victory for life in the midst of numberless death.

CHAPTER TEN

The Englishman's Daughter

❧

Before she was an hour old, the battlefield child sparked conflict. Robert Digby held his tiny daughter in his arms as Claire slept, but the child's grandmother Eugénie refused to embrace her. She held back, thin-lipped and angry. Finally, her fear and disapproval boiled over.

"Digby wanted to go the mayor's office and officially recognise the child as his own, but he was told, 'You must be mad—an Englishman appears on the books at the *mairie* and we're all dead.'" The Englishman also insisted that the child be named Ellen, "after his mother."

After prolonged argument, a compromise was reached: the child would be called Hélène, and since Claire was still too weak to go to the *mairie*, it fell to Eugénie Dessenne—the child's next closest relative, who had done her best to prevent precisely this eventuality—to make the formal declaration of her birth. The arrival of Hélène Claire Dessenne was noted on the municipal ledger at nine o'clock that morning, November 14, signed by Florency Dessenne, her great-uncle, and Claire's cousin Jules Carpentier. The document was witnessed and authenticated by Parfait Marié, acting mayor. With neither parent there to recognise her, Hélène was simply described as *"enfant naturelle,"* a natural child. She would later complain that she was, officially speaking, "a nothing, nonexistent," but in some ways the title was the right one, for nothing could have been more natural, in those unnatural circumstances, than the manner of her creation.

Digby was thrilled with his little daughter. William "Papa" Thorpe, that most paternal of soldiers, was ready to give advice, but Digby proved to be a natural father to the natural child: "He was really proud of her, and he spent all his time attending to her. He would walk around the village with the child, showing her off." People said they could see Digby's colouring and his bright-blue eyes in the little girl: "They were as alike as two drops of water, it was uncanny." Digby called the baby "my little cockatoo," and when he was sure no Germans were in earshot, he sang English songs to her. Marie Coulette was also fiercely proud and defensive of her tiny great-grandchild: "If anyone handled the baby badly, she growled at them and ground her teeth. One day Jean Dessenne, one of Florency's children, accidentally dropped the child, and Marie Coulette fetched him a clout on the head and yelled: 'You be careful with our *t'iote*.'" Claire and Robert, more deeply in love than ever, not married and with no practical prospect of becoming so, took to calling one another "husband" and "wife," and meant it. "She was our secret," one villager said, and for a time, the birth of Hélène seemed to reunite the community. But before long, the murmuring began again, louder than before.

The winter was a harsh one, and the Germans seemed bent on starving and freezing Villeret to death. On New Year's Eve, the German military police staged a raid on the Trocmé wood: "thirty people from Villeret who were collecting fallen wood for their fires were arrested and thrown into prison in Le Câtelet." During the six months before Hélène's birth, with the most intensive fighting elsewhere on the front, the village had been forced to accommodate relatively small groups of Germans, but the year's end saw a sudden influx of additional troops. The soldiers usually stayed about a week to recuperate and then headed to the front, returning a few weeks later in very different shape. Gone were the affable soldiers who had distributed leftovers and flirted with the girls. "They came back exhausted from the Somme front, their numbers decimated and their morale in tatters." The heavy troop concentration continued until the end of January, when many battalions "headed to Verdun to take part in the offensive of February 1916."

Crouching in his trench that winter just a few miles from Villeret, Ernst Rosenhainer recorded: "Rain, nothing but rain. The trenches gradually turn into watery ditches. We have to take hoes and spades and try to stabilize the trench walls, again and again. Nothing is safe from the rats. They devour the bread along with the backpacks and at night they flit across our covers. We suffer greatly from the wet." Rotated out of the line, the German lieutenant gazed on the destruction wrought by Allied shells as he marched back to the rear camp. "How much prosperity, happiness and peaceful comfort have been lost," he wondered. Rosenhainer felt a twinge of something like regret as he marched away to the Verdun killing fields, leaving the muddy maze he had helped dig into the fields of Picardy. "How much labor and love had gone into finishing those trenches; how much hard work by the sweat of our brow. But also a lot of blood."

Looking at the faces of the German soldiers imprinted with the grim shadows of trench warfare, some villagers felt doubly resentful of the English fugitives. Here were warriors, albeit enemies, facing hardship and death just over the horizon, while their English counterparts were being kept in safety and enjoying, in one case, all the pleasures of family life. "*They* were OK, they had enough to eat, they were warm, they even had women. These men were just fine in Villeret."

Some in the village declined to see the men as cowards and deserters, and gave them the benefit of the doubt: "They refused to give themselves up, hoping from day to day to get through the front lines and rejoin their comrades," one sympathetic villager recorded. But even their most staunch supporters were beginning to wonder whether the men would ever leave, and their descendants are wondering still: "They had five, ten opportunities to get away. Why did they stay so long? It's a reasonable question."

It is. The villagers themselves had found ways to evade the German attempts to monitor and control their movements, and spy networks successfully moved their agents around the occupied zone. As late as 1916, other stranded soldiers were still managing to struggle through Belgium to safety. "What I never understood," ponders Marie Dessenne, one of Florency's daughters, "is why my father, who knew all the back roads, all the routes for smuggling contraband, did not help them to get away and into Belgium . . . Perhaps there were too many German troops around." From time to time, the younger soldiers headed off on brief reconnaissance trips to test the possibility of escape. Even after the birth of Hélène, Digby would sometimes slip away, alone, for as much as a day at a time. "They wanted to get through by going north, but always came back to Villeret, where they had made some close attachments," the town notary later recalled, delicately.

Claire's passionate relationship with Digby had cast the other soldiers, in some eyes, in a new and threatening light. No longer were they simply unfortunate allies in need of help, but instead potential predators, young vagabonds with nothing to lose. "They were being looked after, warm and snug, with full bellies, while others did the fighting. And when night fell, they went running after the girls." Undoubtedly, some of the women were simply jealous of Claire and her handsome, attentive lover. The attitude of the remaining Villeret men may have been tinged with envy as they watched an outsider capture the most beautiful girl in the place, getting away with what was rightfully theirs. As one villager remarked: "We would have had stones thrown at us if we went chasing after girls in Hargicourt; but this Englishman, he turns up and goes off with a village girl. That wasn't right."

On February 2, 1916, the 2nd Squadron of the 2nd Regiment of Uhlans arrived in Villeret and made the village their rear camp. Now inured to the bewildering ebb and flow of soldiers, the people were not unwelcoming. "The inhabitants had no complaints about this troop, which remained in place until mid-June, for the Germans contented themselves with making all the able-bodied men work in the fields and on the roads." The first cavalrymen to thunder into the village in pursuit of Robert Digby back in August 1914

had been the harbingers of mass invasion, and the same was true
of the horsemen of 1916: over the coming months, German troops
poured into the region and into Villeret in ever-increasing numbers.

The writer Ernst Jünger was one of them. He recalled the local
inhabitants as "timid, pitiful creatures who had suffered bitterly
from the war" and described how the battle-bruised German troops
would descend on the villages behind the lines and take them over
"like a mighty parasite."

> There were only a few uneasy and unkempt civilians to be
> seen. Everywhere there were soldiers in worn and torn coats,
> with tanned faces and thick beards, who went to and fro with
> long swinging strides, or lounged in small groups by the cot-
> tage doors assailing newcomers with chaff . . . All the avail-
> able space had to be made full use of. The gardens were
> partly occupied with huts and temporary dwellings of one
> sort and another . . . Dragoons watered their horses in the
> village pond, infantry training went on in the gardens, and all
> over the meadows soldiers lay and sunned themselves. Noth-
> ing was kept that did not serve a military purpose. Hedges
> and fences were broken down or removed altogether to give
> better communications. Roofs fell in and all that was burn-
> able went for fuel . . . In the whole village there were no
> boundaries and no personal possessions.

Through his illegal smuggling, Florency Dessenne had managed
to put aside some substantial savings before the war—a box of gold
louis d'or coins, which was hidden behind the stove. In the early
days, the additional food needed for the soldiers could be begged
and borrowed, but now it had to be bought at considerable ex-
pense. "I spent the lot, to feed the Englishmen," Florency Dessenne
would later claim.

The wisdom of teaching Digby and his companions to live as
French peasants was now apparent, for there were almost no hiding
places left. The German troops were steadily stripping Villeret and

other villages down to skeletons. In Bertry, Patrick Fowler was beginning to suffer, not surprisingly, from his long incarceration in the Belmont-Gobert armoire. At night he was able to get out and stretch his legs, so long as there were no Germans in the house, but during the day he remained cooped up in the dark. Fowler was already forty when he began his strange captivity, and despite the attentions of the Bertry pharmacist, who was let in on the conspiracy, he was often ill. When there were Germans in residence, the women would leave the shelved side of the cupboard open, to give the impression that it was shelved throughout, and a hole was cut in the side, through which food could be passed without opening the door. The house was often searched, but Fowler was never detected, partly thanks to his protector's canny understanding of the male soldier's psychology: "When a German was making straight for the cupboard, Madame Belmont-Gobert would play her last card. She would draw attention to the photograph of her second daughter, Euphémie. Euphémie was good-looking. Furthermore, she was safely away in Marseilles, and she was a sure draw. The Germans forgot the cupboard and crowded round the photograph with eager inquiries as to where the young lady was to be found." Even at night, with soldiers billeted in the house, Fowler could not relax, for the hungry men would sometimes "creep down to steal the potatoes that were kept on top of the wardrobe." Madame Belmont-Gobert began to suffer nervous attacks from the strain, particularly when the family was ordered out of the house and into a smaller building. The armoire, with Fowler crouched inside, was loaded onto a horse and cart with the help of her son-in-law, Louis Basquin. Ailing and terrified, Fowler felt his depression lighten briefly when he learned that a fellow cavalryman of the 11th Hussars, Corporal Herbert Hull, was also in hiding in Bertry. The two men met one night in the town cemetery, and talked of planning an escape to Holland. But late in 1915, Hull was betrayed, tried, and shot. Fowler, surely more convinced than ever that a similar fate would soon be his, returned sadly to his cupboard.

In Villeret, the British fugitives were no longer hiding from the enemy but living alongside them, cheek by jowl, sharing food, rooms, and even conversation. In an increasingly perilous situation, this was a time for the English soldiers to shrink into the remaining shadows, but the previous eighteen months spent in Villeret had also had its effect on the fugitives. Old "Papa" Thorpe and new "Papa" Digby might be happy to sit out the war pretending to be French villagers, but the younger soldiers were finding life in Villeret increasingly dull and frustrating. "They became bored, and began to take risks," the mayor noted sourly. Each of the soldiers had learned enough patois to conduct a conversation with the villagers and respond to orders from the German overseers, but to anyone with an ear to hear, the foreign accent beneath the French words was "perfectly obvious."

One morning, as the villagers were being marched to the fields to work, Willie O'Sullivan sauntered out of the line and casually asked one of the guards, in patois, if he could have a light for his cigarette. This was duly produced, and O'Sullivan strolled, winking, back to his place in the column. Many in the village had long looked askance at the young Irishman's antics, considering him "rash" at best, and possibly "mad." The village elders were aghast, remonstrating that such "imprudence must certainly destroy us all." Digby accosted O'Sullivan that night, berating him as an idiot who would end up killing everybody. A fistfight was prevented only by the intercession of Willie Thorpe. In the first days of flight, Digby had exercised his "natural authority over the others," but this had subtly begun to wane since his absorption by the Dessenne family. Thorpe, Donohoe, and Martin still looked up to Digby as "chief of their band," but the other men no longer felt the same compulsion to follow his lead. The hot-headed O'Sullivan, in particular, was determined to challenge Digby and "seemed to enjoy playing with fire." He egged on the other young men, and, to show off to the village girls, they made it "a favourite sport to light their cigarettes from the cigars of soldiers passing through the village, while speaking *picard* to them."

Digby did his best to soothe the mounting resentment over such behaviour, by apologising to the village leaders and stressing his "deep gratitude for all their help" at every opportunity. But opinion

Robert Digby

Claire Dessenne

Villeret in 1914

VILLERET (Aisne). - Rue d'Hargicourt

Edit. Landrieux

Villeret, rue d'Hargicourt

Ellen Digby, Robert
Digby's mother

Colonel Robert Digby,
Robert Digby's father

Thomas, Robert (standing), and Florence Digby

The Pêcherie on the Hargival estate, where the soldiers hid for three months in 1914

Jeanne Magniez, the châtelaine of Hargival, with Flirt and Baddy

Jeanne (in Red Cross
uniform) and Georges
Magniez

Jeanne Magniez and a German officer, possibly Wilhelm Richter

Eugénie Dessenne,
Claire Dessenne's mother

Jules "Le Boeuf"
Dessenne, Claire
Dessenne's father

Marie-Thérèse Dessenne, wife of Florency Dessenne, Claire's uncle

The Lelong family: Elise, Léon, the village baker,
and their daughter Clothilde, with Léon's mother seated

Suzanne Boitelle, Elise Lelong's half-sister

Victor Marié, the spy

Achille Poëtte, the postman

Karl Evers, *Kommandant* of Le Câtelet (front center); Flemming, his adjutant (front left); Bode, the judicial clerk (far left); Hans Grumme, the military judge (back center); and Deutsche, the organizer of forced labor (front right)

Le Câtelet, 1914

Le Câtelet, 1918

Hélène Dessenne, aged about eight, and Claire Dessenne

Hélène Digby (née Dessenne)

A reunion: Thomas Digby, Florence Digby, Georges Cornaille,
and Hélène Cornaille-Digby

French villagers posing with German soldiers in occupied France.
A propaganda photograph

against the Englishmen, who seemed so careless of the danger to their hosts, hardened dramatically as German soldiers poured into Villeret, making discovery and reprisal ever more likely. Soon, the "village was bursting with troops who lodged everywhere, even the attics—exhausted soldiers returning from the front and fresh troops going back up the line. Without being maltreated, the people were no longer in control of their own homes; every family was often obliged to take refuge in a single room, which was very often itself invaded by the soldiers."

Claire Dessenne struggled to act as calmly and normally as possible in a terrifying situation. When the baby Hélène's finger became infected and started to ooze pus, she accosted a German military doctor who was temporarily lodged in the village and demanded that he treat her baby. "She was afraid of nothing." The same could not be said of her neighbours. "This was the worst time for the village," wrote the mayor.

Major Evers grew more neurotic and dictatorial in his belief that the people were hiding food, guns, and, most important, the enemy. He knew they were mocking him behind their shutters. On April 11, a rabbit was stolen from the private hutches Major Evers had ordered built behind the Legé house, sending the *Kommandant* into a substantial rage. "The thief was robbed," the locals remarked with pleasure. Evers concluded that the rabbit theft was an act of open defiance, one of several in recent months. The weird German military vet had felt compelled to "horsewhip a man in Gouy who failed to salute him," so Evers promptly reissued the diktat that all German officers must be saluted, noting that failure to do so would result in "punishment for the individual and his community." The thirty people already in the Le Câtelet prison for forgetting or refusing to salute, including a seventy-seven-year-old man, were brought out en masse and forced to march around the square, saluting a German corporal as they passed. As an afterthought, Evers announced that the saluting of German staff cars was also obligatory, even when these were empty of passengers, and ordered that local inhabitants should get out of the way whenever a German approached. Here was an echo of the lordly Theillier. "The doffing of hats was not enough, the pavement must also be surrendered to officers."

To many, Evers appeared increasingly unhinged, most notably in his manic and mounting preoccupation with espionage. "These German gentlemen tended to see spies and conspiracies everywhere," one French municipal official in Hargicourt observed, but in the case of Evers, paranoia was approaching psychosis. Through informers, Evers learned that a spy network was in operation across the region, with its hub in one of the smaller villages under his control. Villeret had hitherto caught his attention only as a rustic settlement on the way to the hunting grounds of the Château de Grand Priel, but from early in 1916, he and his counterintelligence agents began to focus their attention on the village. Evers, as it happened, was entirely correct in his suspicions that Villeret was harbouring enemy agents, but these spies were French.

The Marié brothers—Victor and his younger brother, Marius—had been born and raised in the village, a weaver's sons, and they were "Villeret to the bone." Cousins of acting Mayor Parfait Marié, they were as fly and dodgy as he was ponderous and honest, and the brothers were known throughout the region as a pair of notorious rascals. Victor, who was thirty-five years old on the outbreak of war, had a home and family in Cambrai. Marius, ten years his junior, lived in Le Verguier, on the other side of the château from Villeret, where he had a reputation as a bruiser "who always carried a gun and wasn't slow to pull it out." After the war, Marius was described as a "man of rare sang-froid, made of stern stuff, and, what is more, with a most independent cast of mind."

Like Florency Dessenne, the Mariés were contraband smugglers, but on a far more sophisticated scale. Victor's house was purpose-built for secrecy, with concealed hiding places in the roof and a hidden tunnel leading from the cellar. One historian of wartime intelligence described Victor Marié as "one of those characters who love to lead their lives at a swinging pace, audacious, arrogant and possessed of a bold self-confidence that can so often enable such people to outface other, less assured spirits. These qualities aside, he was not above double-crossing anybody, and one of his favourite occupations in life was to run rings around those in authority."

Finding himself on the Allied side of the lines at the outbreak of
war, Victor-Pierre-Joseph-Adonis Marié, whose life up until that
point had been marked by a distinct absence of heroism, slouched
up to a British officer in a rear camp and offered his family, contacts, and knowledge of the land beyond the lines in the service of
the Allies. On a moonless night in the middle of August 1915, Victor, under orders from British intelligence, crossed the lines in a
plane piloted by an English airman and touched down by the Bois
de Vaucelles, near Laon, some ten miles inside occupied France.
With the aid of Marius and his underworld contacts, Victor set
about gathering "information on troop movements," local morale,
ammunition depots, and, "above all, the layout of the light rail-
ways." Plans, statistics, and other information were then sent back
across the line, initially via carrier pigeons dropped by British aircraft at arranged sites, and later through "a system of couriers across
the Dutch border." Victor was the brains behind the operation, and
Marius was the muscle—"strolling within hair's breadth of the German officials, a gun concealed under his arm"—but their widowed
mother, Coralie Marié-Leroy, was the "soul."

The Réseau Victor, Victor's network, gradually spread outwards
from its eponymous founder, who had recruited "about sixty members," some of them underworld denizens like himself, in a matter
of months. The organisation, relying on word-of-mouth and absolute secrecy, fanned out into the villages and towns of the region,
with agents in Saint-Quentin, Le Câtelet, and Cambrai, and extend-
ing deep into occupied Belgium and the Netherlands in what
British intelligence code-named the Beverloo System. On dark
nights, British planes would land to collect information, "touching
down at Havrincourt, near the Coufflet wood, or close to Neuville-
Saint-Rémy." Victor and Marius kept on the move with forged
passes, but at the centre of the web was inconspicuous little Villeret.
Whereas everyone in the village now knew of the English soldiers,
only a tiny handful were aware of Villeret's other dangerous secret.
Among those involved in the spy ring were the formidable widow
Marié; Henri Marié, the brother-in-law of Victor and Marius; and
Joséphine Marié, their sister-in-law. It may have been no more than
accident that the most important Allied spy network in the region

and the largest remnant force of British soldiers both happened to be present in the same small village. But a mind like that of Karl Evers did not deal in coincidences.

On March 30, 1916, a new poster was plastered to the door of the Villeret *mairie*. This was not one of Major Evers's periodic intrusions, but a full-blown proclamation from the commander-in-chief of the German army.

> More persons attached to enemy armies have been arrested in the area of France occupied by our troops, having been given hospitality by local people, and consequently I hereby order that: Persons who, in the course of the war, belonged to or followed the orders of an enemy army and who currently find themselves in the territory occupied by German troops are required to surrender to a German command post or an army unit by April 30, at the latest. Whoever surrenders before the deadline will not be punished and will be treated as a prisoner-of-war. All those arrested after April 30, 1916, will be punished by death or, in less serious cases, by imprisonment. Anyone who has fed, housed, or otherwise aided an enemy soldier, as well as those who have failed to report, promptly, the existence of an individual of this type to the nearest military authority, will be punished by imprisonment (five years minimum), plus a fine of up to 10,000 marks. Mayors or administrators of communes where an enemy soldier is arrested after April 30, 1916, or where an enemy soldier is found hidden, will be imprisoned for up to 15 years. In addition, a fine of up to 15,000 marks will be imposed. Any community suspected of taking part in the above infractions will face a larger fine.

Panic gripped Villeret; many were convinced that the declaration was directly aimed at the village, a prelude to mass arrests: "The secret of the soldiers' presence had got out . . ." "The Germans had got wind of the presence of Englishmen in the region," some villagers declared. With German search parties expected by the hour, six of the seven soldiers bid hasty farewells to Villeret and "immediately headed for Bellicourt," guided by Arthur Tordeux, the poacher who had originally found them in the woods outside Villeret. Only Robert Digby opted to stay. "Two days later, the soldiers were back," reporting that the area around Bellicourt was swarming with troops and quite impassable. The following night, Corporal John Edwards, ever a solitary and mysterious figure, vanished without a word to anyone. "He was a canny fellow," Elise Lelong, the baker's wife, remarked approvingly. "He preferred to take his chances alone, which was a damn fine idea, and we never heard another word about him." The Englishman was picked up by the Germans at Marcoing, before he had managed to get ten miles from Villeret. Edwards was brought before Grumme in Le Câtelet, and successfully convinced the judge that he was a member of the Red Cross. "He escaped death, but was sentenced to 15 years in prison."

Willie O'Sullivan and Harry May were also determined to make their move before the deadline expired. They apparently gave a short speech as they prepared to leave: "We do not want the people here to get into trouble because of us, or that you should be exposed to danger, all of you, who have been so good to us." Elise Lelong carefully recorded and later reported this uplifting sentiment, which does not quite ring true. O'Sullivan had shown scant regard for the villagers' safety when he was asking German sentries to light his cigarettes. The two men were captured at Malincourt, about halfway between Villeret and Bertry, within hours of leaving the village, and held as prisoners-of-war. In custody, all three men flatly refused to say where, and by whom, they had been hidden.

Of the original seven who had been sheltered in Villeret, only four now remained, the original group that had banded together back in August 1914. Willie Thorpe, David Martin, and Thomas Donohoe announced they would stand by Robert Digby and stay in the village, at least until a better opportunity for escape presented itself. Digby was only too well aware of the perils: anxious talk was circulating in the village; if his former comrades were intercepted, they might be forced into revealing the place they had been in hiding; someone in the village could crack and go running to the Germans. Léon Lelong, the gloomy baker, was deputed to "make the four remaining men understand the redoubled and grave danger of the situation." Finally, it was Parfait Marié who came forward and, as head of the community, flatly "invited them to leave the area, to prevent reprisals." There was, it seems, more than a hint of threat in Lelong's advice and Marié's "invitation." The four men now agreed they had little choice, but rather than head north they would go south and try to find a way across the battle lines.

That evening, Digby handed Claire Dessenne a letter addressed to his mother, with instructions that it should be sent to Ellen Digby of Totton, Hampshire, after the war, should he fail to come back. It read:

Dear Mother,

This letter is written by me to introduce you to this young woman if, by chance, I should die. I have been in this place, in hiding, from September 1, 1914 until April 25, 1916. I have a child I love very much, and if all goes well, I will come back with her and my little one to be near you. But if anything should happen to me, then I beg you, my dear mother, to help make a good life for my darling little girl. She is five months old. The whole village respects us both, she and I. Do not think ill of her after my death, but cherish and help her.

Your affectionate son,
Robert

The next night, on April 26, the four men set out with "ample provisions and money" donated by the villagers, as well as a guide, Lucien Lelong, the baker's son, to "attempt the impossible and cross the German lines at Péronne." They were "sent off with a 'bon voyage,'" although the attitude of some was closer to "good riddance."

Claire wept bitterly as Digby prepared to depart. Solemnly, he shook hands with the men of the Dessenne household—Florency

and Léon Recolet—and kissed the tearful Marie-Thérèse and Marie
Coulette, for once silent and subdued. Then Claire and Robert
were left alone with Hélène, a murmuring child blissfully unaware
of her parents' pain. Digby told his lover that, whether or not he
evaded capture, he would return to Villeret one day, to make their
lives together in peacetime. Before a final embrace, Digby handed
Claire a second copy of the letter to his mother, translated into
French. "If all goes well, I will come back with her and my little
one . . ." If all went well, the letter would not have to be delivered;
these few lines were, in truth, Digby's farewell statement of love for
Claire and their daughter, a keepsake if all did not go well, as he had
every reason to expect it would not. The words—unconsciously, of
course—echo those of Rupert Brooke: "If I should die . . ."

A few miles away, on the Hargival estate, another fugitive of the
war emerged from his hiding place. For months the German authorities, out of deference to the charming Madame Magniez, had
ignored the magnificent Thoroughbred everyone knew was hidden
between the haystack and the orchard wall on the Magniez estate.
Indeed, the cavalry officer Wilhelm Richter had even taken rides
with Jeanne Magniez when she was mounted on her husband's fine
horse. But in the new, intensifying atmosphere, Jeanne had become
convinced that the Germans planned to confiscate the animal and
punish her. Perhaps she had received a tip-off. One morning, before
dawn, she led Flirt gently from the orchard and walked him to the
far corner of the estate where, in a different life, she used to ride
with Georges and Anne de Becquevort. Deep in the woods, she removed Flirt's bridle, cocked the old pistol she had retrieved from
beneath the barn, and shot the beautiful horse through the temple.

Georges Magniez was mortified when, many months later, the
news of what had happened reached him at the front, more for the
pain it must have caused his wife than for the loss of his fine geld-
ing: "My great woman has killed Flirt in the night to prevent the
Boche from getting him . . . Such misery, what courage. How she
must have wept. I see Jeanne at night in my dreams. The Boche did
not get Flirt. She had to kill him. The poor woman, dear God, deliver her from this soon . . ."

On April 28, just two days after they had departed, Digby and the three other men trudged wearily back into Villeret under cover of night. It had been impossible to get anywhere near the front line for German soldiers, they said, let alone to cross it. They would stay in Villeret, come what may. Claire was of course delighted to see Digby return, but this was not a view universally shared in Villeret. At least one person now decided something would have to be done.

CHAPTER ELEVEN

Brave British Soldier

❧§❧

The squad of German military police—universally known as the *diables verts* (the green devils) on account of the high green collars on their uniforms—knew exactly where they were going when they marched into Villeret at dawn on May 16. The officer in command of the squad declared he had come "to search for horses on the orders of the *Kommandant* of Le Câtelet," and then headed directly for the hayloft behind Florency Dessenne's house in rue d'En Bas, where Digby and the three other men were hiding. In retrospect, it was agreed that the officer's reference to an official search for horses was no more than "a pretext": the last horses in Villeret had been requisitioned months before, and it is not easy to get a horse into a hayloft.

Thorpe, Donohoe, and Martin were asleep on the hay when the Germans burst in. "They were captured without a struggle." Digby's reactions were swifter. The soldiers were barely inside the loft when he "leapt through a window," crashed to the ground some twenty feet below, and sprinted into the woods before the Germans could open fire. This was the second time Digby had taken refuge in the Trocmé wood, and in the intervening eighteen months he had spent many hours there, poaching rabbits and collecting firewood. He knew the ground as well as any inhabitant of Villeret, and it would have taken a hundred soldiers several days to flush him out. After a brief search, Digby's pursuers abandoned the chase. Thorpe, Donohoe, and Martin were bound and marched the five miles to Le Câtelet, where they were flung into the prison. Evers gave full vent to his temper, and within hours the reprisals began in Villeret. "The military police arrived in a furious mood." Florency and Marie-Thérèse Dessenne, Léon and Elise Lelong, and Achille Poëtte, the postman, were all arrested and taken to Le Câtelet, along with "a number of other inhabitants" suspected of sheltering the British soldiers. Louise Dessenne cowered in a corner as the search party ransacked the building. "They opened every drawer in the kitchen and threw everything on the ground. In one of the drawers there were a few coins in a tin. My sister Marthe bent down to pick them up and this German, I remember the shape of his helmet, he shoved her out of the way and grabbed them himself."

Ignoring the screams of her infant son, the soldiers dragged Suzanne Boitelle from her house. The following day, the Germans returned, this time for Parfait Marié, the acting mayor, who was waiting for them in front of the *mairie* alongside the *garde champêtre,* who was also arrested for good measure.

As the villagers and the three soldiers sat awaiting trial in Le Câtelet, the recriminations got under way among those left behind in Villeret, where sentries were posted around the village and in force along rue d'En Bas, in case the fourth soldier should be unwise enough to reappear. There were those who said that Thorpe, Donohoe, and Martin had wanted to be caught, since, like Digby, "they had plenty of time to escape, but allowed themselves to be captured easily." Some were ready to accuse them of treachery, noting that their capture had been followed immediately by the arrests of all the principal conspirators. Rumours began to fly. "Evidently, under interrogation, one of the Englishmen had turned traitor and spilled the beans. Why, he even accused Monsieur Lelong of being the one who had made the fake passes that had been found on the fugitives." But others in the village eyed their neighbours and wondered whether the traitor was not still among them.

On May 18, Major Evers summoned to Le Câtelet every mayor in the district save Parfait Marié, who was languishing in a cell just a few yards away, and delivered a long and furious harangue on the fate that awaited any other official or community foolish enough to harbour enemy spies. "It was a most virulent sermon," the mayors reported, "and utterly pointless."

The trial—if such it could be termed, since none of the defendants had legal representation—opened at midday on May 20, in the château of Le Câtelet, with Judge Grumme—nude fisherman and "Big Red Turkey"—presiding. The villagers were convicted and swiftly sentenced. As the senior village official, Parfait Marié was sentenced to ten years' hard labour and a five-thousand-franc fine. For sheltering the Englishmen, Florency and Marie-Thérèse Dessenne each received a sentence of ten years' forced labour and a combined fine of ten thousand marks; the Lelongs got eight years' hard labour each and a five-thousand-mark fine. Achille Poëtte was sentenced to forced labour for an indefinite period, and Suzanne Boitelle, for providing food and shelter to the men, was ordered to pay a fine of a thousand marks and spend eighteen months in a German prison. Suzanne did not, as it happened, have two marks, or francs, let alone a thousand, and was not about to give the German invaders a single sou. "I am not going to pay this fine," the pistol-eyed woman told Judge Grumme, who immediately and indignantly added another five months to the young mother's sentence. The *garde champêtre* was acquitted, but an additional fine of five thousand marks was imposed on the village as a whole.

Some thought the sentences were oddly lenient. Villeret had already been stripped of every valuable, so it was clear to all that "the monetary punishments were strictly theoretical." German proclamations had threatened the death penalty for anyone sheltering fugitive soldiers, and the fate of Auguste Chalandre and others had shown this was no idle threat. "The affair of the Englishmen ought to have proved fatal for a number of the inhabitants," wrote Henri Lelong, mayor of Villeret in 1928. Judge Grumme had always had a reputation as a more humane man than his colleagues—"he was odd rather than evil," thought Henriette Legé—but Henri Lelong was not alone in wondering why the lives of the villagers were spared. Had a deal been struck? If so, it did not include clemency for the British soldiers. Thorpe, Donohoe, and Martin could not deny that the deadline for surrender had passed some three weeks earlier, but they vehemently rejected the charges of espionage. Thorpe's defence was passionate, and characteristic: he was the father of three children, he pleaded, and his life should be spared. None of the three accused spoke German, no translator was on hand, and there is no evidence the military judge had a clue what was said by the men in their own defence. At five o'clock that evening, Grumme passed sentence on all three: death by firing squad, with sentences suspended until confirmation was received from the superior military authorities in Saint-Quentin, who would render a decision on May 26, six days hence. The condemned men were marched back to their cells.

As in most wartime military "spy trials," the names of the convicted men and the sentences they had received were officially classified as secret, so as not to alert the enemy that its agents had been apprehended. Like most such rules, this one did not work, and news of the death sentences spread swiftly.

While the trial was under way, Robert Digby was hiding in the woods outside Villeret, plunged into "abject misery." On the day of the arrests, Evers had posted a sentry beside the Dessenne household and placed Villeret under surveillance; any attempt on his part to see Claire or their child would be an invitation to even worse disaster. His supporters in the village knew where he was, but dared not get news or food to him without alerting the sentries. He was cold, he was hungry, and he was alone. Digby had spent five days hiding in the undergrowth and wondering what to do when a familiar figure appeared in the Trocmé woods, calling out his name. It was Emile Marié, Parfait's father, who had taken over as acting mayor the day his son was arrested.

Emile was a figure of some amusement in Villeret, nicknamed "The Fat One" since he had managed to stay remarkably portly during the months of privation, while everyone else grew emaciated. He was a retiring man, nearly seventy years old, and the last place he wanted to be was in a dank wood with a dangerous fugitive in the middle of a war. He also wanted his son back. Emile Marié explained to Digby that he had been summoned to a meeting with the *Kommandant* in Le Câtelet, who had "promised to spare the life" of the fourth fugitive soldier if he surrendered promptly. In his next breath, however, the terrifying Major Evers had talked of "dreadful reprisals against the village and those who had helped the enemy soldiers." Whoever betrayed Digby had certainly informed Evers about Claire and Hélène, and when the *Kommandant* spoke of retribution he was surely making a direct threat to the two people the Englishman loved most. Claire and Hélène were effectively hostages.

War forges a few heroes and villains, but often it thrusts ordinary, frail people into a moral no-man's-land, forcing upon them choices or compromises they could never have anticipated. As the recent history of Villeret showed, some had responded to those choices with an instinctive courage, while others had not. A few seemed guided by some inner compass of rectitude, but at least one person, for whatever reason, had chosen what seemed an easier, safer, and less lofty path. Now it was Digby's turn to choose. He could have kept running, leaving behind Villeret, his lover, and their child. With his proven survival skills he could easily have reached a neighbouring district in the occupied zone, outside the vindictive reach of Karl Evers. Alone, he might even have made a clean escape. The alternative was self-sacrifice, in the hope that this would protect the woman and child he adored and the village that had sheltered him. Emile had told him of the sentences already handed down to the other three men, and he must have known that to put himself in the hands of Evers would invite almost certain death. A few months earlier, he might still have chosen the first route, and turned his back on Villeret. Until he found himself in the village, there was little in Digby's past to suggest he had the makings of a hero, or a martyr. But when he faced his choice, he does not seem to have seen a choice there at all.

On May 22, Digby emerged from the woods and walked slowly back into Villeret.

He could not stop to say farewell at the Dessenne household, for fear of drawing further attention to his lover and child. Claire did not have to watch him pass along rue d'En Bas for the last time. That morning, she had been rounded up with the other able-bodied villagers and marched off to the fields under guard. One of the Dessennes recalled that on "the day of the arrest she had to work, just like every other day, there was no respite. But she knew that Emile Marié had persuaded Digby to give himself up. She knew what was going to happen. She was distraught."

Digby knocked on the door of the Marié home, and "Emile Marié, the new mayor of Villeret, led him off to the command post."

> And I to my pledged word am true,
> I shall not fail that rendezvous.

A few hours later, Digby was facing the Le Câtelet military court, accused of spying and passing on German military secrets on behalf of enemy powers. He flatly denied the charges but admitted that it was he, and not Léon Lelong, who had forged the passes carried by the four British soldiers. In less than an hour, the trial was over. Just as Digby had anticipated, Evers's promise of clemency was not honoured. Indeed, it may never have been made. Robert Digby was sentenced to die by firing squad.

Marie Coulette retrieved the soldiers' uniforms from their latest hiding place, and had them delivered to Le Câtelet prison, where the four soldiers were reunited in a single cell. Digby put on the British army-issue boots he had not worn since he first stumbled into Villeret. Made from Indian roan leather, the British boot was as distinctive as it was comfortable. To have worn them while he was on the run would have given him away at once, but now they could replace the worn pair of *sabots* he had borrowed from Florency Dessenne.

The following day, Judge Grumme received word from the military council at Saint-Quentin, confirming the sentences on Thorpe, Donohoe, and Martin. At four-thirty that afternoon, the judge appeared in the fetid cell and "read aloud to the first three Englishmen the sentence of death." The execution, he said, would take place the following day.

Henri Serpebois, the local saddle-maker and mechanic and the only civilian in Le Câtelet who still had a horse and cart, was summoned to the *Kommandant's* office and told to stand ready to transport three execution posts to the moat beneath the ruins of the ancient castle. Ernest Lambert, the carpenter, was also brought before Major Evers: "He told me to make three coffins—I had already furnished him with 1,200," Lambert later recalled grimly. "He also told me to plant the three execution posts, which were three old carriage shafts." News that the Englishmen were to be put to death the following day had spread rapidly through Le Câtelet and on to Villeret. There were those who said that French civilians should have refused to carry out such dishonourable work. Henri Serpebois, however, did not resist. His young son had contracted pneumonia in 1914, and the child's life had been saved by the attentions of a German doctor. "From that moment he always had a certain respect for the Germans." But Ernest Lambert was made of less malleable stuff, and moreover had a certain position to uphold in society. "He had a sharp tongue and an exuberant personality, and he was seen almost as a sacred figure in the village." Lambert had nine children, a mass of wiry black hair, a large heart, and, most eye-catchingly, a hunchback. "The local people often came to touch his hump, to bring them good luck. Ernest never minded." Lambert loudly objected that providing coffins for the *Kommandant* was one thing, but planting posts to shoot three Allied soldiers was another. "The officer told me that I would install those posts because my life depended on it. I left, escorted by two soldiers."

As Lambert began sawing the pine planks to make the coffins, Willie Thorpe, Thomas Donohoe, and David Martin made their own preparations. The Abbé Morelle from Gouy, who had bandaged Digby's wounds in 1914, arrived wearing his soutane and broad-brimmed black hat and was permitted to pray with Donohoe, the only Catholic. He was followed to the jail by the Protestant *pasteur* of Nauroy, Cheminé, who spent several hours talking quietly with Thorpe and Martin, the Ulster Protestant. When the priests departed, anguish set in. "That night was a dreadful one, for the three Englishmen let out a stream of curses and lamentations." The sounds of despair wafted over to the German canteen, where the German "officers were indulging in a debauch." Grumme staggered to his feet, and "the military judge, very drunk, came over to crow cynically at their misfortune, dancing around in front of them and yelling about the coffins that were being made for them." In the neighbouring cells, the prisoners from Villeret—Suzanne Boitelle, Parfait Marié, and the others—as well as "several other inhabitants of Le Câtelet, who also found themselves incarcerated," listened to the abuse in shocked silence. Grumme was joined by other "officers, who came to insult their victims." If the bizarrely cruel performance by the "humane" Grumme was intended to cause the condemned men still greater distress, it seems to have had the opposite effect.

No longer cursing, the three men sat down to write letters of adieu to their families. Donohoe and Martin were not letter-writing men, so Robert Digby helped them, although he felt certain— wrongly, as matters turned out—that the letters would be "confiscated from the hands of Abbé Morelle and Pasteur Cheminé" as soon as they left the cells. Together the men wrote to Jeanne Magniez, their earliest protector. As Henri Godé, mayor of Le Câtelet, observed: "It was a touching detail, to the honour of the three soldiers, demonstrating the dignity of that tragic night." This letter was smuggled out, along with the others written in the condemned cell, and "delivered to Madame Magniez after the war."

"They had not forgotten her," the official municipal historian observed approvingly. But, oddly, she seemed to want to forget them. Jeanne Magniez kept everything relating to her war, including complimentary little notes from German officers. This letter, however, appears to have been destroyed. Perhaps, for whatever reason, it was too painful to keep. The letters were given to the *curé*, who forwarded them to Henri Godé for safekeeping.

David Martin wrote to his father in Athern Street, the Belfast home where he had grown up, and Thomas Donohoe bade farewell to Bridie, his girl still waiting for him in the distant hills of County Cavan. The Irishmen could have no idea, but less than a month earlier, Irish nationalists had staged an armed uprising in Dublin. The Easter Rebellion was the first of a series of events that would culminate in the establishment of the Irish Free State, predecessor of the Republic of Ireland, placing a border between the homes of Catholic Thomas Donohoe and Protestant David Martin. Ireland's sectarian troubles might eventually have made enemies of Donohoe and Martin, but few closer friendships have been forged by war.

William Thorpe was a more literate man, having passed his certificate of education just a few months before coming to France. Garrulous to a fault, Willie had much to tell his beloved wife and children, but for heartbroken "Papa" Thorpe the words would not come. His letter was a simple mantra of pain, love, and loss. On two sheets of paper, "over and over again," he wrote just three sentences:

> Darling wife and children. Brave British soldier. Not afraid to die.

CHAPTER TWELVE

Remember Me

At three o'clock on the afternoon of May 27, 1916, the hunchbacked carpenter Ernest Lambert was waiting by the moat beneath the crumbling ramparts of Le Câtelet's medieval fortress. Serpebois had delivered the coffins, and Lambert had planted the execution posts in the chalky soil, a yard from the wall. "It was a beautiful afternoon," he later recalled. Lambert surveyed the newly made coffins, "not much more than pine boxes," and he felt a wave of disgust. "I took care to hide them in the bushes, so the Englishmen would not have to see them when they arrived." An hour before the time of execution, the *garde champêtre* walked slowly along the main street, ringing his bell. The villagers of Le Câtelet had been ordered to stay inside their homes, but half an hour later, Sister Saint-Etienne, one of the four remaining Sisters of Providence who had tended the wounded in the earliest days of the war, appeared furtively from around the castle wall "with some flowers to place at the foot of the execution posts." Lambert watched nervously as the nun approached in her long blue chasuble and black veil, and suffered the confusion of conscience that had plagued Villeret for the previous two years. "I merely pointed out to her that I would be held responsible for laying the flowers, and she took them away again." The carpenter sat down in the bright sunshine to wait for the condemned men and their executioners, and wondered if he was doing the right thing. "I had no choice," he told himself. "I could not have refused."

The final hours in the cell were spent "praying, singing songs, and writing to their families." As the guard assembled outside the prison, Thorpe, Donohoe, and Martin solemnly shook hands with Robert Digby, and were marched outside. Dressed in khaki once more, they had their hands tied and were loaded onto a low cart. Defiant now, after the terror of the previous evening, they "left the cells singing Scottish tunes, hymns, and parodies of German songs," but then fell silent as the cart creaked over the cobbles, "surrounded by German military police and followed by a squad of 24 infantrymen." Henriette Legé, eight years old, stood at the window of her father's study and watched the grisly procession pass: "The street was deserted. I remember it was quite quiet, then the horses' hooves, and then still again." Her father studied the faces of the condemned men: "Their expressions were resolute, and they nodded their heads to us as they passed, in salutation."

Lambert watched the troop approach in the haze of the late afternoon sun. "The Englishmen arrived, their heads high and their expressions proud. They faced the firing squad bravely." Before they were bound to the posts, the three men shook hands once more. David Martin was lashed to the middle post, with Thorpe at his left shoulder and Donohoe to his right. None wore blindfolds. Somewhat strangely, they chose this moment to offer a chorus of thanks to one of their earliest protectors: "At the foot of the execution posts, they blessed Madame Magniez of Hargival." Then the firing squad of twelve men stepped forward.

According to one account, at this moment Thorpe's spirit buckled under the strain, and he began sobbing for the children he would never see again: "Papa put on a poor show in the face of death," it was said. But that view was flatly contradicted by Lambert, who was, he pointed out, "the only French eyewitness to the execution." According to the carpenter, Thorpe died as he had lived, more for fatherhood than soldiering, but courageously: when the executioners opened fire, the other two men were killed instantly, but "one of the men, the smallest and oldest (Willie, the father of the family), was only wounded. So, in silence, without any other supplication, he lifted up three fingers of one hand, spread apart, to signify that he had three young children. The commander of the firing squad walked up to him, and finished him off with a revolver bullet in the ear."

Down in the town, every inhabitant was listening intently through the crepuscular stillness, from behind shutters and doors. Léon Legé recorded: "Many heard the report of the rifles which put an end to the worldly sufferings of these poor martyrs of war. They died bravely; one of them cried out a few words in his own language: 'Long Live England! Down with Germany!' "

If their ears had not been ringing from the gunfire, Lambert and the German executioners might have heard the stifled sobs of an angry little French boy, for Lambert, whatever he might believe, was not the only local witness to the execution. Georges Mercier, the six-year-old son of a Le Câtelet labourer, was hiding under a bush with his older cousin Eugène, two hundred yards up the slope, with a clear view down to the castle wall. As the rifles fired, he had tried to leap up and shout—he did not know exactly what he meant to shout, simply the worst thing he could think of to shame those "murdering bastards"—but Eugène pulled him down and clamped a hand over his mouth.

The head of the firing squad was anxious to finish the business, and no sooner had the three men slumped to the ground than Lambert was pushed forward. "Despite the horror, I was made to put the bodies into the coffins at once, even though the corpses were all warm, almost living, their muscles still contracting. The Germans told me to hurry and angrily berated me for having hidden the coffins from sight out of humanity; they kicked me brutally." In constructing the coffins, Lambert had not calculated for the lanky Irishman David Martin. Little Willie Thorpe and Thomas Donohoe fit snugly enough, but Martin's legs hung over the end. No matter how he tried, the carpenter could not close the lid. The head of the execution squad shoved him aside: "With two blows of his heel, the officer broke the man's legs and stuffed them inside the box."

The coffins were loaded onto Serpebois's wagon, and "a quarter of an hour after the execution the funeral cortège returned and deposited the bodies at the cemetery." The German troops dispersed. Pasteur Cheminé read from the Bible as Ernest Lambert bent his arched back under a darkening sky and buried three soldiers in Le Câtelet's tiny graveyard, beside the Escaut River that flowed down towards Hargival.

An hour after the execution, the prisoners from Villeret—Parfait Marié, Achille Poëtte, Suzanne Boitelle, and the Dessennes, Florency and Marie-Thérèse—were taken in chains from the Le Câtelet prison and led towards the train station for the journey to Germany, to begin serving their long prison sentences. Marie-Thérèse was still breast-feeding little Robert. "He was weaned in the most brutal way." Suzanne Boitelle, deprived of one child as the war began and now separated from another, was given permission to embrace three-year-old Guy before she, too, was led away, sobbing. Elise Lelong, the ever-superior baker's wife, reprimanded her half-sister for her weakness. "Stop crying. What, weep in front of these people?" she said, pointing theatrically at the German guards. "I would rather make myself sick from the effort I am making to keep the tears back." Suzanne Boitelle needed no lessons in courage from Elise Lelong, but, unfortunately, her response is not recorded.

The following day was Sunday, and the Abbé Morelle, clad in black vestments of mourning, made his way slowly to the church. The grave of the three soldiers was "covered in an immense pile of flowers," and "the church was packed." Major Evers could stop them from watching an execution, but he had not yet forbidden the people to worship, and every able-bodied person was there: the teacher Cabaret, the lawyer Legé, the mayor Godé, the carpenter Lambert, and the mechanic Serpebois. The entire community, including many not seen in church for years, turned out to hear "the mass for the dead read by the *curé* for the three Englishmen, in an atmosphere of unspeakable emotion."

Alice Delabranche, the daughter of the pharmacist, recorded the outpouring of sorrow and anger in her diary:

Their grave was submerged in flowers, and some bouquets were tied with the *tricolore* ribbon. The pile of wildflowers and wreaths grew so large that even the German officers came to stare at it, becoming such an object of curiosity that, on the 29th, the *Kommandant* summoned the acting mayor to get him to ban this profusion of flowers and to ensure that no such demonstration was made in the future. A sentry was placed at the entrance to the graveyard, and nobody was allowed to come in.

Every flower, Evers surely knew, was a small blooming of defiance, a gesture of support for the one remaining English soldier who yet languished in the Le Câtelet prison, whose death was set for the next evening.

Robert Digby had heard the volley of gunfire from down by the old fort and the shouts of his friends before they died, and he had listened to the creaking tumbril bringing their coffins back to the graveyard. He had listened the following morning as the church, just a few hundred yards away, reverberated to the singing of a defiant congregation.

The tiny cell window looked out over the valley in the direction of Villeret and beyond it towards the front line, where a war was taking place without him. Digby was quite alone, and yet his family, both the one he was born into and the one he had now made, were tantalisingly close at hand. Somewhere over there were Claire and Hélène, imprisoned, like him, by a battle that must have seemed insignificant beside their private tragedy. And somewhere beyond Villeret on the Allied side of the line, where British troops were already massing for the Somme offensive, was his brother, Thomas, a creature of the trenches, unaware that his kin was only now facing a death which, in its loneliness and inevitability, was perhaps even more ghastly than the sudden oblivion from a direct shell hit. Claire could not even say farewell, since, under the bureaucratic hell forged by Karl Evers, "she could not get a pass." The war had flung them together, and now it had wrenched them apart.

"Another execution post was planted in the castle moat by the carpenter, in exactly the same place." Pasteur Cheminé of Nauroy was "sick at heart and bedridden after the previous execution," but the wretched man hauled himself out of his bed, and at around six o'clock he entered Digby's cell, to "undertake the honour of preparing him for death." Digby did his best to comfort the distraught *pasteur*, who said that the Englishman "displayed much courage, as befits the son of an officer." Digby asked him to act as Hélène's *parrain de guerre,* her "godfather of war," when her own father was dead. Pasteur Cheminé readily agreed.

In front of the priest, Digby maintained a brave stance, but it was to the French jailer, who brought him food, that the Englishman opened his heart: "He said that death meant nothing to him, but that he was broken-hearted to be leaving behind a little girl, born of a love affair with a young woman from Villeret." On a sheet of paper he scribbled his "last wishes," and handed it to the *pasteur* to pass on to Henri Godé, the mayor, with a plea to send the message on to his family if he could; in the note he again "expressed the desire that his parents should recognise the child, as he himself had done."

Tuesday May 30, 1916, was another glorious early-summer day, clear and still, "with butterflies everywhere."

The slaughter at Verdun still raged, and the pace of bloodletting had accelerated on the Somme front since British troops had taken over that sector from the French a few months earlier. On the very day Digby prepared to die, one English officer could watch from a distance as the armies exchanged shells and find that the "colour effects were a sheer joy to watch: according as a shell burst in coal, chalk or soil, there was a dust fountain of black, white or terracotta, or a mixture of two of these; and there were woolly air bursts that rolled out in whorls—grey-black, pure white, and lemon. Sometimes there was a hint of the human soil on which shells were falling when a large, flaccid thing rose in the spout, and one was sorry for the men there, whichever side they were on."

Le Câtelet and Villeret were but a few miles from the colourful carnage, yet here death still possessed an intimacy, and a face. This was, one diarist noted, "a day of dread and anguish that the people will always guard in the memory, over and above the days of invasion." Word leaked out that Major Evers had tricked Digby into surrendering with a promise that his life would be saved. The Englishman "didn't take into account the deceitfulness of the Germans, who never missed an opportunity to cover themselves with opprobrium," one villager observed grimly. Evers was determined to make the soldiers, and Villeret, pay dearly for their defiance. The lawyer Legé concluded: "The *Kommandant* appears to have exaggerated or falsified the facts, to take revenge against the English soldiers who had lived under his nose for two years, a fact which had certainly humiliated him, putting a dent in his Teutonic pride." The infamy of the Germans was familiar, but there were other, even more chilling rumours circulating, to the effect that "the *Kommandant* did not appear to have played the principal role" in the events leading up to the capture of the British soldiers. The villagers passed on the hearsay quietly, or jotted oblique notes in their journals, but they all agreed: it was French, and not German, perfidy that had passed Digby into the hands of his executioners.

Pasteur Cheminé, ashen and distressed, reappeared at Digby's cell, prayed silently, and then departed. Digby picked up the pen again. As dusk approached, he wrote three letters. The first was to his mother, the strait-laced Ellen Digby, after whom he had named his child. For nearly two years, Digby had lived entirely without military discipline, fighting a battle unlike any soldier of the Great War: he had lived like an animal in the woods, ditched his uniform and gun, found love, and fathered a child. The errant romantic in Digby had always tussled with the obedient soldier-son; had he obeyed his training and the dictates of duty he would not have fallen in love, and perhaps would not now be facing death. Digby's heart had brought him to the condemned cell, but this last letter to his mother reflected his other, conventional side: it is a stoic's statement, precisely tracing the expected cadences of patriotism, martial martyrdom, and mother-love. The English officer who would later pass the letter on to Ellen Digby found its sentiments "brave and noble," but the suppression of emotion is agonising.

> Dear Mother,
>   Sad news for you. I surrendered to the German authorities on the 22nd of May, 1916. I have been hiding since the 2nd September, 1914, in the village of Villeret. Lost my army on the 27th August, 1914, after having been wounded in the left forearm at Villers, not far from here. I went to the hospital to have it attended to and in the meantime my army retired. Misfortunate. I have just received my verdict and am not disappointed, as it is what I expected from them. Condemned to death to be shot at 10 5 p m. this evening. Be brave and do not let this trouble you too much, as I die happy for King and Country. Give a farewell kiss to my brother Thomas and my darling sister Flo. Good-bye. God bless you, and render you happy in your old days. The last dying wish of your son,
>
> Robert Digby

"Misfortunate"; "sad news": "I have a rendezvous with Death." For a man who was about to be executed on bogus charges, who could not even say adieu to the woman and child he loved, this was stunning English understatement. His words also echo Alan Seeger's lofty embrace of martyrdom. "If it must be, let it come," the American foreign legionnaire had written home just a few months earlier. "Why flinch? It is by far the noblest form in which death can come. It is in a sense almost a privilege . . ."

Digby knew his audience, and Ellen Digby did not like fuss.

The condemned man's words in his next letter were equally carefully chosen. Eugénie Dessenne, Claire's mother, had disapproved of Digby from the outset. She had done her best to scupper the affair and made no secret of her view that the Englishmen had plunged her village and family into mortal danger. Digby had every reason to dislike and distrust Eugénie, but after his death Claire would need her mother's support. It was time to call an armistice, and Digby addressed his old adversary as the grandmother of his child.

My dear Grand-mère,

Tomorrow morning, when you wake up, think of poor Robert who is dead. I will have been shot at 10:05 (German time) against the walls of the château. I will die happy and contented for my country and my King, and also for France. One thing makes me happy, which is to know that you have not suffered the same fate as I. Poor Claire and my child will now be left behind without me, but never think ill of her or of my little one. Look after her well, and tell your family to do the same. I want her to have a good grandmother in her life.

Midway through the letter, Digby suddenly switched tone and began speaking to Claire and Marie Coulette, his most forthright defenders. Although the letter was addressed to Eugénie Dessenne, it was intended to be understood by her mother and daughter. His self-control wavered.

Claire, I know you will read this letter to your grandmother. I wish I had never stayed in Villeret to bring such misery into your lives. Look after yourselves always, and reflect that your husband died bravely for a just cause. Remember me to Florency and Marie-Thérèse and tell the child not to weep for me, for I have brought her into a world of such unhappiness. Remember me to all in Villeret. I have asked the pastor of Nauroy (who has been with me for the last four hours) if he will place my body in the graveyard at Villeret after the war. That is my wish.

Goodbye, and thank you.

Your friend,
Robert

The tone of this letter, written in French, was distinctly strange. Addressing Eugénie, Digby appeared contrite and remorseful, but this was also a letter of instruction, leaving its recipient in no doubt that her duty lay in protecting the daughter and granddaughter he was leaving behind. There was also just the hint of a threat implicit in the observation that Eugénie had "not suffered the same fate" as he. The fact that Eugénie Dessenne and her family had escaped punishment, despite their intimate association with the conspiracy, had not gone unnoticed in Villeret either. Was Robert Digby sending Eugénie a coded message?

It was past eight o'clock and the cell was growing murky when Robert Digby began to write to Claire Dessenne. This was the shortest of the three letters, and the saddest. He wrote quickly, again in French, for time was running short. In two years he had become what no one who knew him before 1914 could have anticipated: a Frenchman, with a French family in a tiny French village.

> My darling Claire,
>
>   This is the last letter of my life. I am condemned to die by firing squad at five past ten tonight. Farewell, and never forget Robert, who dies happy and satisfied for France and for my own country. I kiss you. Embrace my baby girl and later, when she is grown, tell her the truth about her father, who has died contented. Send the letter I have already written for my mother. I have given another letter for my family to the pastor, because the Germans have intercepted the letters of my comrades.
>
>   Au revoir,
>
> Your loving,
Robert

The letter ended abruptly, for the execution squad had assembled in the street outside the jail. Pasteur Cheminé, "sick with horror," entered the cell to administer a final blessing. Whereas his comrades had been carried to their deaths on a wagon, Digby marched in his standard army-issue English boots. The villagers, once more, peered silently from behind shutters. "All you could hear was the tramp of the boots on the cobbles," remembered little Henriette

Legé. Digby had no companion with whom he could sing fortify-
ing songs, and he had much to occupy his mind. Lambert was waiting, and this time he had been unable to hide the coffin. If Digby
saw it, his oddly serene expression did not change. "He was very
calm, and allowed himself to be strapped to the post without a
word," wrote Ernest Lambert.

The old war-scarred fortress was, and remains, a tranquil place at
twilight, when, as one local writer noted in the years just before the
war, "birds from all over the countryside gather under the great
trees and bushes covering the ramparts to sing a most delightful
chorus: the warbler, the chaffinch, the goldcrest, the nightingale,
and the blackbird. If a sound breaks the solitude here, it is not the
fanfare of war, the crackling of the fusillade, and the cries of the
wounded, but birdsong, sweet and harmonious."

It was late, but the chorus was still in full flow when eight German soldiers stepped forward, took aim, and killed Robert Digby.

The eye of one member of the firing squad came to rest on the
dead soldier's shiny boots. "They were beautiful brown boots,
brand-new," remembered Lambert. As the carpenter was laying
Digby in the coffin, the German stopped him and began to unlace
what the French called *brodequins* and the British "bluchers"—after
the Prussian Field Marshal von Blücher—and all sides revered
equally, for, as the soldier-novelist Frederic Manning wrote: "If a
sword were the symbol of battle, boots were certainly symbols of
war."

"I stopped him by slamming the lid with a bang. In a rage, the
soldier kicked me hard in the kidneys: I felt the pain for ages afterwards." The hunchback carpenter later admitted what everyone in
the village knew: that he had taken the boots himself. "They were
precious things at that time."

Major Evers, angered by the public emotion over the executed
men and as ever a slave to an "archaic militarist mentality," had
given orders that no more than one wreath could be placed on each
grave, "or a fine would be imposed." Alice Delabranche, the pharmacist's daughter, recorded the *Kommandant*'s reaction to the fresh
wave of grief. "There were too many flowers, he said, and he or-

dered the municipality to ensure a more reasonable display in future, with just a few bouquets from time to time." Le Câtelet was rebellious, for "instead of terror he inspired contempt," and henceforth, "whenever Evers was passing, everyone would slam doors and windows and leave the street deserted. The *Kommandant* was furious, but the inhabitants, enraged by this succession of futile murders, did not stop their demonstrations."

Digby's last wish, to be laid to rest in Villeret, his home, was denied to him. On the orders of Major Evers, he was buried apart from his comrades, away from the road, in the farthest corner of Le Câtelet cemetery, to prevent any more demonstrations of floral insubordination and exhibitions of public mourning. The citizens obeyed the letter of the command and flatly defied the spirit: only one wreath was laid on each of the four graves, but each was a massive one, a vast canopy of flowers gathered from the surrounding fields and hedgerows that completely obscured the mounds of freshly dug earth. After the flowers had wilted, the people put up a simple wooden cross over Digby's grave, with his identity disks attached, to mark the spot in the corner of a foreign field: "In that rich earth a richer dust concealed."

CHAPTER THIRTEEN

The Somme

For weeks before the great battle started, wrote the mayor of Villeret, "one sensed that the British and French offensive on the Somme was coming soon." The British now had tanks, the Germans had swapped the Gothic pointed *Pickelhaube* headgear for more modern steel helmets, but the blood-letting was medieval. A week before the attack, the British guns began shelling the German lines preparatory to the largest single battle man had ever fought, one of the most famous and futile attacks in military history. The noise could be heard in Sussex, a hundred miles away. In Villeret, it was deafening. Every building shivered, every shutter shook, and the air itself seemed to warp and reverberate as a million shells were hurled at the German line by 1,537 artillery pieces. The guns were "louder than ever before, and everything rattled," wrote the pharmacist's daughter. The children of Villeret—among them Hélène Dessenne, the Englishman's daughter, and Marie Sauvage's half-German child—were clutched to their mothers. Some villagers hid in the cellars, others took to the woods. "It was a deafening thunder, all night, rolling up from the valley. But somehow, I know it sounds strange, you got used to it after a while." In Saint-Quentin, experts would feel the trembling glass in the windowpanes and claim they knew which of the heavy guns were in use. On July 1,

1916, in "heavenly" sunshine, as Siegfried Sassoon recalled, the British advanced along a thirteen-mile front. The volunteers of Kitchener's new army were considered too raw to charge. So they were ordered to walk towards the German lines. Captain Nevill of the 8th East Surreys had bought four footballs while on leave, and offered a prize for the first platoon to dribble one into the German trenches. "A good kick. The ball rose and travelled well towards the German line. That seemed to be the signal to advance." Twenty thousand died before sunset, Captain Nevill among the first.

Villeret was eerily empty of troops on the eve of the struggle, but within hours of the bombardment they began to arrive: heart-shocked men carried in on field ambulances with terrible wounds, bodies torn up by shrapnel and explosive, and after them the troops, struggling up from the assault out of deep chasms of ex-haustion and fear. The Allied attack on the Somme failed, but it took its toll. The villagers had witnessed battle-weary soldiers for two years, but never on this scale, as German men and boys were fed into one side of the churning machine, and British and French into the other. Foulon's stables and barns were packed with hun-dreds of troops, and all vestiges of normal life evaporated: "The mairie, the classrooms, the teachers' homes, and the church were all transformed into field hospitals." The oak trestle on which Alexis Morel had once kneaded bread for the *épicerie* was dragged off for the surgeons to use as an operating table. Just one month after Digby's execution, death arrived in cataracts.

"Day and night the wounded from the Somme poured into Villeret," wrote the mayor, a handful of British and French, who had got farther in the futile advance, dotted among the countless Germans. Villeret, now one vast hospital-mortuary for the Somme, stank of sweat and mortality. "One hundred and thirty German sol-diers died from their wounds and were buried in the community graveyard," beside John Sligo, the sole Englishman. Years later, the children of the village would find neatly severed arm bones and leg bones in the field beside the lazarets, where German doctors had flung amputated limbs from their abominable surgery. Even François Theillier's elegant château, along with its stables and outhouses, was transformed into a vast and rococo barracks for wounded and dying men. With wounds came disease, and the farm where Theillier's mother had once kept beautiful cows in pens with brass trimmings became a "hospital for the contagious," ringing to the groans of slow gangrenous and tubercular death.

One of those who found themselves in Villeret's makeshift hospitals was Ernst Jünger, now a twenty-one-year-old officer. Jünger had already distinguished himself as a soldier of almost impossible courage, who would later earn fame for his lyrical depiction of war and less flattering distinction as an extreme right-winger and early Nazi Party supporter. He had been patrolling a part of the front line known as Nameless Wood when "suddenly a shot from an unseen sniper got me in both legs." He bound his wounds with a pocket handkerchief and "limped over the shell-shot ground to the dressing station . . . The same evening I was moved to the Villeret field hospital." Jünger described the scene of mephitic ghastliness inside a field hospital, where "the whole misery of war was concentrated . . . The surgeons carried on their sanguinary trade at operating tables. Here a limb was amputated, there a skull chiselled away, or a grown-in bandage cut out. Moans and cries of pain sounded throughout the room, while nurses in white hastened busily from one table to another with instruments and dressings."

Moved to the military hospital at Valenciennes, the German writer encountered numerous wounded enemy soldiers and noted that, "as elsewhere, when we met Englishmen, we had the joyful feeling of bold manliness." Jünger won the Iron Cross for his part in the battle, and was wounded twice more, by shrapnel in the left leg and a revolver bullet across his scalp. Reflecting on the Somme carnage, Jünger wrote of how man might be "crushed but not conquered; in such moments the human spirit triumphs." In one way, he might have been describing the more valiant side of Villeret's recent history.

Just a few miles away, at the front, Alan Seeger did not fail his rendezvous. On the Fourth of July, the American poet was martyred, just as he had predicted, when he and his fellow legionnaires tried to storm a disputed barricade across the battle-bog at Belloy-en-Santerre, west of Péronne.

The Battle of the Somme brought such horror and excitement to Villeret that few, other than Claire Dessenne, had much time to dwell on the fate of Robert Digby and the other men. But when the German military police reappeared and arrested Henri and Joséphine Marié, the unanswered and suppressed questions suddenly resurfaced. The Réseau Victor, Villeret's highly effective spy network, had been betrayed, reminding any villagers in doubt that a traitor was still among them. "The activities of these two had been uncovered by the enemy," the mayor reported, but "everyone believed that whoever had denounced the Englishmen had done the same to the Mariés."

German penetration of Victor Marié's espionage network was "a sickening body-blow" to British intelligence. For months the system had worked without a hitch: on prearranged dates, when Victor hung out washing on a particular clothes line, homing pigeons would be air-dropped, to be released back across the lines by Marié and his agents with whatever information had been gathered. "Everything appeared to be in first-class order . . . Victor Marié was on the spot, his system was growing, and the pigeons were returning with valuable information about the location and movement of German reserves." From time to time, Victor had returned to GHQ, via the Netherlands, to brief his spymasters. During one of these visits it was noticed that the French spy was showing "clear signs of strain," so it was decided to boost his morale by decorating him. On July 9, 1916, with the battle raging, Field Marshal Douglas Haig personally presented Victor Marié with the Distinguished Conduct Medal, commending him as a "really bold and plucky fellow." But General Sir Walter Kirke, Marié's handler and the officer in charge of Secret Service operations and counter-espionage, remained deeply anxious. "I have misgiving and much fear that we may lose Marié, when the whole service will go phut," he confided to his diary, with gloomy prescience.

Victor Marié's network, woven over the previous two years with all the intricate skill of a *maître-tisseur*, was unpicked in a matter of hours. Two days after Christmas, eight of his agents were arrested and promptly executed by firing squad in Saint-Quentin; seven more were sentenced to long prison terms; three died in captivity.

Delacourt, the mayor of Vendelles, was seized, along with another network agent, and died in his cell the day before his scheduled execution. The acting mayor of Hargicourt was arrested merely for having been seen in Villeret on the same day as the Marié brothers. The sixty-eight-year-old mother of the principal conspirators, herself a key figure in the network, defied the Germans with typical Villeret gumption: "The widow Marié-Leroy denied everything and furiously resisted all attempts at interrogation, disconcerting the members of the War Council by refusing to speak anything but patois." Baffled and uncertain what to do with this incomprehensible peasant woman, the court simply ordered her to be removed to another occupied village, Preux-au-Bois. Scores of others were rounded up, but no one can be sure how many perished. Henri Marié was condemned as a spy and, "deported in captivity to Germany, deprived of food, and exhausted, he contracted tuberculosis, which killed him a few years later," Villeret's mayor wrote. The gravestone of Henri's thirty-three-year-old sister, Joséphine, one of the key operatives of the Villeret network, tells of a still more ghastly fate. Already a widow after the death in combat of her husband, Paul, Victor's brother, "she was imprisoned in Saint-Quentin and tortured by the Germans, who wanted to wring a confession out of her. Driven to insanity by her suffering, she committed suicide in her jail cell on September 18, 1918," less than two months before the war ended.

The Marié brothers, the ringleaders, proved harder to pin down. Marius simply vanished. Early in August, Victor Marié had set off from GHQ to fly across the lines, and had crash-landed in heavy mist. For three months there was a "deafening and worrying silence." The British pilot of the plane duly reappeared in the Netherlands, but Victor himself was captured and imprisoned at Aix-la-Chapelle. According to the official French history, he was sentenced to death, but managed to escape the day before he was due to be shot, "thanks to the help of a Belgian friend," a shadowy Monsieur Dervaux.

The Battle of the Somme staggered to a halt in the freezing mists of mid-November: more than a million casualties, for an advance of just a few meaningless miles of mud. When the wind was blowing from the west and the weather warm, the smell of putre-faction reached as far as Villeret. The British marked Christmas Day by lobbing over a fresh volley of shells at points where festive Germans might be assembling. The Somme fiasco had somehow em-bittered the war; this could no longer be disguised to anyone as a jolly game of football. As the poet Edmund Blunden wrote: "Both sides had seen, in a sad scrawl of broken earth and murdered men, the answer to the question. No road. No thoroughfare. Neither race had won, nor could win, the war. The war had won, and would go on winning."

In the wake of slaughter came another army: Russian prisoners began arriving in their thousands behind the German lines, herded by guards and pitiful to behold. The villagers watched the Russians arrive, columns of filthy and miserable men, "horribly treated, dy-ing of hunger, pulling up roots as they passed and eating them raw," and then lodged in "camps of famine and brutality, reminiscent of the English convict hulks." Legé, Le Câtelet's lawyer, watched them arrive: "The sight of these poor creatures, ill-dressed, badly shod, dragging themselves along with difficulty, chilled us to the marrow. Most died of hunger, misery, and ill-treatment. Some, according to eyewitnesses, were buried alive." An official order of October 29, 1916, strictly forbade "the display of any sympathy for the prisoners, no matter what nation they are from, talking to them, or giving them food." The old quarry north of Villeret was transformed into a vast Russian prison camp, where these "wretched men, practically naked and dying of hunger," were fenced in behind barbed wire.

Once again, the instinctive generosity of the villagers emerged, and "the inhabitants, despite their own deprivation, managed to smuggle food to these poor people to alleviate their sad fate. Some, caught red-handed in these acts of charity, were beaten with the ri-fle butts of the camp guards." At the end of 1916, four hundred British prisoners arrived at Vendhuile, where they were imprisoned in a camp behind the defunct brewery. In the harsh winter of 1917, many died of cold.

In Germany, the villagers condemned for helping the British soldiers fared little better. Marie-Thérèse Dessenne supplemented the pitiful prison diet by knitting socks in exchange for a little sugar and fresh water, and when she did not work hard enough, the women jailers beat her, sometimes so severely that she was unable to stand. Her husband, Florency, never the most robust character, found imprisonment even worse. Consigned to a salt mine and spending every hour he was not labouring hunting for wild and barely digestible roots in the soil of the prison compound, he grew spectrally thin. In the Siegburg prison, Suzanne Boitelle survived principally on "cooked potatoes, sometimes with a little jam, if there was any." At Easter 1917, she and the other women prisoners buoyed their flagging spirits by dreaming of the banquet they could make themselves if they were free women: "*Pâté de foie gras sur canapé, Saumon président, Haricots Raymond, Pain Perdu,*" to be followed by "music, gramophone records, and singing." When she wrote this fantasy menu, Suzanne still had eight months of her sentence to serve before she could be allowed home. But by then, she had no home.

The Russian prisoners were in Villeret to build the stage set for the next and last great scene of the war, the withdrawal to the Siegfriedstellung, the Siegfried Line, named after the Teutonic and Wagnerian hero, or the Hindenburg Line, as the British then knew it. Having fought with such ferocity to defend this part of the line in the Battle of the Somme, the Germans now prepared to slip away. The strategic withdrawal was a military masterstroke, the strongest network of defences man had ever created, and one of the most reprehensible acts of vandalism in the twentieth century. The German army would take cover behind the vast system of fortifications, incorporating the subterranean Riqueval canal and great rolling fields of thick German barbed wire, constructed in such a configuration that the enemy might be funnelled into positions where they could be more easily massacred by machine-gun fire. The new Hindenburg Line was ninety miles long, and surgically excised twenty-five miles of front, freeing up a dozen German infantry divisions. Everything between the new concrete-and-metal barrier and the old front line was to be destroyed. Villeret, and other towns like it, would be rendered not just uninhabitable, but as hard as possible to traverse. Orchards were to be cut down to deny food to the advancing enemy, larger trees felled to a height of one metre to offer retreating riflemen a convenient ledge from which to fire, fields flooded, bridges smashed, castles and houses burned, the country methodically and utterly ruined, and what remained sown with booby traps of grotesque ingenuity: trinkets wired to bombs, the body of a British soldier invisibly attached to the pin of a hand grenade, time fuses inside "graves" to "an unknown soldier." As the historian of Le Câtelet observed, the scientific destruction "left no place for the population: all that remained was to sweep them from the land, and tear them from the homes they had vainly tried to defend by their presence."

The planned withdrawal to the Hindenburg Line would also, in November 1916, sweep away Major Karl Evers and his hated administration. Evers wanted to leave anyway. The strutting major had always considered himself a cut above the common herd, and after complaining of "social isolation," he applied for and was given a new post as a staff officer in the imperial German government in Antwerp, with the highly prestigious title of *geheimer Justizrat* (similar to a privy councillor) and not much to do. Evers's new job did provide plenty of opportunities to hobnob with the top brass, and whenever a senior VIP passed through Antwerp, such as Archduke Friedrich of Austria, he somehow always contrived to be in the photograph, standing next to the eminent personage.

The major's parting blow came in another verbose proclamation: "A group of inhabitants of the average middle class of the population will be taken to Germany as prisoners in reprisal" for the arrest of German Alsatians by the French government. Several hundred "notables" from the region were rounded up and sent to a prison camp in Holzminden, including the lawyer Léon Legé, who had been unwilling host to Evers for the last two years. The next day, the Evers regime was over. "One beautiful day, Evers and his entourage, after building their pyramid of paperwork, were sent away," taking with them all records of their administration and "the Herculean administrative infrastructure that had spawned so many questionnaires and notes, so much harassment of the population, driving the mayors to distraction, sending guards and inspectors trotting from door to door." The new *Kommandant* of Le Câtelet noted, with surprise and irritation, that "his predecessor had left him no information at all, not even a list of lodgings."

In the chill early spring of 1917, the Germans began the withdrawal, code-named, appropriately, Alberich, after the malevolent dwarf in Wagner's *Ring*. The destruction began with the woods and the smaller buildings. Jeanne Magniez watched in desolation as her cherished Hargival was crushed into dust and splinters. "The letters from my beloved Jeanne have arrived," wrote Georges Magniez. "The Pêcherie has been razed to the ground, and she has had to watch the trees she loved so much being chopped down. The thought of her unhappiness obsesses me, and I can barely face it. I dream of the Pêcherie all night, I was walking there with her and we surveyed this devastation. Six months from now, our paradise will be utterly destroyed. Oh, that the Blessed Virgin might spare her from such suffering."

On February 25, 1917, the people of Villeret and surrounding villages were ordered to assemble in the village square. Mobilisation, evacuation, deprivation, deportation, imprisonment, and the other rigours of war had radically thinned out the village population, but what remained was here: the trustworthy and the doubtful, the kind and the cruel, Claire Dessenne and Marie Sauvage with their daughters, each now over a year old. The stalwart Marie Coulette herded Florency and Marie-Thérèse's children, whose care she had taken over from the day their parents were deported to Germany, and the rest of the Dessenne clan. The remainder of the Lelong family, with Suzanne Boitelle's son Guy in tow, Antoinette Foulon and her father, Emile: all waited in the square for instructions from Emile Marié, "The Fat One," acting mayor in the absence of his son Parfait. Emile ensured that the "principal archives, including the lists of births, deaths, and marriages, were safely packed away." Hélène's meagre little birth certificate would survive the war, and so would the requisition orders filled out by the *Orstkommandant* of Villeret, Lieutenant Scholl, the final acts of petty pillage. Emile Foulon looked on wryly as Scholl helped himself to what little remained of his once-extensive possessions: thirty-six porcelain plates, the last remaining milk cow, and his brass chandelier.

"The inhabitants each took with them a bag containing only essential items. The Germans allowed much of the baggage to be loaded onto their carts, but a quantity of this was lost, or opened and pillaged." The refugees, joined by the handful of staff from Theillier's château on the hill, formed a column and walked slowly out of Villeret and into exile in the Ardennes, "through swirling mists, along muddy and rutted roads, the younger ones on foot, the others on carts loaded with bags." The village was deserted, save for the German soldiers and a "handful of men to look after the animals, who were lodged in the Lescroart farm."

Marie Coulette led her little band away; Claire walked with Hélène in her arms. Louise Dessenne, Claire's six-year-old cousin, would recall: "Our possessions were piled into a small cart, with the smallest children on top. Me, I had to walk to the station, where we were loaded onto cattle cars." Two days later, the family trudged into the refugee camp at Revin, in the Ardennes, but the widow Dessenne wrapped herself in fraying dignity. "She was wearing a shawl over her head, and some people mistook her for a beggar and gave her bread." It was politely but firmly returned: "If these people only knew Marie Coulette of Villeret, they would know that I don't need their bread," she remarked.

The scenes of exodus were repeated at Hargicourt, Vendhuile, Gouy, Le Câtelet, and Hargival. Jeanne Magniez bade farewell to her home, but was permitted to load up a cart with her photograph albums, letters, and a quantity of other luggage. As he led the refugees from his town, Henri Godé, the acting mayor of Le Câtelet, kept the last letters written by Digby, Thorpe, Donohoe, and Martin "secreted on his person, which would probably have led to his being shot, had they been discovered." Alice Delabranche, the daughter of the town pharmacist, was one of the last to leave, with the "rain falling in torrents; we were soaked to the skin, our bags and baskets wet through." As she stumbled away from the village where she had been born, Alice looked back only once: "All you could see of the horizon was flames and smoke."

Ernst Jünger described what followed, as the German forces set about carefully creating a new and vast no-man's-land. "They found with demolishing acuity the main girders of houses, attached ropes and pulled with rhythmic cries of great effort until the whole thing collapsed. Others swung mighty hammers, smashing whatever came in their way, from flower pots on window ledges to the artful glasswork of greenhouses. As far as the Siegfried Line every town was a pile of ruins. Every tree was felled, every road mined, every well polluted, every waterway dammed, every cellar exploded or made deadly with bombs."

Before leaving the ruins of Péronne, a German soldier with an eye to history inserted a placard above the shattered colonnade, in curled and mocking script, correct to the last umlaut: *Nicht ärgern, nur wundern!* (Be not angry, only admire).

In the Château de Grand Priel, stripped of its lavish furniture, where François Theillier had grown fat on the land, high explosive was placed in the cellars that had furnished German officers with his finest wines. The blast left a crater fifty yards across, filled with crushed brick, fragments of carved stone, shattered marble pillars, and the glass from ninety-nine windows. Jeanne Magniez's mansion was torn apart, as her Pêcherie had already suffered, and in Le Câtelet every house in turn was reduced to rubble. "The only way to tell one building from another was by the pattern of tiles on the floor." The mountainous walls of the great medieval citadel where Robert Digby had been shot stood immune to the devastation, but the wooden cross on his grave was flattened in the blast that destroyed the old church.

By day, the destruction billowed blackly across the land, and its red glow lit up the night. "The Boche is certainly burning something behind his lines," wrote a British officer. "Dense clouds of smoke can be seen any day at various points, and flames at night. Is he burning villages in the rear? If so, he is certainly about to retire."

In Villeret, the handful of men left behind "watched the preparations being made for its destruction: holes for mines in the cellars, and in the wells; the placement of charges everywhere." The simple village church was packed with strings of explosives, along with the *mairie*, and the homes of Lelong, Marié, Boitelle, Foulon, and

Marie Coulette, from whose homestead Hélène's first cries had echoed down a quiet and fearful street, were soon to vanish in thunder. Florency Dessenne had hidden his few remaining pieces of gold in a metal box in the garden, in the vain hope that they might be retrievable after the war, but they, too, disappeared into dust, along with Marie Coulette's cooking pots, Emile Foulon's stuffed fox, and his daughter's rose beds. "When they finally withdrew, Villeret flared up like a torch with repeated explosions that blew up every house and public building. The village was completely levelled, not a wall was left standing."

CHAPTER FOURTEEN

The Wasteland

❦

Villeret was blasted off the map, its rubble further pummelled into a chaos of dugouts and muddy craters overgrown with rank brambles of barbed wire, while British troops inched forward and the Germans fought on with the immense fortifications of the Hindenburg Line, the final defence, at their backs. A new front line tore like a harrow through the heart of the village. The sweet-tasting streams that had once watered the fields around Villeret ran rancid and dead, their last remaining fish poisoned by gas and lead.

A French soldier from Hargicourt obtained a pass to survey what had become of his former home and reported "a land crisscrossed with trenches, strewn with ruins, as flat as a carpet. Nothing remains." The old world had vanished, save for some shards of building and the remnants of François Theillier's once-abundant game, which continued to breed among the wreckage. Villeret was formally taken by the British on April 15, 1917. At the end of that month, one Captain Oates, son of the commanding officer of the Sherwood Foresters, popped up from a trench that ran through what had once been Foulon's field, "sniped an unsuspecting partridge through the head, collected it from No Man's land during cover of darkness and presented it to his father for supper." Villeret was now no more than a military reference point, but the warmakers considered it an important one, and when summer came the British surged forward in a sweaty rush towards the ridge above the village on which stood the ruins of the Cologne farm, an objective "about one mile to the west of the Hindenburg line itself [which], if taken, would allow observation over sections of the line." The attack succeeded, capturing "a few, very significant yards of front," but the killing was dreadful.

The pattern was repeated again and again in the shadow of the Hindenburg Line: a small movement back or forth, a gush of blood. And with each attack and counterattack, the ancient contours and meanings of the rolling fields and familiar landmarks dissolved and re-formed. The dense woods where Robert Digby had sheltered were splintered into scorched stumps and stagnant holes. From the British lines the soldiers could "count the number of rather despondent looking trees" in what had once been "Les Peupliers de la Haute-Bruyère," and the German-held copse took on a fantastical and menacing aura. The men said the few poplars still standing were "made of tempered steel and capable of hiding a battalion of evil-intentioned snipers." In festive mood, on December 25, 1917, a German wit in the opposing trench raised a sign reading "Merry Christmas": "A Lewis gun was immediately turned on the sign and shot it down." The woods, the quarry, the mill, the ruined outlying farms and hills were now coordinates on trench maps with new military names: "Ruby Wood," "The Egg," "Sheep Post," "Frog Post." The sweeping vista from Theillier's château contained "Priel Crater"; the lanes where Claire and Digby had courted were "Zulu Boulevard" and "Maxim Road." A large dugout in the middle of the beet fields was considered luxurious and christened "The Leicester Lounge," where behind-the-lines entertainment was provided by a battalion band boasting "Riflemen Breedon, Fawcett and Pollock, late of the Drury Lane Theatre, the Scottish Symphony Orchestra and the Trocadero Hotel." In the ferocious dialogue of the guns, the smell of mortality grew overpowering, and corpses piled up where the lovers had harvested beets together, until more people died around Villeret in a few vicious months than had ever lived there.

In January 1918, Sergeant Edouard Séverin—the mayor of Villeret, currently serving in the French army—crept forward with the former mayor of Hargicourt to inspect what was left of their villages in the *région dévastée*. "The brutes, the depraved brutes! In this vision of destruction, there is not a wall left high enough to shelter a dog. The village is a spectacle of death. Ruins! Ruins! Ruins! They have wrecked everything, the stables, the farms, the church, and even the arbours in the gardens. Villeret is a place of desolation. We could see only the smashed houses, land ripped up by the trenches and bomb craters." The pair pushed on through Villeret, where iron bedsteads twisted by the heat poked up through the debris, and down a shredded incline towards Hargival, the hill where Digby and Sligo had once tried to outrun the Uhlans. "The Boche guns could be heard, bombarding the batteries at Hargicourt. The rain of iron became heavier around us. *'Dangerouss!'* the Tommies cried as we passed. And we left, thinking it would be foolish to take additional risks with that storm breaking overhead."

On March 21, a "breathless cook" ran through the Villeret trenches, screaming that the Germans had attacked in force: "German grenades were bouncing down dugout steps before [the British] knew the battle had begun." From behind the pile of brick that had been the *mairie*, the machine-gunners of the Manchester Regiment fired until it grew dark, and then escaped before the village was overrun once more. Having discreetly shifted forces from the Eastern to the Western Front, the Germans selected the pulverised Somme for their counterattack, advancing with stunning power along forty miles of front. In six days, the British suffered three hundred thousand casualties. But the German advance was stopped, and then, in August, rolled back by the Allied counterattack. Slowly and bloodily, the German army began to fall apart.

Hargicourt and Villeret were not finally "cleared" until the end of September. That month, the New Yorker "doughboys" of the 107th Infantry Regiment battled furiously over Gillemont Farm and the Magniez pastures, with the Germans resisting every step: "Few surrendered. In the ruins, in hedges and in every copse were concealed Boche machine guns, and as the men charged up the slope they received this murderous fire full in their faces. It was rifles, bayonets and bombs against machine guns," wrote G. F. Jacobson of the 107th. The British reached the mighty Hindenburg Line on September 26. At Bellenglise, where the line had seemed strongest, British infantry crossed the canal under a thick fog and crashed through the unbreakable line. "The enemy's defence in the last and strongest of his prepared positions had been shattered," reported British Commander-in-Chief Douglas Haig. So many had been killed that this was now, in large measure, an army of children: as the end of war dawned, more than half of the British infantrymen were under the age of nineteen.

Some of the troops around Villeret had broken at the same moment as the Hindenburg Line. On September 21, the Australian troops crouched on the Hargicourt road were ordered to move up to the front line for another assault. One hundred and nineteen of them, "desperately under strength and in need of rest," convinced that the colonial troops were being forced into the slaughter while British units were held in reserve, had refused to budge. All except one were found guilty of desertion; the war ended before they could be punished.

Suzanne Boitelle was in the Revin refugee camp in the Ardennes, with the other Villeret exiles, when the weary peace finally arrived. She had been released and reunited with little Guy in February 1918. The villagers were delighted to see her, and Emile Marié, who had continued as acting mayor while his son Parfait still languished in a German work camp, was particularly solicitous. After her months of deprivation, Suzanne was earnestly grateful: "He was most welcoming. He gave me everything I needed." Exile had been brutal, and some had not survived the ordeal. The people sensed peace before it was announced. "A few days before the Armistice, the French cavalry appeared a few miles off, the cannon sounded all night, and the Germans fled," Suzanne Boitelle would recall. The next morning, the people of Villeret saw their first French troops in more than four years.

But the war raged around their homes until the end. In Le

Câtelet on September 29, Thomas O'Shea, a New Yorker and a Corporal in the U.S. Infantry, became separated from his platoon "well within enemy lines" and found himself hiding in a shell hole, alongside the ruined medieval castle, with two other American soldiers. The medal roll recorded that, "upon hearing a call for help from an American tank, which had been disabled 30 yards from them, the three soldiers left shelter and started towards the tank, under heavy fire from German machine guns and trench mortars." They rescued three injured soldiers from the tank and then, "in the face of violent fire, dismounted a Hotchkiss gun, and took it back to where the wounded men were, keeping off the enemy all day by effective use of the gun and later bringing it, with the wounded men, back to our lines under cover of darkness." O'Shea died of his wounds on a stretcher, not far from where Robert Digby lay in Le Câtelet graveyard.

On October 9, a "thin, grey-haired man in ragged civilian clothes" suddenly detached himself from a pair of South African infantrymen who were escorting him down the Roman road about ten miles from Villeret, and ran towards a passing horseman. Dancing up and down in front of Major Francis Drake of the 11th Hussars, who had happened to be passing, the wizened little man kept shouting: "That's my troop officer." After four years of concealment, most of it in an oak cupboard the size of a coffin, Patrick Fowler had finally been liberated, only to be arrested by his own side. Half an hour earlier, a wild apparition, "gesticulating wildly" and telling an unbelievable tale of survival, had rushed towards the South African troops entering Bertry. "They had immediately placed him under arrest as a spy, and were marching him back under escort." Drake was "one of the very few men left in France who could have recognised him," and had it not been for their chance encounter on the Roman road, Fowler might have shared the same fate as Digby. The hussars were stationed just a few miles away, and the regiment's commanding officer immediately rode over to Bertry to thank Fowler's saviours; he found Louis Basquin dying of consumption. "Monsieur, you have nothing to thank me for, I was too ill to fight for my country and wished to do my duty. I could do no less." Fowler was reunited with his regiment, but declined to take the leave he was offered. "He was too weak for active work, and saw the war to an end in the officers' mess." Even though the fight was nearly over, he refused to go home. This may have been a reflection of innate heroism, or perhaps the mark of a man who had spent far too long cooped up in a cupboard.

The German grip had to be prized from the land, like a dead man clinging to his gun. At Le Cateau, where Digby's war had started and officially ended, one German machine-gun company battled on until the eleventh hour. At 11:00 a.m. on November 11, the crew fired a final thousand-round burst, "before standing up and taking off their forage caps to the English, and walking away without looking back." Karl Evers beat a hastier retreat. Having helped to burn the files held in Antwerp, he joined the other staff officers in a swift rush back to Germany. By the end of November, Major Evers, onetime Etappen-Kommandant 8/X of the 2nd Etappen-Inspektion, the former king of Le Câtelet, was back in his hometown of Celle, and out of uniform.

The day before the Armistice, Henri Godé, the mayor of Le Câtelet, spotted an advance guard of British troops, the 12th Battalion of the London Regiment, entering the little town of Neuf-maison, where he had been exiled along with the rest of the town's population. Godé accosted the commanding officer, Major Ashmead-Bartlett, and handed over to him the letters written by Digby, Thorpe, Martin, and Donohoe on the eve of their deaths, which he had "kept hidden for a year and a half." Ashmead-Bartlett was deeply moved by the simplicity of these "voices rising from the grave to accuse the Germans."

Suzanne Boitelle knew it was over when the French troops were shot at by Germans retreating into the woods and did not fire back, since they "had not received orders to open fire." The heroine of Villeret was standing near a group of French gunners at eleven o'clock. "They cried out that the Armistice was signed, and everyone went mad, everyone was happy. The soldiers danced around their guns, shouting and singing."

It had taken just two days to get from Villeret to the refugee station, but it took months to get back across the devastated land, poisoned by the excreta of battle. In the words of one resident: "The valley had become the valley of Jehoshaphat, covered by a mantle of war consisting of abandoned arms and ammunition, guns, machine-gun belts, countless shells, grenades, cannons, tanks, tank bridges, bayonets, helmets by the thousand, pitfalls, spades, pickaxes, tin cans, knapsacks, greatcoats, and all sorts of other debris crushed into soil itself, to say nothing of the corpses emerging from the ground and rotting horses." The wealthy and the official were the first to come home, to find "not only no more houses, but no trees lining the roads, no woods, no agriculture. It was as if the entire countryside had been flattened."

Some believed a place so utterly devastated should not be repaired, but merely abandoned as a permanent monument to the horror. Mademoiselle Fournier d'Alincourt gazed on the wreckage of her château, where Robert Digby had been sentenced to death, and despaired: "My heart is torn apart by the sight of my poor destroyed home . . . I will never see it as it was before." Jeanne Magniez, reunited with Georges, returned to find her home similarly ruined. The mansion was a pile of bricks, the courtyard a mess of shell holes and barbed wire. With typical vim, she set about rebuilding Hargival: the house would be smaller, but the stables larger, and the ruined Pêcherie would be preserved in its state of devastation as a *memento mori*. François Theillier never rebuilt the Château de Grand Priel, and he could never bring himself to hunt again on the ground where so much human blood had been spilled.

Much of the original population did not come back to this wilderness, this strip of Armageddon thirty miles wide where more than a thousand different townships and half a million homes had been consumed. By mid-January 1919, the local newspaper reported that the canton of Le Câtelet was undergoing "a repopulation," with a grand total of three of its prewar inhabitants back in their homes. "The land was no longer their land," observed a local writer. "They no longer recognised the changed faces of their villages, denuded of old trees, ancient churches, venerable châteaux, and farms, which gave them their particular character." When once-plump Marie-Thérèse Dessenne was finally released from German prison, she weighed a pitiful eighty-four pounds. Neither she nor Florency set foot in Villeret, but settled instead in Saint-Quentin, where Florency immediately took up smuggling tobacco again.

Léon and Elise Lelong, the baker and his wife, accompanied by Lucien and Clothilde, came back and inspected the remains of what had been their home, but departed almost immediately, never to return. Elise Lelong told her family that they had been "ruined by the war, and by their involvement in the episode with the English soldiers, which had cost them dear." Marie Coulette, predictably, stood her ground. With her daughter Eugénie, her granddaughter Claire, and her great-granddaughter Hélène, the head of the Dessenne family set to work rebuilding their home, with whatever could be scraped together in the way of government compensation. As the reconstruction got under way, they lived in temporary corrugated iron shelters, flimsy shacks, or underground, in the few cellars that had not been mined. Gangs of Chinese labourers were brought in to clear away the barbed wire, rubble, and live explosive. Exile and exposure to Englishmen, Irishmen, Germans, and Russians had done little to broaden the cultural horizons of some in Villeret, who saw the Chinese as "yellow devils . . . with their slit eyes, their sordid and multicoloured accoutrements, their savage expressions, their gesticulations, their confinement like wild animals behind wire, and the total impossibility of understanding a word they said." When Chinese labourers were spotted clearing out what remained of the Cologne farm, "one inhabitant of Villeret opened fire at these exotic rogues."

The rebuilders of Villeret finally erected a large and ugly *mairie*, and a church that was even larger and uglier, in the middle of the village. It was assumed, officially and wrongly, that Villeret would eventually return to its former size, but barely half of its inhabitants came back. Some, like the Lelongs, stayed away out of choice, while others were listed on the Monument aux Morts in front of the new church: four Lelongs, three Mariés, two Boitelles. Of the sixty Villeret men mobilised in those first heady days of war, thirty-three died in battle; only two of those were identified and buried in the village cemetery. Some who had survived the war did not long survive the peace: Victor Marié, the slippery former spy returned to

Villeret in 1919 with his DCM, and died just three years later, at the age of forty-three. The cause of death was rumoured to be poison.

In 1920, Villeret was awarded the Croix de Guerre. "This small village suffered greatly," wrote Mayor Henri Lelong. "Even the last sleep of its dead was not respected, for many of the tombs in its cemetery were destroyed by explosives, the bones inside scattered to the wind. But its children did their duty valiantly, as was demonstrated in the business with the British soldiers and the spying affair, as well by those who left in 1914 and fell on the field of honour."

Paul Boitelle had left Villeret to fight in 1914, leaving a jolly young wife with two healthy sons. He returned to find his home destroyed, just one surviving son, Guy, and Suzanne prematurely aged from imprisonment and semi-starvation. But the Boitelles considered themselves lucky, and Suzanne struggled on: "We women collected all the bricks we could find, and with these we put up temporary shelters. We received war compensation, but it couldn't replace everything we had lost." She bore little resentment towards the Germans, considering them a different race from the Nazi fanatics who would follow. "The soldiers of 1914 were more humane than those of 1940. They were older, understood more, and they were kind to the children, giving them sweets."

For some, little seemed to have changed. Achille Poëtte returned, even thinner than before from his forced toil in Germany. The postman got a new bicycle, and once again his familiar, gaunt shape could be seen toiling up the slope between Hargicourt and Villeret. Parfait Marié restarted his charcoal business, but in spite of himself he hankered for the duties of municipal office. Parfait ran for the position of municipal councillor, and won. In 1923, he travelled to Bohain, to appear before the War Damages Commission, and returned with 69,337 francs and 30 centimes in reparations for the village. His father, old Emile Marié, who had coaxed Digby out of the woods to his death, started to rebuild his house in Villeret, but then abandoned the task, moved to Hargicourt, and became a stranger to the town of his birth.

Richard Sauvage found his wife, Marie, with a two-year-old daughter that everyone said was the child of a German soldier.

Without a word, he left and never came back. Marie remarried, and her new husband recognised the German's child as his own. Claire's father, Hélène's grandfather, Jules Dessenne, also survived the war; "Le Boeuf" was no longer the merry, bovine glutton, but a tired hulk, eyes permanently weepy from gas, who declined to discuss his war or anyone else's. Jules was more philosophical about Hélène's arrival than his wife, Eugénie, had ever been: "I am happy, for I would rather find one more person in the house than one less," he said. Hélène made her first communion in a makeshift church, erected in the middle of the cemetery.

Claire Dessenne seldom talked about Robert Digby, except to her growing daughter. She kept his letters and a grainy photograph, as well as the phrase-book British soldiers had been issued to help them communicate with the natives of France. On weekends, when she had time off from the cloth factory, Claire walked to Le Câtelet and laid flowers on his grave in the corner of the cemetery. His Britannic Majesty's Government, having heard of "the valued service which she had rendered in the course of the Great War," expressed its "deep sense of gratitude for the self-sacrificing efforts" she had made in the form of a bronze medal and a long letter Claire could not understand and never translated. The medal went in a drawer, and was then lost.

Claire did, however, send on to an address in Hampshire the letter Robert Digby had written to his mother, asking that she support his French lover and child. Ellen Digby never replied.

Gradually, the gored and butchered countryside healed over; the trenches were filled and ploughed back into the fields, although the new landscape was emptier and bleaker, shorn of trees and landmarks, a familiar face indelibly marked by shell-shock. The Chinese labour gangs had toiled mightily, but the ground was still riddled with grenades, poison-gas canisters, and shells, and some made a living out of collecting the metal scraps of war. Some years later, Robert Dessenne, the son Marie-Thérèse had named after Digby, was ploughing in the fields when he struck an unexploded shell, and was blown to pieces.

There is a song which the villagers of Villeret sang in 1917 as they were driven into exile and their houses were dynamited. Over the months and years, the words were altered and more verses were added, and the song was passed on from the refugees of Villeret to other exiles from the north. These, in turn, brought it back to their own towns and villages after the war, and it slowly settled into the landscape of collective history until, like the craters in the fields, it seemed always to have been there. The tune was jaunty, and the young men sang it when, a generation later, they marched off to the fresh slaughter of another war, twisted offspring of the first. Some called the song "Le Bébé Rose" (The Pink Baby), but others knew it as "Four Young Englishmen." The old people of the Somme and the Aisne still sing it:

> In the village of Villeret
> There once were four young Englishmen
> Who from the beginning of the war
> Were so well hidden
> That one of them, he fell in love
> With a young and beautiful maid of France
> And from their union was born
> A pretty little baby.
> Oh, what a lovely picture for France and England
> For two allies to be so united in love
> But, sadly, this was wartime
> And the picture could not last.
> A woman who loved a square-headed Hun,
> A thing which freezes the blood with horror and loathing,
> Decided she now wanted for herself
> The handsome young Englishman with the baby.
> But he immediately pushed her away,
> And that is why this German-lover,
> So jealous and so wicked,
> Decided to alert the enemy
> To the hiding place of the Englishmen . . .

The war erased everything in Villeret except memory, for the song continues:

The Germans dragged our allies
Into the village of Le Câtelet
To bring them to judgement.
This the Germans swiftly did
And decided they must die.
The *Kommandant* called for volunteers
To execute these innocent men.
He asked for only 14 killers
But 20 Germans stepped forward.
The Englishmen were made to dig their graves
And our suffering comrades cried out "Vive la France,
Up with the king and our beloved land,
And down with the cursed Hun"

Dessenne, Lelong, Poëtte, Marié, Dubuis, Boitelle are still the
people of Villeret, and they have not forgotten.

CHAPTER FIFTEEN

Villeret, 1930

❦

Hélène Dessenne, the Englishman's daughter with the cornflower-blue eyes, was helping to bring in the beet harvest when a car drew up at the edge of the field on the east side of Villeret. Motor vehicles were still a rare enough sight in the region for the workers to stop and stare. The first person to emerge from the car was its driver, Henri Godé, still mayor of Le Câtelet, his long whiskers greying, spectacles perched on his nose, leaning on a cane. Godé had aged more than the dozen years since he had handed over his hidden letters to the English officer, but he made an incongruous and impressive figure standing in the roadside dust, wearing his best cravat and an air of importance. Behind the mayor emerged a tall stranger wearing a hat. The man was in his forties, with a kind, lined face. He carried a rolled umbrella, although the summer sky was cloudless.

The mayor spoke to Léon Recolet, supervisor of the harvest, who pointed towards the young girl standing alone in the field. The mayor waved and beckoned. "Suddenly everyone was shouting my name—'Hélène! Hélène!'—and I wondered what could be going on." She dropped her hoe and ran over. "As I came closer, I saw this big man with his arms open wide, who was saying softly, '*Ma petite fille*.' He had tears on his face. I don't know why, but I threw myself into his arms and hugged him." Sitting in the back of the mayor's Renault as they bumped along the track into Villeret, the man in the hat tried to explain, in broken French, who he was and why he had come.

Thomas Digby's had been a grim and gruelling war. After the news of Robert's disappearance, he had never quite given up hope that his brother might be alive. The strain had helped to drive his father mad and then into the grave, while his mother retreated ever further into herself. It was not until after the Armistice that she finally received a letter stating that Robert Digby had been shot by the enemy, with a brief note of thanks and commiseration: "Private 9368, killed in action, France and Flanders, 30th May 1916." Ellen Digby never openly showed her grief for her favourite child, but her bitterness turned her hard, and then sour. Secretly she drank too much, and kept her younger son and daughter, Florence, at a distance. The few who dared to call on the sharp-tongued widow Digby would be made to read the letter passed on by Major Ashmead-Bartlett and his note commending her "brave and noble" son. She never mentioned that her son had fathered a French child.

Thomas, back in civilian clothes and perhaps suffering the guilt of the survivor, mourned his brother deeply, and seemed to find some release in poetry. Thomas had never had his brother's flair and dash, and his poetry had the thumping rhythm of the hymnal. Yet the strained rhymes and high diction somehow make Thomas's doggerel more moving than polished verses. He spent months working on his poem for Robert, and he was proud of it. The shy and admiring younger brother had it printed on black-bordered cards and sent to everyone he could think of. He meant every painfully wrought word.

IN MEMORY OF
ROBERT DIGBY
Aged 31 who was shot by the Germans, May 30th, 1916

Friend of my youth, whose early joy,
And recollections as a boy,

Spread o'er my memory sweet.
The bliss which winged those rosy hours,
Among the leafy sunny bowers,
Is ne'er our lot to meet.

Yet we did yield those happy days
From truth's secure, unerring ways
To flow in different channels.
A soldier's life your footsteps trod,
To roam the Empire's foreign sod,
And shine in honour's annals.

Your country called, you went to war,
To fight a foe we all abhor,
Repine not at thy lot.
I prayed for you each darkest hour
To God, who gives us strength and power,
Your danger ne'er forgot.

Alas! I never heard from thee
Each year, a seeming age to me,
And yet I still had hope.
But now I know that you are dead,
Your farewell letter I have read,
And each brave word you spoke.

O brother! in thy pangs of death,
What sighs re-echoed to thy breath,
Before your spirit fled.
Could tears have stayed the tyrant's course,
Could tears avert his brutal force,
Those tears I would have shed.

Well! thou art happy, and I feel,
For still my heart regards your weal,
I must be happy too.

Before I share the gloomy cell,
Whose ever-slumbering inmates dwell
My duty I must do.

Why weep? Your matchless spirit soars,
Among the weeping angels bowers
Beyond the starry skies.
The all of thine that cannot die
Will live through all eternity,
Before God's throne thou lies.

Farewell! brave brother; all is past,
The bugle blows thy Post "The Last,"
Each volley rents the air.
The Gates of Heaven are open wide
For those like thee, who bravely died,
Go! rest forever there.

After the war, Thomas had gone into "gentleman's service," working as a valet for a wealthy family in the Isle of Wight. Thomas made a good manservant, discreet and careful. In 1923, he returned to the north to marry a Northwich woman, Florence Leyland, his first cousin, the daughter of Ellen Digby's brother. It proved a childless marriage, but perfectly happy, for Florence shared her husband's gentle approach to life.

Ellen Digby died in Southampton in 1929, and it was not until he was sorting through her effects that Thomas came across another, very different letter from the one referred to in his poem: written by a man preparing for death, it asked that his lover and daughter be formally recognised and cared for by his family. Ellen Digby had never shown the letter to anyone and had hidden it, for shame. But she had not been able to destroy it. Thomas Digby was astonished, then angry, and finally resolute.

Defying his mother for probably the first time in his life, he bought a second-class ticket for the steamer to France. On arrival in Le Câtelet, he asked a group of boys to show him where the Englishmen had been shot. Georges Mercier, the child witness now grown into a burly teenager, led him to the exact spot and stuck his fingers into the bullet holes in the chalky ramparts of the castle. Thomas Digby took a photograph of Georges standing there, and then gave him a silver franc.

Henri Godé immediately put himself and his car at the disposal of this soft-speaking, well-dressed foreigner with the courteous manners. After Hélène, they collected two more generations of Dessenne women from the fields around Villeret. The teenager babbled away excitedly in the back seat, but Claire Dessenne was too shocked at the sudden apparition of her dead lover's brother to speak a word. Her mother, Eugénie, set her lips to their habitual pursed arrangement, uncertain whether to approve. The strange little party drove to the Villeret mayor's office, where a document remains, handwritten in studied municipal copperplate, stating: "Thomas Digby, born in Bengal, resident of number 2, Randolph Mews, Maida Vale, W9, hereby formally recognises as his own daughter, a child born in Villeret on the 14th November nineteen hundred and fifteen and known by the name of Hélène Claire Dessenne." Hélène was no longer an *enfant naturelle*. On her birth certificate, the name "Dessenne" was struck out, and "Digby" was written in its place.

Villeret, 1999

❦

To save your world you asked this man to die:
Would this man, could he see you now, ask why?
— W. H. Auden, "Epitaph for an Unknown Soldier"

Like the battlefield enthusiasts who still come to sift through fields and ditches in search of wartime relics, I scoured the history around Villeret, gathering the fragments of Robert Digby's story. So many hours were spent in dark, overheated kitchens with the descendants of Lelongs, Mariés, and Dessennes that the generations merged, as I searched for traces of an ancient love story among the farms and villages of Picardy.

In common with most British families, mine has its own First World War memories, and casualties. One great-uncle, Donald Macintyre of the Black Watch, lies—I discovered with a jolt—in the Vadancourt military cemetery, not five miles from Villeret. My mother's uncle, Tim Massy-Beresford, returned from the Western Front full of holes and stories. Uncle Tim was a nineteen-year-old machine-gunner in the trenches at Saint-Eloi in 1915 when a sniper shot him through the chest. As Tim collapsed, with a pierced lung, the officer kneeling behind him dropped dead. "The bullet, having passed through me with bad enough results, had continued straight into his head, killing him instantly," my great-uncle wrote. Tim had recovered from his wound sufficiently to rejoin his unit at the front in 1918, and that September he led an attack down a slope towards the German lines near Cambrai, about fourteen miles north of Le

Câtelet. He was shot first through the right thigh, then in the left leg, and finally across the ribs under his heart. His matter-of-fact tone is reminiscent of Robert Digby: "As I wasn't dead, the only thing to do was to crawl back up the hill."

Uncle Tim's life had been saved by a small, inch-thick pocket diary which he had tucked into a breast pocket. The diary was on permanent display in a glass case in his drawing room: "There is a neat hole in the middle of one side, but as one turns the pages one can see that the thickness slowed up the bullet and gradually deflected it so that it emerged at right angles on the last page." Tim spent twelve months at the front, was wounded four times, received the Military Cross, and, as he ruefully observed many years later, "never actually saw a live German soldier."

That was the sort of Great War I had known about before I came to Villeret: a war of futile gallantry, an inconceivable death toll, and a powerful but diffuse sense of loss. To understand how much had been destroyed, wrote F. Scott Fitzgerald, "you had to have a whole-souled sentimental equipment going back further than you could remember. You had to remember Christmas, and postcards of the Crown Prince and his fiancée, and little cafés in Valence and beer gardens in Unter den Linden and weddings at the mairie and going to the Derby and your grandfather's whiskers."

Like other Britons of my generation, I knew the war remotely, from symbol and song: the annual paper poppies on Armistice Day, the chirpy ditties from the school performance of *Oh, What a Lovely War*, Uncle Tim's diary with the bullet hole, and the architectural emptiness of memorials to the Unknown Soldier.

But in Villeret I had chanced upon a different aspect of this war, more intimate and much more recent. The soldier, for me, was no longer unknown; only his betrayer remained faceless and elusive. Robert Digby was a nonconformist and a romantic. His love affair had imperilled an entire community, but I believe that when his moment of choice arrived, he took the right route. I had come to like him, and to admire him. I felt I owed it to Robert Digby to find the person who had betrayed him and his comrades.

My days and nights were filled with images of Robert, Claire,

Florency, Marie Coulette, and the others of Villeret. As the months went by, I began to see the faces of the long-dead in the living. Perhaps they felt the same way about me: an unlikely Englishman appearing from nowhere, thrusting himself into their homes and lives, eating their food, undermining their defences, asking questions. I showed them photographs of my three children. They laughed and clapped my shoulder and called me "Papa." Some spoke with warmth and intimacy of characters they had never met, of a time known only through the stories of grandparents but permanently inscribed in the collective memory. They talked of the executions as if through personal recollection, of the love affair between Claire and Digby in the present tense, and his death as if it had taken place last week. But there was an invisible barricade, a point where my inquiries were always stopped and turned back. When I asked who had betrayed Robert Digby, eyes were swiftly averted, shoulders shrugged, the subject was discreetly changed, refreshment offered. Suddenly memories would cloud and clutter, and they would break into impenetrable patois among themselves. At first I took this to be a natural aversion to a delicate subject, but over the weeks and months I convinced myself that they knew the answer (or believed they did) but would not (or dared not) reveal it.

Their forebears, those who left some permanent record behind of the Guerre Quatorze, were scarcely more forthcoming, but they all agreed on one aspect of the drama: Digby had been sent to his death by a woman. Writing his account in 1920, Léon Legé, the Le Câtelet notary, declined to name names, but recorded that the British soldiers had been "discovered as the result of some feminine indiscretions," something closer to accident than design. Joseph Cabaret, the schoolmaster, placed the blame with discreet vagueness on the neighbouring village. "The poor soldiers were betrayed by a woman from Hargicourt," he stated flatly, and without elaboration. Alice Delabranche, the daughter of the pharmacist, carefully copied out her entire diary after the war "to avoid any indiscretions," removing the "names of certain people who acted more or less delicately with the Germans." She then destroyed the incriminating original version. The words of "Le Bébé Rose" pointed to a woman "who loved a square-headed Hun" and then set her sights on Robert Digby.

Georges Mercier, the little boy who hid in the bushes to watch the executions, is eighty-eight now, and as angry today as he was then. His voice quavering, but not from age, he recalls the scene. "I wanted to cry out "Bastards!," something like that went through my head, but my cousin Eugène stopped me. He was fifteen, and supposed to be looking after me. If the Germans had seen us, they would have shot us, the sons of bitches. One man was too tall for the coffin, and I saw that whoreson commander of the firing squad break the legs with his boot heel. That chilled my bones."

"Who betrayed them to the Germans?" I ask.

"It was a woman, a neighbour, that's what I heard," he says, rolling the thought around his mouth like a bad taste.

In Saint-Quentin I found tiny Henriette Legé, the notary's daughter who, more than eight decades before, aged ten, had watched the tumbril rolling past her occupied house, and heard the tramp of Digby's passing boots. "I had the misfortune to live in that epoch," she says, remembering how her safe middle-class world had been destroyed. "My childhood was devastated."

A million and a half Frenchmen perished, leaving six hundred thousand widows. After the war, there were not enough men to go around. Henriette was one of half a million young women who never found a husband.

"They said it was a jealous woman. The Englishmen were getting around the village, and a jealous woman betrayed them," she observes, without condemnation.

Suzanne Boitelle died in 1988, but a few years earlier her grandson recorded her memories of the First World War. I listened to them with her youngest son—born just one year after the war and named, intriguingly, Robert—a story of blunt heroism, told in simple staccato sentences, laced with patois: "In 1914 I lived in Villeret. I was arrested because I had sheltered a British soldier in my home. I was twenty-one years old. My husband was away at the war. I was taken before the German war court, and sentenced to a year in prison and a fine of one thousand marks. Since I wouldn't pay the fine, I got five additional months in prison."

Only once did her voice rise in anger, but she remained guarded: "We were betrayed by someone in the village."

Robert Boitelle stared at his mother's medals and citations, British and French, commending her "courage and dignity," and answered the question before it had been asked. "I don't know who did it, but they say it was a jealous woman."

The Villeret Municipal Archives produced no evidence that anyone had ever tried to bring charges against the nameless traitor, but Florency's wife, Marie-Thérèse Dessenne, had her own suspicions, and exacted vengeance of a sort. After the war, Marie-Thérèse became exceptionally pious, performing novenas—nine successive days of prayer—in the hope of having her supplications answered. It was in the midst of one such novena, at the rebuilt cathedral in Saint-Quentin, that she spotted "the betrayer" in a nearby pew. "A woman was also praying, asking forgiveness for her sins. Marie-Thérèse hid next to her, concealed behind one of the cathedral columns. Then, in a loud voice, she shouted: 'Your sins can never be forgiven, you have blood on your hands!' The woman fled in panic. She must have believed it was the voice of God speaking to her."

Some years later, Marie-Thérèse was shopping with her grandson Edgar in Saint-Quentin when she spotted the woman. "Look, that's the one who sent us to prison," she said. The woman started when she recognised Marie-Thérèse, and scuttled away. Edgar recalled the woman's face, "younger than my grandmother," and her "expression of shock." But not her name.

Frustrated, I walked up the hill outside Villeret to the copse where François Theillier's great castle once dominated the skyline. The trees have grown through the remains of smashed brickwork and shards of glass from the château's exactly ninety-nine windows. Stone steps, overgrown by creepers, led down to a deep crater, once a splendid wine cellar, where German explosives had been packed among the wine racks.

At the end of a sunken avenue, no longer lined with lindens, lay a shallow concrete watering trough, made in Paris, an echo of Theillier's hunting passion—placed close enough to the castle for the owner to get a clear shot when a luckless deer stopped to drink. Nearby stood a row of empty and rotting concrete rabbit hutches, the *clapiers* from which a young French cavalry officer snatched a rabbit and shared its remains with three bewildered foreign soldiers named Thorpe, Donohoe, and Martin on an August day in 1914. I pushed through tangled undergrowth and over a pink granite column lying in exact broken segments like disjointed vertebrae, to the point where Theillier's great dining room would have been. Something crunched wetly underfoot: snails; dozens of fat, slowly twitching *escargots de Bourgogne,* bred for a rich man's table, liberated by war, and now multiplying undisturbed amid the ruins.

In Germany I found satisfaction of a sort. After the war, according to the official French account, a judicial investigation was launched into whether Major Karl Evers should be prosecuted for the deaths of the four English soldiers. Evers was still on the staff of the imperial government in Antwerp when the Armistice was declared. He had inconspicuously returned to Celle, to resume his career as a magistrate, with a clutch of medals in recognition of his wartime service—the Iron Cross (second class), the Friedrich August Cross of Oldenburg, and the Order of the Red Eagle. But Evers was never quite the same; he drank heavily, and the bizarre behaviour noted by the people of Le Câtelet became ever more pronounced in peacetime. In 1920, Evers spent an extended period in the sanatorium at Bad Nauheim, suffering from an unidentified "nervous disorder." Soon afterwards, Evers, now the senior judge of Celle, was prosecuted for refusing to leave a pub at closing time. By January 1926, he was residing permanently in Karlsbad Sanatorium under the care of neurologist Dr. Hans Willige. A month later, Evers retired, and by the end of the year, he was dead. She could not have known it, but Marie Coulette, the elderly matriarch of the Dessenne family who had defied Evers for so long, outlived her enemy by a full week.

Of an official investigation into Evers, which might have unlocked the secret of the betrayal, there was barely a trace. In April

1919, the Prussian Ministry of Justice apparently handed over Evers's personal file, following a request by the German Foreign Office, but many of the German First World War records were destroyed by Allied bombing in the second war, and no record of any investigation can be found in either the French or the British archives. There was little appetite for prosecuting German war criminals after 1918. "The inquiry came to nothing," the official historian of the region concluded in 1933, "because Evers was not part of the war council in Le Câtelet and the penalty had been confirmed by the war council in Saint-Quentin." The death sentences had been imposed by a German military court, even if Evers was personally responsible for bringing espionage charges against the four. "We can conclude that Evers, deceived for so long and determined to have his revenge, had made his accusations as damning as possible," the official record states. It was somehow comforting to know that the petty tyrant had ended his days mad and drunk.

The war also left an indelible mark on Patrick Fowler, the soldier who had spent that war inside Marie Belmont-Gobert's armoire. After returning to England, Fowler got a job as a valet and lived on to the age of eighty-eight, reticent about his experiences, and, perhaps aptly after four years spent facing the inside of a cupboard door, slightly unhinged. The Belmont-Goberts, however, fell on hard times. But their plight was discovered by the British popular press and their heroism recounted in the papers. Madame Belmont-Gobert was awarded the OBE, the hussars presented her with an engraved silver plate, the War Office stretched a point and decreed that she was entitled to twopence a day as Fowler's mess allowance, which came to more than two thousand francs, and the *Daily Telegraph* set up a fund to help them out. Finally, she and her daughter were ferried across the Channel to London, "where a magnificent reception was accorded them by the King and Queen, the Lord Mayor and the British public generally, proving to the whole French nation that England knows how to recognise and honour heroism and self-sacrifice." Even the cupboard was venerated. Purchased by a grateful nation, it was placed on exhibition in the Imperial War Museum and then finally transferred to the King's Royal

Hussars Museum in Winchester, where it remains, a thing of inde-
structible peasant simplicity and sturdiness.

The Villeret story was more complicated.

I was starting to give up hope of ever knowing who betrayed
the British soldiers, when the first direct accusation was made. One
Saturday afternoon, I was finishing a bottle of wine after lunch
with Jean-Marc Dubuis, bus-driver of Villeret, whose grandfathers,
Arthur Tordeux and Désiré Dubuis, were the pair of poachers who
had first found the Englishmen in the Trocmé wood. I had stayed
with the Dubuis family half a dozen times already, asking questions
with no apparent effect. Every time I managed to turn the conversation towards the betrayal, Jean-Marc, a cautious and reticent man,
would deftly steer it away again. "One shouldn't talk about it," he
would say. Or "It was a long time ago . . . These things are painful;
the family is still in the village." When I asked him whether he was
referring to Hélène or to the family of the betrayer, he clammed up
completely.

But as he poured himself another glass of wine, Jean-Marc
Dubuis broke off in the middle of a long and complicated com-
plaint about the bus company, and the air in his kitchen held, for a
moment, quite still. "Another woman was in love with Digby," he
said slowly. "He would have nothing to do with her, because he was
in love with Claire, and his baby. This woman did not mean it to go
as far as it did. She did not think they would all be killed."

I glanced at Jean-Marc's wife, Evelyne, who was staring at her
husband, with her mouth open and eyes wide. But Jean-Marc
rolled on.

"She thought they would be arrested and imprisoned. She never
expected them to be shot. But the village made her pay anyway. She
left Villeret, and never came back."

A long, long pause.

"Her name was Lelong, I think it was *Charlotte*. Charlotte Lelong."

At last, a name. A member of the Lelong clan, rivals of the
Dessennes, the baker's family that had quit Villeret after the war,
never to return.

As I was leaving the Dubuis home, Evelyne Dubuis plucked at

my jacket and drew me aside. Hitherto notably unforthcoming on the subject, she whispered, "That may be wrong. I heard the name of the treacherous woman was Antoinette Foulon. She was also in love with Digby. She told Claire Dessenne, 'If I can't have him, then you can't have him either!' " Evelyne paused, suddenly doubtful, too much said. "But then, the person who told me that may have been trying to shift the blame . . ." She closed the door.

Antoinette Foulon, the pretty Villeret schoolmistress who had cooked meals for the fugitives in the earliest days of their concealment, appears on the official Almanac for Villeret in 1913. But in the first census after the war she is gone, replaced by a new teacher. Had Antoinette Foulon betrayed a man who would not be her lover? Or was the *traîtresse* the mysterious Lelong girl?

Jean Dessenne, the mayor of Villeret for twenty-seven years, is the last member of the clan still living in the village. Jean's father, Emile, had acted as lookout while his cousin Claire and Robert Digby were in the hayloft, and his home, another postwar construction, is just a stone's throw away from the site of Marie Coulette's house. Jean Dessenne and I spent hours together in the archives and talking with his neighbours. Yet it took weeks of prompting before Jean, too, vouchsafed a name. "My father knew who had denounced them, but he never said exactly who it was. He did say one thing, however, which was that it was someone within the family. In my opinion he was talking about Léon, Marie Coulette's brother. He had a big mouth, that one, he just didn't know how to shut up, and he was really stupid."

Could it be big, lumbering Léon Recolet who had inadvertently betrayed the men's existence and whereabouts? But if the culprit had indeed been a member of the Dessenne family, there was a more plausible candidate to hand.

Eugénie Dessenne, Claire's mother and Hélène's grandmother, had wanted Digby out of their lives from the moment he first appeared at the back door of Florency's house. She had tried her best to prevent her daughter's affair with the Englishman, and made no secret of her disapproval when the child was born. With the threat of reprisals looming over the entire village, had Eugénie slipped out one night to speak to the *Orstkommandant* at Cardon's house? Was she unsurprised when Major Evers's squad of *Feldgendarmerie* arrived in Villeret on May 16, 1916, and made straight for Florency's hayloft?

If a deal had been struck, that might explain why the Dessennes, with the exception of Florency and Marie-Thérèse, escaped punishment. It might also explain the tone of Digby's last letter to Eugénie, written from his prison cell, at once solicitous and vaguely threatening, and his observation that she had "not suffered the same fate" as he. Did Digby believe that his child's grandmother had betrayed him? The flashing blue eyes of that child, now eighty-eight years old, cloud over when her grandmother's name is mentioned. "She never talked about it. Never."

Like Major Evers, I was beginning to see traitors everywhere. Even the halo over the heroic Jeanne Magniez was fading.

Jeanne and Georges Magniez rebuilt Hargival after the war, but they left standing off the new courtyard a German *Blockhaus* pitted by bullets as a memorial to what had happened there, and a good place to keep the chickens. The ruins of the Pêcherie became overgrown, and Georges and Jeanne grew old together. There were no children, but many dogs and more horses. A photograph of Flirt, the horse she had killed rather than relinquish him to the German army, remained on Jeanne's bedside table.

Jeanne died in 1964 at the age of eighty-three. As I picked my way through the sheaves of papers, letters, and photographs she had left behind, I was tugged by doubt. Jeanne's relations with the German officer class had been warm. Judge Grumme, the German who had sentenced her former wards to death, came back to visit Madame Magniez at Hargival after the war, and she proudly showed him the remains of the fishing lodge where she had hidden the soldiers for so many months. They laughed about it together. Some three decades after Jeanne first met Wilhelm Richter, the once-young German aristocrat was still writing to her in a vein not usually associated with occupying enemy troops: "*Je vous adore de tout mon coeur*" (I love you with all my heart), wrote Richter in 1948, thanking Jeanne for sending photographs which showed that Hargival had become "a veritable paradise of calm and beauty, re-creating what was there before." A year later he wrote again, after Jeanne had sent yet more photographs of the estate: "I see you in spirit at Hargival in your great château, or riding out, tall in the saddle, on a successor to the Son of Steel. *Je vous adore, comme toujours . . .*"

I was uneasy, too, at the way the condemned men had chosen to bless Jeanne Magniez as they faced the execution squad. Had her friendship with a German officer spilled over into intimacy, and then complicity? Had Jeanne Magniez made the decision that it would be safer for the English soldiers, and for her, if they were taken into captivity?

Philippe Delacourt inherited Hargival estate from Jeanne, his aunt. Together we set off, down a narrow, rutted track, towards the spot where the Pêcherie had once stood; as we walked, Philippe pointed to a dented British soldier's helmet from the Great War hanging on a nail on the wall of the barn, and the finials missing from the top of the gate into the orchard, "shot off by bored German officers." Every year, the Delacourts plough up more rusting unexploded shells. "Sometimes they go off." After a heavy rain, the air smells rusty.

A small cellar with a vaulted brick roof is all that remains of the Pêcherie, where Digby and the other men had hidden in the first days of the war as unsuspecting German officers used the building for target practice. When Philippe dug out the old building, he had found the earth thick with thousands of spent cartridges.

"Who betrayed Robert Digby?" I asked, without exactly meaning to. "Was it a woman?"

Philippe scratched his ear and smiled, and instead of replying, he pointed to the green fields. "Do you see the ripples and indentations in the meadow? That is the pattern left by falling bombs."

Like the villagers of Villeret, the land is permanently marked by a war fought a lifetime ago. Explosive remnants, the ancient secrets that explain its contours, lie buried just beneath the surface.

Thomas Digby died leaving no children apart from the French daughter he had formally adopted. The other Digby sibling, Florence, died a spinster. Hélène Digby was the last of the line.

But Thomas's brother-in-law and cousin, Thomas Leyland, was still living in Northwich, the last survivor from his generation. I found the old man in a tiny, freezing house in the back streets of the town. Drinking brick-red tea and huddled around a single-bar electric fire, we talked of two long-dead brothers, he in the rolling accents of the north.

"Robert was great wi' pigeons. There was nowt he couldn't train a pigeon to do. They said he was the best pigeon-handler ever seen in these parts." Thomas Leyland continued: "The father, he had a breakdown, got violent, and Tommy was let out of the army on account of it. He always said he got a special letter from the king on account of his father being a colonel. It wasn't till after the war we found out what happened to Robert in France. He got in with this French family, see, when they found him in the garden, with his arm all shot up. And in time he fell for the daughter, and they had a baby. Aunt Nell—that's what we called his mother, Ellen—was very wicked over it, they say. Didn't want nowt to do with the girl. She was a hasty-tempered woman, that one."

Thomas Leyland chuckled at the scandal of another era and slurped his tea. I wearily prepared myself to ask the question I had voiced a hundred times in French, certain I would learn nothing new: "Do you know how the Germans found out where Robert Digby was hiding?"

"Oh aye," he answered brightly. "The postman gave him away."

The old man continued, oblivious to my astonishment: "Seems this postman might have fancied the unmarried daughter and he was jealous, on account he didn't want our Robert to have her. So he told the Germans where to look. All the village said it was the postman."

Achille Poëtte, the lanky postman, had certainly carried a torch for Claire. After the war he had always been particularly solicitous of Hélène, calling out to her whenever he passed by the Dessenne household. But Achille had spent eighteen months in a forced-labour camp for his part in the plot to conceal the Englishmen, whereas a traitor would surely have been granted clemency. Achille's son Robert, born four years after the war, was defensive on the subject: "The Englishmen were betrayed by someone. I don't know who. This is always a delicate subject, you understand."

My conversation with Thomas Leyland had opened a whole new avenue of possibility. Breeding carrier pigeons is a beloved hobby in northern England, just as it is in northern France, but Digby was more than merely a gifted amateur when it came to pigeon-handling. He was, in Thomas Leyland's words, "a real pro."

Major Evers had been rightly convinced that messages were being sent across the front by carrier pigeon. Villeret had been at the heart of the French spy network, gathering vital intelligence on German troop movements to be passed on to the British army's GHQ. Could Robert Digby have been acting as a messenger for the Réseau Victor?

There was always something about Robert Digby that seemed too large for his uniform as a shilling-a-day private soldier: his command of languages, his superior level of education, the ease with which he had established links with the local people, and his concealment and survival skills. It seemed highly unlikely that he had intentionally stayed behind the lines—his wound was proof enough that little planning was involved—but it seems just possible, having found himself in that position, he had remained out of choice rather than necessity, becoming a part of the local espionage network. We know the Marié brothers were reporting to British army intelligence, and through them Digby could easily have established contact with the Intelligence Corps at GHQ. His accidental cover, as a French peasant with a girlfriend and a baby in tow, was a good one; and if caught, he could always maintain that, like his comrades, he was just another fugitive soldier. On the other hand, if Digby had been involved in the espionage network, why did he take the risk of staying in Villeret, where there were so many other British fugitives and no safety in numbers? Perhaps the answer is that he had fallen in love.

There was no way to find out for certain whether Digby had been, or had become, a spy behind the lines. Victor Marié died in 1922, his brother, Marius, in 1952, and their mother in 1931—the family tomb in Villeret graveyard pays elaborate tribute to their wartime espionage, exalting "those who sacrifice themselves for their country," and even inflating Victor's medal to a Victoria Cross.

The British remember Victor Marié rather differently, for his former spy-masters were of the firm belief that the person who betrayed the Réseau Victor to the Germans, blowing one of the Allies' most important spy networks, was the man who had created it. "True to character, Victor Marié defected to the German Secret Service, with the result that GHQ's Beverloo system was destroyed." This would explain the ease with which he had "escaped" from the prison at Aix-la-Chapelle. The British believed Victor had turned traitor after he was captured in December 1916, but it seems likely that he had begun working for the Germans many months earlier. Indeed, when Haig pinned a medal to Victor Marié's chest and commended his bravery in July 1916, the turncoat had probably already started to pass information to the other side. No wonder he had seemed anxious.

The discovery of Victor Marié's treachery raised yet another disquieting possibility: if Digby had indeed worked with Victor as part of the Réseau Victor, he may also have been one of the dozens of spies subsequently betrayed by the smuggler and double agent. Most documents relating to the Réseau Victor were burned on the eve of Nazi occupation by French municipal officials, well aware that reprisals were likely against those who had resisted in the first war. Only a handful of references have survived in the French intelligence archives, none alluding to a British agent on the ground in 1914–16. The British intelligence files, if such exist, remain under seal.

In 1933, the Scottish writer John Buchan wrote a First World War novel entitled *A Prince of the Captivity*. My father had read it to me when I was a child, and I now read it again with eerie recognition.

During World War I, Buchan had served as a second lieutenant with the Intelligence Corps, attached to the British GHQ in France, with responsibility for censorship, publicity, and propaganda. He may not have been directly involved in spying, although he liked to hint that he had "performed fantastic duties which a romancer would have rejected as beyond probability," but he was privy to some of the most secret workings of the British military machine.

The novel tells of a British army officer, Adam Melfort, who is disgraced and stripped of his rank after being condemned for a cheque forgery committed by his wife. As a gentleman, he cannot bring himself to reveal the real culprit, but to salvage his reputation after his release, Melfort embarks on a secret mission behind enemy lines. He is flown into occupied northern France in January 1915, and for months, disguised as Jules, the local village idiot, and with the complicity of a handful of local conspirators, he collects vital military information, "notes of German troops and concentrations, and now and then things which no-one knew outside the High Command, such as the outline for the Ypres attack in the spring of '15 and the projected Flanders offensive which was to follow the grand assault on Verdun." Melfort passes the information back to British intelligence by various "devious ways."

"Sometimes the neighbourhood was black with troops moving westward, and then would come a drain to the south and only a few *Landsturm* companies were left in the cantonments. There was such a drain during the summer of '16 when the guns were loud on the Somme . . ."

Melfort adapts himself entirely to the life of a rural farm worker, "but there would come times when he listened to the far-off, grumbling guns in the west with a drawn face. His friends were there, fighting cleanly in the sunlight, while he was ingloriously labouring in the shadows."

The local *Kommandant*, a man "with an eye like an angry bird, and no bowels of compassion for simple folk," begins to suspect the "shaggy young peasant" is more than he seems. The espionage network is exposed by a traitor and unravelled, and Adam Melfort is forced to flee for his life. "There were wild rumours in the village. Jules the simpleton had, it appeared, been a spy, an Englishman, and a confederate had betrayed him." (Melfort escapes, carries out a number of other heroic exploits, and finally regains his reputation and rank.)

At GHQ during the war, John Buchan had made the acquaintance of one Major Cecil Cameron, an officer in the Special Intelligence Section. Cameron had himself been jailed before the war, for a crime committed by his wife, but at the time Buchan met him, he was responsible for coordinating spy networks in the occupied territories, such as the Réseau Victor, and infiltrating agents behind the German lines. If Digby was a spy, then Cameron, who killed himself in 1924, could have been his spy-master.

The name chosen by Buchan for his fictional French village, where a British agent hides for half the war before betrayal unravels his spy network, was Villers.

Robert Digby may not have been a spy, but it became clear that many in Villeret, including some of his most staunch allies in the village, had believed that he was.

In 1919, the *Bulletin de l'Aisne* published a list of prisoners-of-war that included an account provided by Marie-Thérèse Dessenne, the wife of Florency, describing how she had been condemned to ten years' imprisonment in Germany. "Madame Dessenne left behind four little children, the youngest only a few months old, when she was arrested . . . She had taken in an entire squad of English spies without having a clue what she was getting mixed up in."

I had hitherto assumed that whoever turned Digby in had done so for reasons of personal jealousy—a *crime passionnel* linked to his love affair with Claire Dessenne. The possibility that the villagers had discovered Digby was a spy, and had perhaps learned of the existence of the Réseau Victor at the same time, added another dimension.

The village elders—Parfait Marié; his father, Emile; Léon Lelong, the baker—clearly had most to lose by the discovery of a spy network in their midst. Emile's behaviour was certainly open to question. It was he, after all, who had persuaded Digby to give himself up. His intervention might explain why his son had been imprisoned rather than executed, and also why, after the war, he had chosen to exile himself to Hargicourt. Had Emile Marié revealed the soldiers' whereabouts as an act of self-defence, to protect the village and his son, or were they all in it together?

Emile's name had a galvanising effect on Georges Cornaille, the elderly member of one of Villeret's oldest families. Monsieur Cornaille, sharp of memory but hard of hearing, had nodded politely but vaguely as I ran through the facts of the betrayal and my list of suspects. When I came to the name Emile Marié, however, he sat up as if someone had prodded him with a fork, and snapped: "Claire wanted him dead; it was Emile who sold Digby to the Germans." Then he seemed to fall asleep.

The one person whose life was most directly affected by the treachery displayed no animosity, and little curiosity, as I rifled through the past trying to find her father's killer. Hélène was always hospitable when I would appear at her door with a fresh batch of inquiries. We spent hours over orange juice and photographs, as her husband, Hubert, fussed in the kitchen. She could no longer move around without her walking frame, and although her eyes remained bright, their brilliance was fading. When we talked about the father she had never known, she seemed almost childlike, entranced. "They said we were as alike as two drops of water. He spoke five languages, you know. He was a champion rugby player, and so handsome. He was an officer, like his father. He was so in love with my mother." Sometimes she cried. "My father was so proud of me, it was he who looked after me all the time. He would promenade through the village dressed in civilian clothes, holding me in his arms."

As the Englishman's daughter, Hélène had enjoyed a special childhood status: "In the village, after the war, I was known to everyone as *la t'iote anglaise* (the little English girl). People opened their doors to me, I was welcomed everywhere. That made the other children jealous."

We pored over photograph albums: Hélène as a pretty child and a handsome young woman, reunions over the years in France and Britain with gentle and generous Thomas Digby; formal posed pictures of her wedding to Hubert, her home, and her son. She had kept the French phrase-book issued to Robert Digby and the other soldiers of the BEF, but of her father only one image survived, clipped from a photograph of the battalion rugby team, folded and copied so many times it has become an indistinct blur, a myth with a moustache.

When I asked Hélène if she thought her father had been a spy, she merely smiled and shrugged, as if only too happy to see another layer of honour settle over the paternal legend. When I uncovered and passed on details of her father's life she had never known before, she would clap her hands and exclaim in pleasure.

The lives of Hélène and Claire Dessenne had not been easy or lucky ones. After the war, Claire had refused to look at another man, turning down all offers, and there had been many. It was not until Hélène herself married Hubert Cornaille, from the neighbouring village of Le Verguier, at the age of eighteen, that Claire had allowed herself to be courted again. But Robert Digby never strayed far from her memory. She finally married the foreman of the local textile mill, an arrangement of friendship more than passion. Often mother and daughter would walk over to Le Câtelet to stand at the grave of lover and father, where the rustic wooden cross was eventually replaced by a symmetrical hewn headstone, donated and engraved by a British government commission: "Remembered in honour." Hélène recalled that her mother "always took a beautiful blue hydrangea to put on the grave, but she didn't cry in the cemetery. She only wept at home."

Hélène had experienced her own anguish in the next war, when Hubert had gone off to fight the Nazis, only to be captured, imprisoned, and forced to labour for another German regime, building civilian bunkers. "We went five years without seeing one another. Our best years," Hélène said. "When Hubert left for the war I was about to have our son. He saw the child only once when he was a baby, and the next time he saw him the boy was six years old."

Despite her suffering, Hélène showed little desire for revenge. She confirmed that her mother "had it in for Emile Marié" after the war, but when I spoke of the betrayal she would smile in an almost mystical way, for a god cannot be brought down by a mortal. "Why do you want to know?" she once asked me softly, but did not wait for a reply. "I don't mind if you find out. But you understand, this was wartime, and we were in an occupied land. What happened, happened." There was something of her father in that stoical under-statement.

The evidence was still no more than circumstantial and cast doubt on the actions of nearly a dozen individuals: Eugénie Des-senne, the resentful grandmother; Léon Recolet, the foolish uncle; courageous but complicated Jeanne Magniez; Achille Poëtte, the overtalkative postman; the schoolmistress Antoinette Foulon; Emile Marié, onetime acting mayor; and even Victor Marié, the spy and quisling. A case could be made against each of them.

Yet my strongest suspicions kept returning to where they had started, with the baker and his wife, Léon and Elise Lelong. Char-lotte Lelong, the half-remembered name given to me by Jean-Marc Dubuis, was very close to Clothilde Lelong, and it was common practice in Villeret to be christened with one name and known by another.

The baker's daughter was much the same age as Claire. I discov-ered that she had left the village and married a soldier from the south immediately after the war, with what seemed, to my increas-ingly suspicious mind, like great haste. Léon Lelong had personally begged the soldiers to leave in 1916, with more than a hint of des-peration, and even provided his own son to act as a guide on their last, abortive attempt to get out of the village. But, perhaps most compellingly, of all the people affected by the events in Villeret, the Lelongs were the only ones to hold a grudge against Robert Digby.

"My grandmother told me that the affair with the Englishmen had cost her dear," recalls Michel Lelong, Lucien's son, now himself aged seventy-four. "Before the war, my grandparents were well off, but they were practically ruined by this business, which left them so strapped for cash they ended up living with my father. They seldom talked about it, but my father said that helping the Englishmen had caused them great problems. He always said that 'we were be-trayed,' but I don't know who by."

If the Lelongs had alerted the Germans to the presence of Digby and the others, why had the baker and his wife been so severely punished, condemned to eight years' hard labour each and a five-thousand-mark fine? As Michel pointed out, "They were prisoners of war, deported to Germany." The sentence meted out by Judge Grumme to the poor Lelongs was surely enough to prove their innocence.

Except that it was never carried out.

Emile Marié had taken pains to preserve the municipal archives when Villeret was evacuated in 1917. After a long and dusty search, Jean Dessenne found them for me, still tied together with string, in a box in the town-hall cellar. Much of the material was missing, and there was no reference anywhere to the English soldiers, save for a single sheet of paper headed "Political Prisoners," on which appeared the names of all those who had been convicted "for espionage, protecting and assisting Allied prisoners." Here were listed Parfait Marié, Suzanne Boitelle, and even Henri Marié, arrested for his role in the Réseau Victor, again suggesting a direct link between the British soldiers and the spy ring in Villeret. But of Léon and Elise Lelong there was not a mention.

Suspicion rising, I next ordered up the British medal lists of French and Belgian civilians decorated for their roles in the First World War. "My grandmother always said that the British had been very grateful, and thanked her profoundly for what they had done," Michel Lelong had said. Here, once again, were the names of all those who had been convicted by the German military court in Le Câtelet—each had been awarded a bronze medal by the king, "as a testimony of Britain's thanks for the timely help which you gave to our distressed comrades, and as a token of gratitude for such assistance to his subjects." The Lelongs were not on the list.

Clearly, the Lelongs' account of their wartime sufferings, accepted as historical fact by their descendants, was open to question, but I needed more solid evidence. In the archives of the Société Académique de Saint-Quentin, I found it.

Elie Fleury, a Saint-Quentin journalist and local historian, had spent the war making copious notes of everything he had witnessed, or had been told by others, during the occupation. From these he compiled a book entitled *Sous la botte* (*Under the Boot*), in which he gave a brief account of "The Englishmen of Villeret." But he also left behind a sheaf of handwritten notes describing a meeting he had had with Elise Lelong, the baker's wife. The date at the top leapt off the tattered page: June 1, 1916, two days after Digby's execution.

The Lelongs had each been sentenced to eight years' hard labour by the German court, but as Fleury casually noted in his looping hand, on the very day that Thorpe, Donohoe, and Martin were executed, the couple had been released, their fine reduced from five thousand to three thousand francs. Elise Lelong had then obtained an official pass to travel to Saint-Quentin, at a time when it was virtually impossible to get even as far as the next village. Once there, she arranged a meeting with a local politician, Charles Desjardins, who brought her to see Elie Fleury. Ostensibly, Elise had come to Saint-Quentin to try to raise money to pay the fine, but in reality it appears that she was also intent on making certain that her version of history entered the unofficial record, which would later become the official one. Her account of those events painted her and her husband in the best possible light, as brave resisters who had fought to the last to save the Englishmen. "The attitude of the Lelongs was perfect," Fleury dutifully noted, relating a number of heroic speeches supposedly uttered by Elise that sound distinctly fake: "Yes, we have fed and cared for our allies, and we'd do it again if we could," she was quoted as telling Judge Grumme. "What would you think of your women if they turned over your soldiers to the enemy?" It was Elise who recited Willie O'Sullivan's unlikely speech extolling her kindness, "you who have been so good to us." Even more unbelievably, she claimed that she and her husband had been unaware that Digby, Thorpe, Donohoe, and Martin had returned to the village after their last, failed attempt to get away. "We would have gone to warn them that the patrol was coming if we had known they were back," she said. This does not ring true. Since their son, Lucien, had acted as a guide to the men throughout this abortive escape attempt, the Lelongs knew the men were back before anyone else.

"It was clear that one of the Englishmen had decided to spill the beans," the journalist recorded. "For he accused Monsieur Lelong of making the forged identity papers." The Lelongs' sentence had been reduced, and they were spared deportation and imprisonment, because Digby had "confessed" that the forgeries were his work. But is it likely that a condemned man would single out one of his erstwhile protectors for betrayal, when virtually the entire village had taken part in the conspiracy to protect them? Is it not more likely, instead, that the soldiers were trying to implicate the Lelongs to gain revenge on those they thought had betrayed them?

The Lelongs had sheltered the men as long as any family in Villeret, but unlike the Dessennes and Suzanne Boitelle, they had been let off with a simple fine. Wealthy by local standards, the baker and his wife had been able to pay the money to the German authorities "without difficulty," according to Fleury. By contrast, Elise's half-sister, Suzanne Boitelle, had seen her sentence increased because she would not and could not pay up. Why had the Lelongs not stepped in to help Suzanne pay off her fine and escape a longer jail sentence?

Every other contemporary account refers to a "betrayal" by someone in the village; but on this subject Elise Lelong, and her conduit Fleury, remained resoundingly silent. She did reveal, perhaps unwittingly, how desperate she and her husband had been to get the Englishmen out of the village by May 1916. To Fleury, Madame Lelong insisted that she had bravely stood by the Englishmen, but as I knew from her son, she was actually furious over the damage and danger they had brought on the family, and remained so for the rest of her life.

In his handwritten account, Elise Fleury had noted down the names of others in the village who had aided the Englishmen, but then, perhaps at Madame Lelong's suggestion, he had scored them out again. One name with a pencil line through it was "Foulon." In the final published version the other names were omitted, and the Lelongs were left alone, as the central heroes of the drama.

Suddenly something Florency Dessenne's daughter had told me clicked into place. "One day, about ten years after the war, my father came into the house and said: 'I've just read an article about the history of the Englishmen in Villeret, and there's not much truth in it. It's as if we didn't do anything at all, and most of it is a downright lie.' " Fleury's flawed account, giving all credit to the Lelongs and none to anyone else, was serialised in the *Bulletin de l'Aisne* in 1926.

The mystery of what happened in 1916 is so bent with age, so overgrown with eighty intervening years of village gossip, that it will never be possible to untangle it completely, but a possible explanation finally seemed to be emerging from the dust of the archives, and the fog of memory. The weight of motive, proof of malice aforethought, the burden of documentary evidence, and strong hints of a cover-up all seemed to point in the same direction.

No guilty verdict can ever be passed in the strange case of Robert Digby, but perhaps the story went something like this: The Lelongs stoutly defended the English soldiers until something turned them against the fugitives. Maybe it was their realisation that there was a spy network operating out of the village, possibly involving Digby and the other soldiers. More likely, given the evidence suggesting a spurned woman lay at the heart of the affair, their daughter, Clothilde (or Charlotte), had been rejected by Digby in favour of Claire Dessenne, giving the Desenne-Lelong family rivalry a more sinister turn. Léon and Elise then tried to persuade the men to leave; only half did so. When it became clear that the rest were staying put, the Lelongs may have quietly alerted the Germans, perhaps hoping the soldiers would be tipped off before the Germans arrived and escape into the woods, as Digby did. "They had all the time in the world to escape," Elise Lelong complained to Fleury. "But they allowed themselves to be captured easily." After a few days in jail, averting suspicion, the Lelongs were released by Major Evers, and their sentence was reduced to a payable sum. Just days after Madame Lelong had been arrested and convicted of harbouring an enemy spy, Evers issued her a pass, and she hurried to Saint-Quentin to gather the cash to pay him, but also to provide the town's history-maker with a carefully constructed and, with hindsight, highly questionable rendering of events. Did she also, having removed the name Foulon from the list of Villeret's wartime heroes, put it about that Antoinette Foulon, the school-teacher, was the traitor—a rumour that persists to this day?

In 1913, Carl Jung had a vision that a "monstrous flood" of blood would inundate Europe, wrecking civilisation and spreading as far as the mountains of his native Switzerland. Fifteen years later, the great psychologist dreamed he was driving away from the Western Front with a French peasant, on a horse-drawn wagon, when shells began to explode all around them. Jung woke up, and concluded: "The happenings in the dream suggested that the war, which in the outer world had taken place some years before, was not yet over, but was continually to be fought within the psyche."

I never told Hélène that I suspected her father had rebuffed the advances of another Villeret girl and had then been betrayed by her parents, the baker and his wife. One afternoon in late June, I went to see Hélène for the last time. A handful of neighbours, her son, and his wife had been invited to bid me goodbye. We sat rather formally in her parlour, sipping fizzy pink wine. I had been welcomed heartily, and now felt—as another stray Englishman must once have done—that I had stayed long enough. As the marching song went: "Oh, we don't want to lose you, / but we think you ought to go." Whilst Hélène's guests interrogated me gently with small talk, she sat quietly in the corner in her rocking chair, her eyes bright, swaying gently back and forth. When I rose to say farewell, she took both my hands in hers and kissed me once on the cheek.

The dusk chorus of birdsong was already under way when I climbed the overgrown ramparts of the ancient fortress at Le Câtelet. Robert Digby and his comrades had been executed at the foot of this crumbling hillock, man-made for war; on its summit there stands a German *Blockhaus*, as squat and solid as the day it was built for a war fought at the furthest tip of living memory. Beside the bunker is an ancient oak tree. It must have been mature and tall during that war, for it was used as a lookout point, the tallest tree on the highest point in the landscape, from which the sentries could see across the valley as far as Villeret. The German soldiers hammered iron spikes into the trunk, as steps to climb up. Over the decades, the tree has grown and gnarled around the metal, clutching the alien rungs and dragging them into its body. Such are the memories of war, grown into the landscape. The scars weep rust and sap down the bole. One day, if the tree lives long enough, the bark may cover them up completely. But they will still be there.

Notes

PROLOGUE

5 "What passing-bells": Wilfred Owen, "Anthem for Doomed Youth," in Jon Silkin (ed.), *The Penguin Book of First World War Poetry*, p. 193.

1. THE ANGELS OF MONS

10 "Who has matched us": Rupert Brooke, "Peace" (Sonnet 1), *Collected Poems*, p. 5.

10 "The evening was": Sir Edward Spears, cited in John Terraine, *Mons: The Retreat to Victory*, p. 70.

11 "You make a mistake": Arthur Osburn, cited in Richard Holmes, *Riding the Retreat: Mons to the Marne, 1914 Revisited*, p. 282.

11 "It was heart-rending": Ernst Rosenhainer, *Forward March: Memoirs of a German Officer*, p. 13.

12 "broken torrent": Alan Hanbury-Sparrow, cited in Holmes, *Riding the Retreat*, p. 163.

12 "an unthought-of": Ibid., p. 197.

12 "the whole valley": Ibid., p. 169.

12 "We must allow": John Keegan, *The First World War*, p. 112.

12 "Amongst all the": *The Times*, Aug. 30, 1914.

12 "That pained look": John Lucy, cited in Holmes, *Riding the Retreat*, p. 205.

13 "a most extraordinarily": Cited in Lyn Macdonald, *1914–1918: Voices and Images of the Great War*, p. 21.

13 "good many cases": General Sir Horace Smith-Dorrien, cited in Terraine, *Mons*, p. 203.

13 "a perfect débâcle": Kenneth Godsell, cited in Holmes, *Riding the Retreat*, p. 196.

14 "did not trouble": Walter Bloem, cited in ibid., p. 180.

14 "We saw no organised": Henry Hamilton Fyfe, *Daily Mail*, Aug. 30, 1914.

14 "scallywags and minor": John Lucy, cited in Holmes, *Riding the Retreat*, p. 33.

14 "adepts in musketry": British Official History, cited in ibid., p. 96.

15 "It was the coward's chance": Sir Philip Gibbs, cited in Terraine, *Mons*, p. 204.

16 "Where shall the traitor rest": Sir Walter Scott, *Marmion: A Tale of Flodden Field* (Edinburgh, 1808).

16 "the pleasure of seeing": *Royal Hampshire Regimental History*, vol. II, p. 9.

16 "The stillness was": Arnold Robinson Burrowes, *The 1st Battalion: The Faugh-a-Ballaghs in the Great War*, p. 4.

16 "as if every gun": *Royal Hampshire Regimental History*, vol. II, p. 11.

16 "We marvellously": Private F. G. Pattenden, 1st Bn. Hants Regt, 11th Infantry Brigade, Public Records Office WO 95/1495, p. 2.

17 "I am too full": Ibid.

17 "lost my army": Robert Digby to Ellen Digby, cited in Major S. Ashmead-Bartlett, *From the Somme to the Rhine*, p. 128.

18 "Private Robert Digby": 1st Battalion Casualty Roll, *Regimental Journal* (of Hampshire Regiment), Oct. 1914.

18 "The weather was perfect . . . dense as the crowd": Colonel J. H. Cowper, *The King's Own: The Story of a Royal Regiment*, vol. III, p. 9.

18 "A full 7 to 10 minutes": Anonymous account in King's Own Lancaster archives, possibly written by Colonel Bois.

18 "greatly reassured": Cowper, *The King's Own*, p. 90.

18 "could not possibly . . . New life came": Anon./Bois, King's Own Lancaster archives.

19 "a valiant attempt": Cowper, *The King's Own*, p. 10.

19 "Some tried": Ibid., p. 12.

19 "Of those who got up": Anon./Bois, King's Own Lancaster archives.

19 "terrible sight": Captain H. C. Hart, Narrative of the Retreat from Mons, Aug. 24, 1914, PRO: CAB45/196.

19 "There was no reconnaissance": Field Marshal the Viscount Bernard Montgomery, *Memoirs*, p. 32.

19 "terrible work": Montgomery, cited in Nigel Hamilton, *Monty: The Making of a General, 1887–1942*, p. 76.

19 "There was nothing": Cowper, *The King's Own*, p. 15.

20 "singing and cheering": Burrowes, *The 1st Battalion*, p. 4.

20 "Although I am sure": Barbara Tuchman, *The Guns of August* (London, 1962), p. 82.

20 "Outnumbered and": Cowper, *The King's Own*, p. 9.

20 "I do not understand": Burrowes, *The 1st Battalion*, p. 6.

21 "as if in a trance . . . physically unable": Ibid.

21 "To our rear": General Sir Aylmer Haldane, cited in Peter T. Scott, *Dishonoured*, p. 33.

2. VILLERET, 1914

22 "nature is beautiful": Charles Poëtte, *Promenades dans les environs de Saint-Quentin*, p. 318.

23 "What with the war": Cited in Denis Winter, *Death's Men*, p. 23.

24 "How many workers": Villeret Municipal Archives, Aug. 16, 1914, dossier 4H2, Télégrammes d'août 1914.

24 "Extend help to": Ibid., Aug. 17, 1914.

24 "The rich folk": Interview with Bernard Bétermin, Feb. 4, 1999.

25 "frank and united": Dominique Grenier, *Introduction à l'histoire générale de la province de Picardie*.

25 "*Chacun s'n pen*": Information from Lydia Delectorskaya, cited in Hilary Spurling, *The Unknown Matisse*, vol. I, p. 13.

25 "Before the war": Departmental Archives of the Aisne, 15R 1041, Dommages de Guerre, dossier 411, Morelle-Dessenne, Samuel Alphonse.

26 "thoroughly mediocre": Account of Monsieur Duchange, cited in Evelyne Dubuis, *Villeret à travers les âges*, p. 43.

26 "would not want": Ibid., p. 45.

26 "Oh, France, beautifully": *L'Invasion de 1914 dans le canton du Câtelet par des témoins* (henceforth referred to as *Le Câtelet*), p. 9.

27 "295 francs": Departmental Archives of the Aisne, 15R 1041, Dommages de Guerre, dossier 505, Morel-Saby.

27 "They had the unspeakable": *Le Câtelet*, p. 12.

27 "They had only one". Ibid.

28 "It is very sad": Macdonald, *1914–1918*, p. 22.

28 "as rich as": Information courtesy of Monique Séverin, Société Académique de Saint-Quentin.

29 "polished brass": Monique Séverin, "Le Château de Priel," unpublished account, in Archives of the Société Académique de Saint-Quentin.

29 "He had to sit . . . I've just seen": Interview with Jean-Paul Plume, Feb. 1, 1999.

30 "bearing the inscription": *Le Câtelet*, p. 15.

31 "an abandoned factory": Interview with Louise Vanassche, née Dessenne, Dec. 13, 1999.

31 "swung around": Henri Lelong, "Notes sur l'histoire de la commune de Villeret pendant la guerre de 1914–1918," unpublished account, 1928, in Archives of the Société Académique de Saint-Quentin, p. 1.

31 "It was the last": Ibid., p. 2.
32 "hand-to-hand combat": Arthur-Daniel Bastien, *Avec le Corps de Cavalerie Sordet, Témoignage d'un dragon de 1914* (n.d.), private archive of Jean-Paul Plume, p. 12.
32 "sent to war": Ibid., p. 2.
32 "With the Germans": Ibid., p. 12.
33 "charge, without hesitation": Ibid., p. 14.
33 "The dragoons made . . . The lieutenant": Ibid.
33 "The infantry scattered": Ibid., p. 15.
33 "The convoy of soldiers": Ibid., p. 16.
34 "nerves at full": Ibid.
34 "Having thanked": Ibid., p. 18.
34 "As night fell": Ibid.
34 "The Germans don't . . . three new occupants": Ibid., p. 19.
34 "I gave them a gift": Ibid.
35 "I will never": Ibid., p. 35.

3. BORN TO THE SMELL OF GUNPOWDER

36 "Here's another": Cited in Spurling, *The Unknown Matisse*, vol. I, p. 10.
36 "Children of": Ibid., p.11.
37 "powerful personage": Poëtte, *Promenades*, p. 323.
37 "Jean, seigneur": Laon Departmental Archives, Fonds Piette, no. 808.
37 "rude and rough": Gabriel Hanotaux, cited in Spurling, *The Unknown Matisse*, vol. I, p. 13.
37 "foreigners, notably": Poëtte, *Promenades*, p. 346.
37 "What an unforgettable": *Le Câtelet*, p. 16.
38 *"Où sont les"*: Ibid., p. 29.
38 "the other two": Ibid., p. 22.
39 "sat playing cards . . . Only two cavalrymen": Ibid., p. 20.
39 "The English": Ibid., p. 21.
39 "Hundreds of soldiers": Ibid., p. 22.
40 "Hand over": Ibid.
40 "Bring us": Ibid., p. 24.
40 "He knew he had": Ibid., p. 25.
41 "The German officers": Ibid.
41 "cleaned out . . . The body of the horse": Ibid., p. 26.
41 "that imbecile": Interview with Georges Mercier, Sept. 28, 1998.
41 "they wanted to": *Le Câtelet*, p. 17.
42 "had the audacity": Ibid., p. 38.
42 "rode about": Major-General Sir Edward Spears, *Liaison 1914*, p. 519.
43 "My God": Interview with Louise Vanassche, Dec. 13, 1999.
43 "I always tried": Interview with Marcelle Sarrazin, Jan. 12, 2000.
43 "Marie Coulette": Interview with Jean Dessenne, Feb. 3, 1999.

4. FUGITIVES

47 "set off to try": *Le Câtelet*, p. 94.

47 "*Nach Paris*": Ibid., p. 17.

47 "home before": Cited by John Keegan, *Daily Telegraph*, Nov. 6, 1998.

47 "The French are": *Le Câtelet*, p. 41.

47 "wept with joy": Léon Legé, Journal, in Archives of the Société Académique de Saint-Quentin.

47 "It's over": *Le Câtelet*, p. 48.

47 "Villeret became": Lelong, "Notes sur l'histoire," p. 1.

47 "cavalry division": *Le Câtelet*, p. 41.

48 "there was an exchange": Lelong, "Notes sur l'histoire," p. 1.

48 "We were trapped": Adapted from the account of J. Magniez in *Le Câtelet*, p. 94.

49 "For her": Interview with Philippe Delacourt, Jan. 31, 1999.

51 "taking advantage": *Le Câtelet*, p. 14.

51 "It couldn't": Magniez, cited in ibid., p. 94.

51 "For several days": Ibid., p. 49.

51 "Pillage took": Ibid., p. 51.

51 "We heard a loud": Interview with Henriette Legé, Jan. 31, 1999.

52 "I decided . . . The mayor": *Le Câtelet*, p. 94.

53 "They lived a quiet": Ibid.

55 "clever, and wild": Telephone interview with Thomas Leyland, Feb. 13, 1999.

56 "as a God": Interview with Thomas Leyland, Mar. 3, 1999.

56 "an odd sort . . . He was a *yallus*": Telephone interview with Thomas Leyland, Feb. 13, 1999.

56 "If you want . . . He was quite": Interview with Hélène Cornaille, Mar. 17, 2001.

56 "natural gentleness . . . very common": Interview with Thomas Leyland, Mar. 3, 1999.

5. BEHIND THE TRENCHES

60 "the cannons": *Le Câtelet*, p. 54.

60 "We came through": Rosenhainer, *Forward March*, p. 88.

60 "A mighty blow": Mlle Hénin, Journals, cited in *Le Câtelet*, p. 52.

61 "a vast": Quoted in Helen McPhail, *The Long Silence*, p. 55.

62 "telling everyone": *Le Câtelet*, p. 57.

62 "when soldiers . . . delivered a lecture": Ibid., p. 55.

62 "Of medium height": Joseph Cabaret, Journal, in Archives of the Société Académique de Saint-Quentin.

62 "Initially, he displayed": Legé, Journal.

62 "He was wicked": Madame Salandre, cited in *Le Câtelet*, p. 55.

63 "little people": Cabaret, Journal.

63 "a young squirt": *Le Câtelet*, p. 55.

63 "a ferocious": Ibid., picture caption, p. 65.

63 "responsible for overseeing": Ibid., p. 61.

63 "He was a fantastic drunk": Ibid.

63 "liked to creep up": Ibid., p. 68.

63 "the Big Red": Ibid., picture caption, p. 65.

63 "His attitude was": Legé, Journal.

63 "Barbarians": Interview with Henriette Legé, Jan. 31, 1999.

63 "terrorised the population": Legé, Journal.

64 "The windows looked out": *Le Câtelet*, p. 55.

64 "Every time": Interview with Henriette Legé, Jan. 31, 1999.

64 "All eggs are": *Le Câtelet*, p. 57.

65 "He saw all": Interview with Jean Dessenne, Sept. 28, 1998.

65 "all enemy soldiers": Spears, *Liaison 1914*, p. 382.

65 "the manhunt": *Le Câtelet*, pp. 54, 89.

66 "1. All mayors": Cited in ibid., p. 89.

67 "The officers": Magniez, cited in ibid., p. 94.

67 "An inhabitant": Ibid.

67 "I have strongly": Ibid., p. 18.

68 "On November 1": Ibid., p. 94.

68 "château was infested . . . lent some female": Ibid., p. 92.

68 "On horseback with": Ibid., p. 94.

69 "I sent the poor": Ibid.

69 "I brought them": Ibid.

70 "chickens on various": Departmental Archives of the Aisne, 15R 1041, Dommages de Guerre, dossier 356, Emile Alphonse Foulon.

70 "because the local . . . to change methods": *Le Câtelet*, p. 95.

71 "Why should they": Spears, *Liaison 1914*, p. 519.

71 "a veritable garrison": Elie Fleury, *Sous la botte*, vol. II, p. 89.

71 "it would be more": *Le Câtelet*, pp. 95–96.

71 "live as country": Lelong, "Notes sur l'histoire," p. 5.

72 "like a poplar": Interview with Georges Mercier, Sept. 28, 1998.

72 "It was feared": *Le Câtelet*, p. 95.

72 "They were each": Lelong, "Notes sur l'histoire," p. 5.

6. BATTLE LINES

73 "as everywhere": *Le Câtelet*, p. 62.

74 "You got the feeling": Ibid., p. 65.

74 "Lelong agreed": Ibid., p. 96.

74 "They had to be": Interview with Jean Dessenne, Feb. 3, 1999.

74 "She was a hard": Interview with Louise Vanassche, Dec. 13, 1999.

74 "She picked up": Interview with Etienne Dessenne, Oct. 30, 1999.

74 "they slept in": Interview with Louise Vanassche, Dec. 13, 1999.

75 "Our house was . . . Once Florency": Ibid.

76 "strong character": Interview with Michel Lelong, Jan. 28, 1999.

76 "Their curtains": Interview with Louise Vanassche, Dec. 13, 1999.

76 "The Englishmen were": Ibid.

77 "We all lived": Ibid.

78 "The bread oven": Interview with Michel Lelong, Jan. 28, 1999.

78 "like two pistols . . . she considered": Interview with Robert Boitelle, Oct. 14, 1999.

79 "They were harshly": Lelong, "Notes sur l'histoire," p. 5.

80 "the occupation of Villeret": Ibid.

80 "December 16": Departmental Archives of the Aisne, 15R 1041, Dommages de Guerre, dossier 505, Morel-Saby.

80 "in dread of": Spears, *Liaison 1914*, p. 519.

81 "The most private": *Le Câtelet*, p. 71.

82 "At this time": Lelong, "Notes sur l'histoire," p. 2.

82 "They were confined . . . they walked around": *Le Câtelet*, p. 95.

7. RENDEZVOUS

84 "our garrison now": Lelong, "Notes sur l'histoire," p. 2.

84 "an old man of 82": *Le Câtelet*, p. 77.

85 "It's nothing to do": Interview with Louise Vanassche, Dec. 13, 1999.

85 "They never altered": Legé, Journal.

86 "He would play": Interview with Hélène Cornaille, Sept. 28, 1998.

87 "It's almost like": Ibid.

88 "pure hell of it": Interview with Thomas Leyland, Feb. 1999.

88 "The landscape": Siegfried Sassoon, *Memoirs of a Fox-Hunting Man* (London, 1937), p. 372.

88 "I still had": Thomas Digby, poem dedicated to Robert Digby, 1930.

88 "Far behind": Winter, *Death's Men*, p. 80.

89 "the three pretty bells": Article by Abbé Pierre Gourmain, June 13, 1858, on building of church, Archives of the Société Académique de Saint-Quentin.

90 "slow pulsation": Ernst Jünger, *The Storm of Steel*, p. 1.

90 "a shell landed": Interview with Marcelle Sarrazin, Jan. 12, 2000.

90 "The Germans made . . . under the surveillance": Lelong, "Notes sur l'histoire," p. 2.

90 "They left the village": Ibid., p. 5.

91 "The officers have heard": *Le Câtelet*, p. 66.

91 "a return to": Ibid., p. 56.

91 "cases of extreme": Ibid., p. 81.

91 "With the cellars": Ibid., p. 67.

91 "You are required": Mlle Hénin, Journals, cited in ibid., p. 67.

92 "The continual surveillance": Lelong, "Notes sur l'histoire," p. 2.

92 "a tool by which . . . Let them eat": *Le Câtelet*, p. 71.

92 "in June 1915": Lelong, "Notes sur l'histoire," p. 2.

92 "miracle of": Quoted in McPhail, *The Long Silence*, and by John Ezard, in *The Guardian*, Aug. 21, 1999.

93 "Our Englishmen": Interview with Jean Lelong, Jan. 1, 1999.

93 "He had a photograph . . . He was a serious": Interview with Hélène Cornaille, Aug. 11, 1998.

93 "He was particularly": Interview with Louise Vanassche, Dec. 13, 1999.

93 "He was a nobleman . . . He was so handsome": Interview with Hélène Cornaille, Sept. 28, 1998.

94 "She loved Digby": Interview with Marcelle Sarrazin, Jan. 12, 2000.

94 "was always laughing": Interview with Jean Dessenne, Feb. 3, 1999.

94 "It usually wasn't": Interview with Louise Vanassche, Dec. 13, 1999.

94 "Germany *kaput*! . . . Her hair was": Interview with Hélène Cornaille, Sept. 28, 1998.

95 "reaching to the floor": Interview with Hélène Cornaille, Aug. 11, 1998.

95 "Even when she": Interview with Etienne Dessenne, Oct. 30, 1999.

95 "One day": Interview with Marcelle Sarrazin, Jan. 12, 2000.

96 "When he sat": Interview with Etienne Dessenne, Oct. 30, 1999.

96 "She had a mouth": Interview with Hélène Cornaille, Sept. 28, 1998.

96 "Can't read": Military service book of Henri-Florency Dessenne, 1902, courtesy of Etienne Dessenne.

96 "My father would leave": Interview with Louise Vanassche, Dec. 13, 1999.

96 "My father really": Interview with Marcelle Sarrazin, Jan. 12, 2000.

97 "a weed": Interview with Jean Dessenne, Feb. 3, 1999.

97 "it was his wife": Interview with Hélène Cornaille, Sept. 28, 1998.

97 "They fell for": Interview with Jean Dessenne, Feb. 3, 1999.

97 "had never known": Interview with Hélène Cornaille, Mar. 17, 2001.

98 "God said behave": Interview with Monique Godé, Aug. 18, 1998.

99 "Claire was much": Interview with Jean Dessenne, Feb. 3, 1999.

99 "Marie Coulette was": Ibid.

99 "Emile, Claire's": Interview with Jean Dessenne, Sept. 28, 1998.

99 "Claire did everything": Interview with Jean Dessenne, Feb. 3, 1999.

99 "She looked askance": Interview with Marcelle Sarrazin, Jan. 12, 2000.

100 "without stopping": Edgar Dhéry, quoted in *Bulletin de l'Aisne*, Jan. 10, 1918.

100 "In this new": Field Marshal Lord Kitchener's personal message to troops of the BEF, cited in Burrowes, *The 1st Battalion*, p. 2.

100 "with its undulating": Poëtte, *Promenades*, p. 316.

101 "In the shuddering revulsion": Frederic Manning, *Her Privates We*, p. 50.

101 "ironic proximity": Paul Fussell, *The Great War and Modern Memory*, p. 69.

101 "There was no . . . the waltz": Interview with Hélène Cornaille, Feb. 17, 2001.

8. AREN'T THOSE THINGS FLOWERS?

103 "play up": Sir Henry Newbolt, "Vitaï Lampada" (1898).

104 "You'd think": Manning, *Her Privates We*, p. 61.

105 "They went through . . . But it was": Magniez, quoted in *Le Câtelet*, p. 95.

105 "The very same day . . . Had my two": Ibid.

106 "A little soldier": Erich Maria Remarque, *All Quiet on the Western Front*, p. 69.

107 "imbued with the ancient . . . gold earrings": *Le Câtelet*, p. 134.

107 "offer around cigars": Ibid., p. 137.

107 "It was hard": Ibid., p. 144.

107 "Under the circumstances": Rosenhainer, *Forward March*, pp. 87–88.

107 "Some soldiers": Mlle Hénin, Journals, cited in *Le Câtelet*, p. 140.

107 "After a time": Ibid., p. 137.

108 "Under the rules": Account of M. Lebergue, in ibid., pp. 117–18.

108 "Under the regime": Cited in McPhail, *The Long Silence*, p. 128.

109 "I'm paid 1,000 marks": *Le Câtelet*, p. 119.

109 "shipped back": Ibid., p. 124.

109 "Country walks": Legé, Journal.

109 "Grumme was": Interview with Philippe Delacourt, Jan. 31, 1999.

109 "Evers himself dreamed . . . an entire weekend": Account of M. Peingnez, mayor of Beaurevoir, Archives of the Société Académique de Saint-Quentin; also cited in *Le Câtelet*, pp. 63–64.

110 "When a sheep": *Le Câtelet*, p. 75.

110 "For four years . . . working horses": Ibid., p. 62.

111 "She terrified": interview with Giselle Godé, Aug. 18, 1998.

111 "treated, on principle": Bundesarchiv Militärarchiv Freiberg Bestands- und Archivsignatur PH/3/534.

112 "A German soldier": *Le Câtelet*, p. 100.

112 "research team": Cited in McPhail, *The Long Silence*, p. 51.

112 "a fugitive English soldier": *Le Câtelet*, pp. 93–94.

113 "a woman who": Geraldine Beys in *Voix du Nord*, Nov. 20, 1994.

114 "Any men who": *Le Câtelet*, p. 91.

114 "Everyone knew": Interview with Hélène Cornaille, Sept. 28, 1998.

114 "He made himself": Interview with Hélène Cornaille, Mar. 17, 2001.

9. SPARKS OF LIFE

115 "We felt Spring's": Rosenhainer, *Forward March*, p. 102.

116 "It was agricultural": Jünger, *The Storm of Steel*, p. 111.

116 "Our relations with": Ibid., p. 119.

116 "The little pleasures": Ibid., p. 67.

116 "question of parentage": Poëtte, *Promenades*, p. 329.

117 "Every case . . . They took what": *Le Câtelet*, p. 144.

117 "Almost all": Interview with Marie-Louise Dessenne, Sept. 28, 1998.

117 "In times of war": W. H. Auden, *The Age of Anxiety* (New York, 1947), p. 111, cited in Fussell, *The Great War*, p. 270.

117 "We don't talk much": Remarque, *All Quiet on the Western Front*, p. 68.

118 "open and intelligent . . . very model": *Le Câtelet*, p. 140.

118 "He didn't hide": Ibid.

118 "Mon Vieux": Letter from W. Richter to J. Magniez, Dec. 20, 1948; private archives of Philippe Delacourt.

119 "daily communion": Letter from G. Magniez to J. Magniez, n.d. [c. May 1915]; private archives of Philippe Delacourt.

119 "It is madness . . . A memorable night": Georges Magniez, Journals, Mar. 12 and 13, 1916; private archives of Philippe Delacourt.

120 "At last I have": Letter from G. Magniez to J. Magniez, n.d. [c. May 1915].

120 "Every enemy invasion . . . all smiles": *Le Câtelet*, p. 143.

121 "filthy Prussian": Ibid., p. 115.

121 "the invaders were": Lelong, "Notes sur l'histoire," p. 3.

122 "She and the": Interview with Hélène Cornaille, Aug. 11, 1998.

122 "It was all Claire's": Interview with Jean Dessenne, Feb. 17, 2000.

122 "Claire was only": Interview with Jean Lelong, Sept. 28, 1998.

123 "corpse fields": F. Forstner, *Das Reserve Infanterie Regiment 15* (Berlin, 1929), pp. 226–32, cited in Keegan, *The First World War*, p. 218.

123 "The pilot jumped": Interview with Bernard Bétermin, Jan. 26, 1999.

123 "all available aircraft . . . Few planes": Trevor Henshaw, *The Sky Their Battlefield* (London, 1995), p. 240.

124 "We were about to": Interview with Michel Lelong, Nov. 28–29, 1999.

125 "We were very proud": Interview with Jean-Marc Dubuis, Aug. 11, 1998.

125 "What was an English": Interview with Jean Dessenne, Sept. 28, 1998.

10. THE ENGLISHMAN'S DAUGHTER

126 "Digby wanted": Interview with Hélène Cornaille, Sept. 28, 1998.

126 *"enfant naturelle"*: Birth certificate of Hélène Cornaille, née Dessenne, Villeret Municipal Archives.

127 "a nothing": Interview with Hélène Cornaille, Sept. 28, 1998.

127 "He was really": Ibid.

127 "They were as alike": Interview with Hélène Cornaille, Aug. 11, 1998.

127 "my little": Interview with Hélène Cornaille, Feb. 2, 1999.

127 "If anyone handled": Interview with Hélène Cornaille, Sept. 28, 1998.

127 "She was our": Interview with Bernard Bétermin, Aug. 11, 1998.

127 "thirty people": *Le Câtelet*, p. 123.

127 "They came back . . . headed to Verdun": Lelong, "Notes sur l'histoire," p. 2.

128 "Rain, nothing": Rosenhainer, *Forward March*, p. 96.

128 "How much prosperity": Ibid., p. 98.

128 "How much labor": Ibid., p. 102.

128 "They refused to": Legé, Journal, p. 1.

128 "They had five": Interview with Jean Dessenne, Feb. 3, 1999.

129 "What I never": Interview with Marcelle Sarrazin (née Marie Dessenne), Jan. 12, 2000.

129 "They wanted"; Legé, Journal, p. 1.

129 "They were being": Interview with Jean Dessenne, Feb. 3, 1999.

129 "We would have": Interview with Jean Barras, Jan. 1999.

129 "The inhabitants had": Lelong, "Notes sur l'histoire," p. 3.

130 "timid, pitiful": Jünger, *The Storm of Steel*, p. 33.

130 "There were only": Ibid., p. 2.

130 "I spent the lot": Quoted in interview with Etienne Dessenne, Oct. 30, 1999.

131 "When a German": Spears, *Liaison 1914*, p. 520.

131 "creep down": Ibid., p. 521.

132 "They became bored": Lelong, "Notes sur l'histoire," p. 5.

132 "rash . . . mad": Interview with Bernard Bétermin, Aug. 11, 1998.

132 "imprudence must": Fleury, *Sous la botte*, vol. II, p. 90.

132 "natural authority . . . chief of their": Interview with Hélène Cornaille, Mar. 17, 2001.

132 "seemed to enjoy": Cabaret, Journal.

132 "a favourite sport": Fleury, *Sous la botte*, vol. II, p. 90.

132 "deep gratitude": Interview with Hélène Cornaille, Mar. 17, 2001.

133 "village was bursting": Lelong, "Notes sur l'histoire," p. 3.

133 "She was afraid": Interview with Hélène Cornaille, Sept. 28, 1998.

133 "This was the worst": Lelong, "Notes sur l'histoire," p. 3.

133 "The thief was": *Le Câtelet*, p. 77.

133 "horsewhip a man": Alice Delabranche, Journal, May 4, 1916, in Archives of the Société Académique de Saint-Quentin.

133 "punishment for": Ibid., May 5, 1916.

133 "The doffing of hats": Mlle Hénin, Journals, cited in *Le Câtelet*, p. 84.

134 "These German gentlemen": Edgar Dhéry, mayor of Hargicourt, interviewed in *Bulletin de l'Aisne*, Jan. 10, 1918.

134 "Villeret to the bone": Lelong, Notes sur l'histoire," p. 6.

134 "who always . . . man of rare": Fleury, *Sous la botte*, vol. II, p. 90.

134 "one of those": Michael Occleshaw, *Armour Against Fate: British Military Intelligence in the First World War*, p. 229.

135 "information on": Lelong, "Notes sur l'histoire," p. 6.

135 "above all": *Le Câtelet*, p. 102.

135 "a system of": Inscription in Marié family mausoleum, Villeret Cemetery.

135 "about sixty members . . . touching down": Ibid.

136 "More persons": Order from General von Below, Mar. 30, 1916.

136 "The secret": *Le Câtelet*, p. 96.

136 "The Germans had . . . Two days later": Lelong, "Notes sur l'histoire," p. 5.

137 "He was a canny": Elise Lelong, as reported to Elie Fleury, in Fleury, *Sous la botte*, vol. II, p. 90.

137 "He escaped death": Delabranche, Journal, May 24, 1916.

137 "We do not want": Elise Lelong, in Fleury, *Sous la botte*, vol. II, p. 90.

138 "make the four": Ibid.

138 "invited them": Legé, Journal.

138 "Dear Mother": Letter from Robert Digby to Ellen Digby, n.d.; private archives of Hélène Cornaille.

138 "ample provisions": Fleury, *Sous la botte*, vol. II, p. 90.

138 "attempt the impossible": *Le Câtelet*, p. 96.

138 "sent off with": Fleury, *Sous la botte*, vol. II, p. 90.

139 "My great woman": Georges Magniez, Journals, Mar. 18, 1916; private archives of Philippe Delacourt.

11. BRAVE BRITISH SOLDIER

141 "to search . . . a pretext": Fleury, *Sous la botte*, vol. II, p. 90.

141 "They were captured . . . The military police": Fleury, *Sous la botte*, vol. II, p. 90.

142 "a number of": Legé, Journal.

142 "They opened": Interview with Louise Vanassche, Dec. 13, 1999.

142 "they had plenty . . . Evidently": Fleury, *Sous la botte*, vol. II, p. 90.

143 "It was a most": *Le Câtelet*, p. 96.

143 "I am not going": Interview with Suzanne Boitelle.

143 "the monetary punishments": Fleury, *Sous la botte*, vol. II, p. 91.

143 "The affair of": Lelong, "Notes sur l'histoire," p. 6.

143 "he was odd": Interview with Henriette Legé, Jan. 31, 1999.

144 "abject misery": Lelong, "Notes sur l'histoire," p. 6.

145 "promised to spare": *Le Câtelet*, p. 97.

145 "dreadful reprisals": Cabaret, Journal.

146 "the day of ": Interview with Hélène Cornaille, Mar. 17, 2001.

146 "Emile Marié": *Le Câtelet*, p. 97.

147 "read aloud": Delabranche, Journal.

147 "He told me": Ernest Lambert, cited in *Le Câtelet*, p. 98.

147 "From that moment": Interview with Louis Locqué, Aug. 18, 1998.

147 "He had a sharp": Interview with Giselle Godé, Aug. 18, 1998.

147 "The local people": Interview with Jean Modeste, Aug. 18, 1998.

147 "The officer told": Ernest Lambert, cited in *Le Câtelet*, p. 99.

148 "That night": Fleury, *Sous la botte*, vol. II, p. 91.

148 "officers were indulging": Delabranche, Journal.

148 "the military judge . . . several other": Cabaret, Journal.

148 "officers, who": Legé, Journal.

148 "confiscated from": Fleury, *Sous la botte*, vol. II, p. 97.

148 "It was a touching . . . delivered to": Henri Godé, cited in *Le Câtelet*, p. 97.

148 "They had not forgotten": Ibid.

149 "over and over . . . Darling wife": Ashmead Bartlett, *From the Somme to the Rhine*, p. 128.

12. REMEMBER ME

150 "It was a beautiful": Interview with Louis Locqué, Aug. 18, 1998.

150 "not much more": Delabranche, Journal.

150 "I took care . . . I merely pointed out": Ernest Lambert, cited in *Le Câtelet*, p. 98.

151 "I had no choice": Interview with Jean Modeste, Aug. 18, 1998.

151 "praying, singing songs": Cabaret, Journal.

151 "left the cells": Fleury, *Sous la botte*, vol. II, p. 91.

151 "surrounded by": Delabranche, Journal.

151 "The street was . . . Their expressions": Interview with Henriette Legé.

151 "The Englishmen arrived": Ernest Lambert, cited in *Le Câtelet*, p. 98.

151 "At the foot": *Le Câtelet*, p. 98.

151 "Papa put on": Fleury, *Sous la botte*, vol. II, p. 91.

151 "the only French": *Le Câtelet*, p. 98.

151 "one of the men": Ernest Lambert, cited in *Le Câtelet*, p. 98.

152 "Many heard": Legé, Journal.

152 "murdering bastards": Interview with Georges Mercier, Sept. 28, 1998.

152 "Despite the horror": Ernest Lambert, cited in *Le Câtelet*, p. 98.

152 "With two blows . . . a quarter of an hour": Interview with Georges Mercier, Sept. 28, 1998.

153 "He was weaned": Interview with Marcelle Sarrazin, Jan. 12, 2000.

153 "Stop crying": Fleury, *Sous la botte*, vol. II, p. 91.

153 "covered in . . . the mass for": Cabaret, Journal.

153 "Their grave": Delabranche, Journal.

154 "she could not get": Interview with Hélène Cornaille, Aug. 16, 1998.

155 "Another execution post . . . displayed much courage": Delabranche, Journal.

155 "godfather of war": Interview with Hélène Cornaille, Mar. 17, 2001.

155 "He said that . . . last wishes": Ibid.

155 "expressed the desire": *Le Câtelet*, p. 99.

155 "with butterflies": Interview with Henriette Legé, Jan. 31, 1999.

155 "colour effects": J. C. Dunn, *The War the Infantry Knew, 1914–1919*, p. 202.

156 "a day of dread . . . the *Kommandant* did not": Legé, Journal.

157 "brave and noble": Ashmead-Bartlett, *From the Somme to the Rhine*, p. 128.

157 "Dear Mother": Quoted in ibid.

157 "If it must be": Alan Seeger, cited in *The Dictionary of Literary Biography* (Gale, 1986), p. 373.

158 "My dear Grand-mère": Robert Digby to Eugénie Dessenne, May 30, 1916; in private collection of Hélène Cornaille.

159 "My darling Claire": Robert Digby to Claire Dessenne, May 30, 1916; ibid.

159 "sick with horror": *Le Câtelet*, p. 98.

159 "All you could": Interview with Henriette Legé, Jan. 31, 1999.

160 "He was very calm": Ernest Lambert, cited in *Le Câtelet*, p. 99.

160 "birds from all over": Charles Gomart, quoted in Poëtte, *Promenades*, p. 30.

160 "They were beautiful": *Le Câtelet*, p. 99.

160 "If a sword": Manning, *Her Privates We*, p. 142.

160 "I stopped him": *Le Câtelet*, p. 99.

160 "They were precious": Interview with Jean Modeste, Aug. 18, 1998.

160 "archaic militarist": *Le Câtelet*, p. 99.

160 "or a fine": Cabaret, Journal.

160 "There were too many": Delabranche, Journal.

161 "instead of terror": *Le Câtelet*, p. 99.

161 "In that rich earth": Brooke, "The Soldier," *Collected Poems*, p. 9.

13. THE SOMME

162 "one sensed": Lelong, "Notes sur l'histoire," p. 5.

162 "louder than ever": Delabranche, Journal.

162 "It was a deafening": Interview with Jean Moreau, Feb. 1, 1999.

163 "heavenly": Siegfried Sassoon, *Memoirs of an Infantry Officer* (London, 1930), p. 71.

163 "A good kick": Private L. S. Price, quoted in Martin Middlebrook, *The First Day on the Somme* (London, 1971), p. 124.

163 "The mairie": Ibid.

163 "Day and night . . . One hundred and thirty": Lelong, "Notes sur l'histoire," p. 3.

164 "hospital for": Interview with Monique Séverin, Feb. 3, 1999.

164 "suddenly a shot": Jünger, *The Storm of Steel*, p. 115.

164 "the whole misery": Ibid., p. 116.

164 "as elsewhere": Ibid., p. 52.

165 "The activities": Lelong, "Notes sur l'histoire," p. 12.

165 "everyone believed": Interview with Bernard Bétermin, Aug. 11, 1998.

165 "a sickening . . . clear signs": Occleshaw, *Armour Against Fate*, p. 230.

165 "really bold": Field Marshal Douglas Haig, *Diaries*, vol. 10, July 9, 1916.

165 "I have misgiving": General Sir Walter Kirke, *Diaries*, July 20, 1916, in the Imperial War Museum.

166 "The widow": Inscription on Marié family mausoleum, Villeret Cemetery.

166 "deported in . . . she was imprisoned": Lelong, "Notes sur l'histoire," p. 7

166 "deafening and worrying": Occleshaw, *Armour Against Fate*, p. 230.

166 "thanks to the": Inscription in Marié family mausoleum.

167 "Both sides": Edmund Blunden, *The Mind's Eye* (1934), p. 38.

167 "horribly treated": Legé, Journal.

167 "camps of famine": *Le Câtelet*, p. 110.

167 "The sight of . . . the display of ": Legé, Journal.

167 "wretched men . . . the inhabitants": Lelong, "Notes sur l'histoire," p. 8.

168 "cooked potatoes": Interview with Robert Boitelle, Oct. 14, 1998.

168 "*Pâté de foie gras*": Postcard from Siegburg prison, June 30, 1917, signed Comtesse G. de Monge; private collection of Robert Boitelle.

169 "left no place": *Le Câtelet*, p. 145.

169 "social isolation": Personal file of Karl Evers, Niedersächsisches Hauptstaatsarchiv Hannover (Archive of the Federal State of Lower Saxony), 173 Acc 67/78 Nr. 10 I, Fol 75–76.

169 "A group of ": Proclamation cited in *Le Câtelet*, p. 127.

169 "One beautiful day": Ibid., p. 70.

170 "his predecessor": Delabranche, Journal, Nov. 2, 1916.

170 "The letters": Magniez, Journals, c. Mar. 1916; private archives of Philippe Delacourt.

170 "principal archives": Lelong, "Notes sur l'histoire," p. 4.

171 "The inhabitants": Ibid.

171 "through swirling mists": Delabranche, Journal.

171 "handful of men": Lelong, "Notes sur l'histoire," p. 4.

171 "Our possessions": Interview with Louise Vanasschc.

171 "She was wearing": Interview with Jean Barras, Sept. 9, 1998.

171 "secreted on his person": *Royal Hampshire Regimental History*, vol. II, p. 24.

171 "rain falling . . . All you could": Delabranche, Journal.

172 "They found with": Jünger, translation here by Thomas Nevin, *Ernst Jünger and Germany: Into the Abyss, 1914–1945* (London, 1997), p. 52.

172 "The only way": Interview with Henriette Legé.

172 "The Boche is": Diary of Colonel J. D. Wyatt, Gloucestershire Regiment, 10 Mar 1917, Department of Documents, Imperial War Museum.

172 "watched the preparations . . . When they finally": Lelong, "Notes sur l'histoire," p. 4.

14. THE WASTELAND

174 "a land crisscrossed": Edgar Dhéry, in *Bulletin de l'Aisne*, Jan. 10, 1918.

174 "sniped an unsuspecting": L. de Grave, *The War History of the 5th Sherwood Foresters, 1914–18* (London, 1929), cited in Mitchinson, *Riqueval: The Hindenburg Line*, p. 104.

175 "about one mile": Ibid., p. 106.

175 "a few, very": Ibid., p. 109.

175 "count the number . . . made of tempered": Ibid., p. 110.

175 "A Lewis gun": Ibid. See also F. Petre, *The History of The Royal Berkshire Regiment*, vol. II (London, 1926).

175 "Riflemen Breedon": Mitchinson, *Riqueval*, 104.

176 "The brutes . . . The Boche guns": *Bulletin de l'Aisne*, Jan. 31, 1918.

176 "breathless cook": Oldham, *The Hindenburg Line*, p. 169.

176 "Few surrendered": G. F. Jacobson, *The History of the 107th Infantry, U.S.A.* (New York, 1920). Cited in ibid., p. 162.

177 "The enemy's": Cited in Terraine, *The Great War*, p. 362.

177 "desperately under": Mitchinson, *Riqueval*, p. 113.

177 "He was most . . . A few days": Interview with Suzanne Boitelle, recorded by her grandson, c. 1982.

178 "well within . . . in the face": Medal roll of 107th U.S. Infantry, 27th Division.

178 "thin, grey-haired": L. R. Lumley, *History of the 11th Hussars, 1908–1934* (London, 1936), p. 396.

178 "one of the very few": Ibid., p. 405.

178 "Monsieur, you": Ibid., p. 406.

179 "before standing": W. Nicholson, cited in Winter, *Death's Men*, p. 235.

179 "kept hidden": *Royal Hampshire Regimental History*, vol. II, p. 24.

179 "voices rising": Ashmead-Bartlett, *From the Somme to the Rhine*, p. 127.

179 "had not received": Interview with Suzanne Boitelle, recorded by her grandson, c. 1982.

180 "The valley . . . not only no": *Le Câtelet*, p. 171.

180 "My heart is": Mlle Fournier d'Alincourt to Elie Fleury, Mar. 17, 1919, in Archives of the Société Académique de Saint-Quentin.

180 "a repopulation": *Bulletin de l'Aisne*, Jan. 16, 1919.

180 "The land was": *Le Câtelet*, p. 171.

181 "ruined by the war": Interview with Michel Lelong, Jan. 28, 1999.

181 "yellow devils": *Le Câtelet*, p. 175.

181 "one inhabitant": Ibid., p. 176.

182 "This small village": Lelong, "Notes sur l'histoire," pp. 8–9.

182 "We women": Interview with Suzanne Boitelle, recorded by her grandson, c. 1982.

183 "I am happy": Interview with Hélène Cornaille, Aug. 28, 1998.

183 "the valued": Commemorative letter from Secretary of State for Foreign Affairs to Suzanne Boitelle, Sept. 30, 1920.

184 "In the village": From the song "Quatre Petits Anglais," as recalled by Elvire and Emile Vasseur, and reproduced courtesy of Bernard Bétermin.

15. VILLERET, 1930

186 "Suddenly everyone": Interview with Hélène Cornaille, Feb. 2, 1999.

187 "Private 9368": HMSO (1920) Oart. 41: Hampshire Regiment casualty list.

187 "brave and noble": Ashmead-Bartlett, *From the Somme to the Rhine*, p. 128.

187 "In Memory of": Thomas Digby, privately distributed, courtesy of Thomas Leyland.

189 "gentleman's service": Interview with Thomas Leyland, Mar. 13, 1999.

190 "Thomas Digby": Document in Villeret Municipal Archives.

EPILOGUE. VILLERET, 1999

191 "The bullet": Tim Massy-Beresford, "Recollections of a Rifleman," unpublished memoir (c. 1982), p. 9.

192 "As I wasn't dead": Ibid., p. 20.

192 "There is a neat": Ibid., p. 22.

192 "never actually saw": Ibid., p. 23.

192 "you had to have": F. Scott Fitzgerald, *Tender Is the Night* (New York, 1934).

193 "discovered as": Legé, Journal.

193 "The poor soldiers": Cabaret, Journal.

193 "to avoid any indiscretions": Alice Delabranche to Charles Desjardins, July 11, 1928, in Archives of the Société Académique de Saint-Quentin.

194 "who loved": "Quatres Petits Anglais," courtesy of B. Bétermin.

194 "I wanted to": Interview with Georges Mercier, Sept. 28, 1998.

194 "It was a woman": Interview with Georges Mercier, Jan. 2, 1999.

194 "I had the misfortune": Interview with Henriette Legé, Jan. 31, 1999.

194 "In 1914": Interview with Suzanne Boitelle, recorded by her grandson, 1980.

195 "We were betrayed": Ibid.

195 "courage and dignity": Secretary of State for Foreign Affairs to Suzanne Boitelle, Sept. 30, 1920.

195 "I don't know": Interview with Robert Boitelle, Oct. 14, 1998.

195 "A woman was": Interview with Edgar Vanassche, Dec. 13, 1999.

195 "Look, that's the one": Ibid.

196 "nervous disorder": Letter from Professor Hans Willige, Aug. 9, 1926, in Niedersächsische Hauptstaatsarchiv Hannover: Hann. 172 Acc 67/78 Nr. 10 I24.

197 "The inquiry came": *Le Câtelet*, p. 99.

197 "where a magnificent reception": Spears, *Liaison 1914*, p. 524.

198 "One shouldn't": Interview with Jean-Marc Dubuis, Aug. 11, 1998.

198 "It was a long time": Interview with Jean-Marc Dubuis, Aug. 16, 1998.

198 "These things are painful": Interview with Jean-Marc Dubuis, Aug. 11, 1998.

198 "Another woman": Interview with Jean-Marc Dubuis, Aug. 17, 1998.

199 "That may be wrong": Interview with Evelyne Dubuis, Aug. 17, 1998.

199 "My father knew": Interview with Jean Dessenne, Feb. 3, 1999.

200 "She never talked": Interview with Hélène Cornaille, Feb. 2, 1999.

200 *"Je vous adore"*: Letter from W. Richter to J. Magniez, Dec. 20, 1948; in Delacourt private collection.

201 "I see you": Letter from W. Richter to J. Magniez, Sept. 5, 1949; in Delacourt private collection.

201 "shot off by": Interview with Philippe Delacourt, June 6, 1998.

202 "Robert was": Interview with Thomas Leyland, March 13, 1999.

203 "The Englishmen were betrayed": Interview with Robert Poëtte, Oct. 17, 1998.

204 "those who sacrifice": Inscription in Marié family mausoleum, Villeret.

204 "True to character": Occleshaw, *Armour Against Fate*, p. 231.

205 "performed fantastic": Andrew Lownie, *John Buchan: The Presbyterian Cavalier* (London, 1995), p. 129.

205 "notes of German": John Buchan, *A Prince of the Captivity*, p. 42.

205 "Sometimes the neighbourhood": Ibid., p. 44.

205 "but there would come": Ibid., p. 45.

205 "with an eye like": Ibid., p. 40.

205 "There were wild rumours": Ibid., p. 48.

206 "Madame Dessenne": *Bulletin de l'Aisne*, Oct. 16, 1919.

207 "Claire wanted": Interview with Georges Cornaille, Feb. 29, 2000.

207 "They said we were": Interviews with Hélène Cornaille, Aug. 11, 16, 1998.

207 "My father was": Interview with Hélène Cornaille, Aug. 20, 1998.

207 "In the village": Interview with Hélène Cornaille, Mar. 17, 2001.

208 "always took a beautiful": Ibid.

208 "We went five years": Interview with Hélène Cornaille, Feb. 2, 1999.

208 "had it in": Interview with Hélène Cornaille, Mar. 17, 2001.

208 "Why do you": Interview with Hélène Cornaille, Aug. 11, 1998.

209 "My grandmother told": Interview with Michel Lelong, Jan. 28, 1999.

210 "They were prisoners": Interview with Michel Lelong, Jan. 29, 1999.

210 "Political Prisoners": Liste des prisonniers politiques; document in Villeret Municipal Archives.

210 "My grandmother always": Interview with Michel Lelong, Jan. 28, 1999.

210 "as a testimony": Secretary of State for Foreign Affairs to Suzanne Boitelle, Sept. 30, 1920.

211 "The attitude of . . . We would have gone": Handwritten note, Archives of the Société Académique de Saint-Quentin, partially reproduced in Fleury, *Sous la botte*, p. 89.

212 "It was clear . . . confessed": Ibid.

212 "without difficulty": Ibid.

212 "One day": Interview with Marcelle Sarrazin, Jan. 12, 2000.

213 "They had all the time": Fleury, *Sous la botte*.

214 "monstrous flood . . . The happenings": Carl Jung, *Memories, Dreams, Reflections*, p. 203; cited in Fussell, *The Great War*, p. 113.

A Select Bibliography

BOOKS

ENGLISH

Ashmead-Bartlett, Major S. *From the Somme to the Rhine*. London and Norwich, England: London and Norwich Press Limited, 1921.

Brooke, Rupert. *Collected Poems*. Edinburgh: Turnbull and Spears, 1918, 1924.

Buchan, John. *A Prince of the Captivity*. Edinburgh: B & W Publishing, 1933, 1996.

Burrowes, Arnold Robinson. *The 1st Battalion: The Faugh-a-Ballaghs in the Great War*. Aldershot: Gale and Polden, 1926.

Cobb, Richard. *French and Germans, Germans and French*. Hanover, N.H.: University of New England Press, 1983.

Cowper, Colonel J. H. *The King's Own: The Story of a Royal Regiment*. Lancaster: privately published, 1957.

Dunn, Captain J. C. *The War the Infantry Knew, 1914–1919*. London: Little, Brown, 1938, 1997.

Ellis, John. *Eye-Deep in Hell: Trench Warfare in World War I*. Baltimore: Johns Hopkins University Press, 1976.

Fussell, Paul. *The Great War and Modern Memory*. Oxford: Oxford University Press, 1975, 2000.

Gaines, Ruth. *A Village in Picardie*. New York: E. P. Dutton, 1918.

Gilbert, Martin. *First World War*. London: Weidenfeld and Nicolson, 1994.

Hamilton, Nigel. *Monty: The Making of a General, 1887–1942*. London: Hamish Hamilton, 1981.

Holmes, Richard. *Riding the Retreat: Mons to the Marne, 1914 Revisited*. London: Jonathan Cape, 1995.

Keegan, John. *The First World War.* London, New York: Random House, 1998.

Liddell Hart, Captain B. H. *The Real War, 1914–1918.* London: Little, Brown, 1930.

Lownie, Andrew. *John Buchan: The Presbyterian Cavalier.* London: Constable, 1995.

Macdonald, Lyn. *1914: The Days of Hope.* London: Penguin, 1987.

———. *1914–1918: Voices and Images of the Great War.* London: Michael Joseph, 1988.

Manning, Frederic. *Her Privates We.* London: Hogarth, 1929, 1986.

McPhail, Helen. *The Long Silence: Civilian Life Under the German Occupation of Northern France, 1914–1918.* London: I. B. Tauris, 1999.

Mitchinson, K. W. *Epéhy.* Battleground Europe Series. London: Pen Sword Books, 1998.

———. *Riqueval: The Hindenburg Line.* Battleground Europe Series. London: Pen Sword Books, 1998.

Montgomery, Field Marshal the Viscount Bernard. *Memoirs.* London: Collins, 1958.

Mottram, R. H. *The Spanish Farm Trilogy 1914–1918.* London: Chatto & Windus, 1924.

Nevin, Thomas. *Ernst Jünger and Germany: Into the Abyss 1914–1945.* London: Constable, 1997.

Occleshaw, Michael. *Armour Against Fate: British Military Intelligence in the First World War.* London: Columbus, 1989.

Oldham, Peter. *The Hindenburg Line.* Battleground Europe Series. London: Pen Sword Books, 1997.

O'Shea, Stephen. *Back to the Front: An Accidental Historian Walks the Trenches of World War I.* New York: Avon, 1996.

Scott, Peter T. *Dishonoured: The Colonels' Surrender at St Quentin, the Retreat from Mons, August 1914.* London: Tom Donovan Publishing, 1994.

Silkin, Jon, ed. *The Penguin Book of First World War Poetry.* London: Penguin, 1979.

Spears, Major-General Sir Edward. *Liaison 1914: A Narrative of the Great Retreat.* London: Eyre & Spottiswoode, 1930.

Spurling, Hilary. *The Unknown Matisse: A Life of Henri Matisse.* Vol. I, 1869–1908. London: Hamish Hamilton, 1998.

Terraine, John. *The Great War.* London: Hutchinson, 1965.

———. *Mons: The Retreat to Victory.* London: B. T. Batsford, 1960.

Tuchman, Barbara. *August 1914* [*The Guns of August*]. London: Constable, 1962.

Winter, Denis. *Death's Men: Soldiers of the Great War.* London: Allen Lane, 1978.

FRENCH AND GERMAN

Bastien, Arthur-Daniel. *Avec le Corps de Cavalerie Sordet: Témoignage d'un dragon de 1914*. Private archive of Jean Plume. n.d.

Becker, Annette. *Oubliés de la Grande Guerre*. Paris: Editions Noêsis, 1998.

Blancpain, Marc. *La Vie quotidienne dans la France du Nord sous les occupations (1814–1944)*. Paris: Hachette, 1983.

Congar, Yves. *Journal de la Guerre 1914–1918*. Paris: Editions du Cerf, 1997.

Dubuis, Evelyne. *Les Anglais de Villeret pendant la Grande Guerre*. Privately published. n.d.

——. *Villeret à travers les âges*. Privately published, n.d.

Fleury, Elie. *Sous la botte: Histoire de la ville de St-Quentin pendant l'occupation allemande, août 1914–février 1917*. Saint-Quentin: Fleury, 1925–26; Saint-Quentin: Editions de la Tour Gile, 1997.

Jünger, Ernst. *The Storm of Steel*. New York: Howard Fertig, 1996.

Kirschen, Sadi. *Devant conseils de guerre allemandes*. Brussels. Russel, 1919.

L'Invasion de 1914 dans le canton du Câtelet par des témoins. Saint-Quentin: Société Académique de Saint-Quentin, 1933.

Poëtte, Charles. *Promenades dans les environs de Saint-Quentin*. Saint-Quentin: Imprimerie de Charles Poëtte, 1898.

Pourcher, Yves. *Les Jours de guerre: La Vie française au jour le jour, 1914–1918*. Paris: Librairie Plon, 1994.

Remarque, Erich Maria. *All Quiet on the Western Front*. Translated by Brian Murdoch. London: Jonathan Cape, 1994 (first published 1929).

Richard, Patrick. *Quand leurs ailes se brisaient: Combats aériens 14–18*. Privately published, distributed by the Communauté des Communes du Vermandois, 1999.

Rosenhainer, Ernst. *Forward March: Memoirs of a German Officer*. Translated by Ilse R. Hance. Shippensburg, Pa.: White Mane Books, 2000.

ARCHIVES
ARCHIVES DE LA SOCIÉTÉ ACADÉMIQUE DE SAINT-QUENTIN

Annuaire administratif de l'Aisne. 1913.

Cabaret, Jean. Journal: Principaux événements qui se passèrent au Câtelet pendant la guerre.

Delabranche, Alice. Journal: Souvenirs de la guerre de '14, remis à la Société par Charles Journel. Juillet 1928.

Dessailly, Oscar, maire de Vendhuile. Extrait d'une lettre adressée à Charles Journel, 8 août 1932.

Fleury, Elie. Note manuscrite. Le Témoignage de Mme Elise Lelong au sujet des anglais de Villeret. Mai 1916.

Fournier d'Alincourt, Mlle. Extrait d'une lettre adressée à Elie Fleury, 17 mars 1919.

Legé, Léon, notaire au Câtelet. Journal.

Lelong, Henri. "Notes sur l'histoire de la commune de Villeret pendant la guerre de 1914–1918." 1928.

Peingnez, maire de Beaurevoir. Journal.

ARCHIVES DEPARTEMENTALES DE L'AISNE, LAON

Fonds Piette. No. 808, dossier sur la commune de Villeret: Huit Anglais à Hargival, puis à Villeret. Anonyme, n.d.

L'Abbé P. Gourmain. Article sans titre, daté du 13 juin 1858, racontant l'inauguration de l'église de Villeret.

Registres paroissiaux et de l'état civil de Villeret:

   1E1023/12 (1891 à 1896).
   1E1023/11 (1883 à 1890).
   1E1023/10 (1875 à 1882).
   1E1023/9 (1869 à 1874).

Dommages de Guerre, commune de Villeret. Dossier No. 15R 1041:

   Dossier 280, Dessenne-Boitelle.
   Dossier 356, Foulon-Margerin.
   Dossier 361, Mlle Lecart, institutrice.
   Dossier 375, Mazoyer-Birnbaum.
   Dossier 404, Lelong-Dholent Fernand fils.
   Dossier 411, Morelle-Dessenne.
   Dossier 424, commune de Villeret.
   Dossier 494, Gravet-Thuet.
   Dossier 505, Morel-Saby.
   Dossier 543, Société Secours Mutuels.
   Dossier 568, Prévot-Cardon.

ARCHIVES MUNICIPALES DE VILLERET

Liste des prisonniers politiques.

Liste des travailleurs civils contraints de travailler en colonne pendant plus de 3 mois sans interruption.

Dossier 4H2, télégrammes d'août 1914.

Dossier 4H6, sépultures militaires.

BIBLIOTHEQUE MUNICIPALE DE SAINT-QUENTIN

Bulletin de l'Aisne:

   8 décembre 1917: "Un drame près de Guise."
   28 février 1918: "Les Allemands et les violations de sépulture."
   10 et 31 janvier 1918: "Une interview de Monsieur Edgar Dhéry—Le

Conseiller Général du Câtelet, maire d'Hargicourt, est rentré en France Libre."

4 avril 1918: "Les Poisons boches de l'Aisne."

2 mai 1918: "Des nouvelles de chez nous—Nos Ruines—Villeret."

16 mai 1918: "Le boche Wilhem qui tire sur une femme sourde."

16 janvier 1919: "On apprend que l'arrondissement de St-Quentin se repeuple."

23 et 30 janvier 1919: Articles de Elie Fleury, sans titre, racontant l'histoire de Mme Contant.

20 mars 1919: "Les Anglais fusillés."

22 mai 1919: "L'Episode de La Fère."

16 octobre 1919: "Nos Bourreaux."

18 décembre 1919: "Bellicourt: un anamite tue deux personnes."

29 juillet 1920: "Procès des publicités Bouillons Kub."

28 octobre 1920: "Le Gouvernement anglais récompense Gustave Pieux."

17 aú 27 décembre 1920 (numéro spécial): "Les Héroïnes de la guerre: Mme Marguerite Contant"—Elie Fleury.

PUBLIC RECORDS OFFICE, KEW

WO 95/1439, BEF General War Staff, Diary.
WO 95/1449, 4th Division, War Diary and casualty lists.
WO 95/1477, HQ, 10th Brigade, War Diary.
WO 95/1486, HQ, 11th Infantry Brigade, War Diary and Appendices.
WO 95/1495, 1st Battalion, Hampshire Regiment, War Diary.
WO 95/1501, 12th Brigade, War Diary.
WO 95/1506, 12th Infantry Brigade, War Diary.

Acknowledgements

I am hugely indebted to those who helped me to research this book: Thomas Weber in Germany, Tony Blair in Britain, and, above all, Sylvie Deroche in France, whose dedication to this project was truly heroic. Jean-Luc Gibot and Evelyne Dubuis first alerted me to the story; Monique Séverin of the Société Académique de Saint-Quentin was a fund of information and encouragement; Monique Godé provided regular spiritual and gastronomic sustenance. The following historians gave me invaluable advice at various junctures: Niall Ferguson, Helen McPhail, Julian Putkowski, Annette Becker, K. W. Mitchinson, Nicolas Offenstadt, and Gerd Krumeich. Others who have helped along the way include Tim Livesy and Andrew Gadsby of the Foreign Office; Harry Hunt of County Cavan; Joanna Macintyre; Tony Millett; Michael and Trish Massy-Beresford; Paul Cooper; Susan Bell; Françoise Braud; Patrick Beresford of the King's Royal Hampshire Museum; Peter Donnelly, archivist of the King's Own Lancaster Regiment; John Darroch, archivist of the Royal Hampshire Regiment; Major Hume Grogan, administrator of the British Legion.

Hélène Cornaille Digby was unfailingly generous with her time and her memory, as were so many others: Jean Barras; Raymond Beresse; Bernard Bétermin; Robert Boitelle; Georges Cornaille;

ACKNOWLEDGEMENTS

Hubert Cornaille; Philippe Delacourt; Lucie Delacourt; Etienne Dessenne; Jean Dessenne; Jean-Marc Dubuis; Marie Fourny; Giselle Godé; Henriette Legé; Michel Lelong; Jean Lelong; Barry Leyland; Thomas Leyland; Léon Locquet; Monsieur Martin; Georges Mercier; Marcel Moreau; Jean-Paul Plume; Robert Poëtte; Marcelle Sarrazin; Jean-Marie Simon; Edgar Vanassche; Louise Vanassche. My gratitude also goes to some who have asked not to be named, out of modesty or discretion.

My agent, Ed Victor, and my publishers, Michael Fishwick and John Glusman, have been encouraging, generous, and patient far beyond the call of duty. Kate Johnson and Aodaoin O'Floinn made the editing process a pleasure. My love and thanks, finally and always, to Kate Muir for her endless supply of support, tolerance, and fine judgement.

Index

About the Author

❧

Ben Macintyre is the author of *Forgotten Fatherland: The Search for Elisabeth Nietzsche* and *The Napoleon of Crime: The Life and Times of Adam Worth, Master Thief*. A senior writer and columnist for *The Times* of London, he was the newspaper's correspondent in New York, Paris, and Washington. He now lives in London.